Teaching Guide

BOOK 2 • LESSONS 31 – 60

Reading Eggs Teaching Guide – Book 2

ISBN: 978-1-76020-085-5

Published by Blake Education Pty Ltd
ABN 50 074 266 023
Locked Bag 2022
Glebe NSW 2037

Ph: (02) 8585 4085
Fax: (02) 8585 4058

Email: info@blake.com.au
Website: www.blake.com.au

Publisher: Katy Pike
Series editor: Sara Leman and Megan Smith
Editors: Sandra Iannella and Stacey Belgre
Designed and typeset by The Modern Art Production Group
Printed by Green Giant Press

Introduction

Reading Eggs

Since the launch of the website in 2008, Reading Eggs has grown to be an integral part of how children learn to read in many schools and homes across Australia and the world. Millions of children have successfully used the program and it's a key learning tool in more than 10 000 schools worldwide. The program has continued to grow and improve with many additional lessons, features, books and teaching resources. The Reading Eggs website now has a vast range of literacy resources including teaching tools, posters, lesson plans, worksheets and more than 2000 e-books, making it the most comprehensive reading program on the web.

Reading Eggs Teaching Guide

The four books in this series cover the 120 Reading Eggs lessons that are the core of the learn-to-read program. Each lesson has now been fully cross-referenced to all other components in the program and to the Australian Curriculum. Whether it's handwriting lessons for the Interactive Whiteboard, apps for student practice on their iPads, whole class alphabet activities, comprehension teaching posters, memorable songs, flashcards or more books to read, you will find a vast range of resources to use in your classroom. Every lesson comes with four student worksheets that focus on a specific skill including phonemic awareness, phonics, sight words, vocabulary, comprehension and handwriting.

Reading Eggs Lessons 31 - 60

This book covers lessons 31 – 60. Each lesson is supported by two pages of teaching notes with learning objectives, curriculum links, classroom activities and a Reading Eggs lesson sequence that links to the four student worksheets. Also included for each lesson are the related Reading Eggs activities, interactives, songs, apps and e-books that can be used to reinforce the content and skills covered in each lesson.

My program

From lesson 11 onwards, the additional *My Program* books appear, with four books for every lesson. These carefully levelled books are a balance of fiction and nonfiction titles, each with their own short comprehension quiz. *My Program* books provide students with the real reading practice they need to improve their reading fluency, vocabulary and comprehension skills. In later lessons, other parts of the program including the Skills Bank spelling lessons, Driving Tests and Storylands appear as part of each student's *My Program* board.

Contents

Reading Eggs Teaching Guide Books 1 to 4 Overview

Lesson	Phonic Letters and Sounds	Phonically Decodable Words	High Frequency Sight Words
Reading Eggs Teaching Guide Book 1 Overview			
1 - the letter m	m		
2 - the letter s	s		
3 - words I and am, and the letter i	a, m, am, i	Sam	I, am
4 - the letter t	t		
5 - the word and sound at	a, t, at	bat, cat, fat, pat, rat, sat, mat, hat	at, a, I, am
6 - the letter b	b	bat	
7 - the letter c	c	cat	
8 - the letter f	f, at	cat, bat, fat, mat, sat	
9 - the word a	a, m, t, at, am	am, Sam, cat, bat, fat, mat	I, a, am
10 - Review	a, b, c, f, i, m, s, t, am, at	am, Sam, at, bat, cat, fat, mat, sat	I, am, at, a
11 - the letter n	n	cat, sat, bat	I
12 - the letter p	p, am	pat	am
13 - the sound ap	a, p, ap	Sam, pats, cat, bat, fat, sat, zap, map, cap, tap, nap, rap, lap, gap	I, am, a
14 - the letter h	h	hat, ham	
15 - the letter r	r	rat, ram, rap	
16 - the sound an	a, n, an	ran, fan, can, van, pan, ant, Sam, bat, cat, rat	I, am, a, an, can, man
17 - the letter z	z	zap	
18 - the letter e, the sound ee	e, ee	bee, tree, see, seed, weed, Zee, three, tee	see
19 - the words see and the	s, ee	Sam, can, see, man, fan, pan, tap, cap, hat, bat, cat, sat, rat, mat, fat, zap, map	see, the, I, can, man, at, am
20 - Review	n, p, h, r, z, e, ap, an, ee	see, can, hat, man, bee, bat, Sam	see, the, can, man, you, I
21 - the letter v	v	van	see, the
22 - and		see, ant, band, rat, hat, sand, hand, land, mat, bee, bat, cat, Sam	and, see, the
23 - the letter d	d	Dan, dad	you
24 - the words in and had		rat, cat, hat, sat, fat, map	in, had, I, can, see, the, a
25 - the letter j	j	jam	see, you, the, can
26 - the sound ad	ad	dad, bad, had, pad, mad, sad, cats, rats, bees, ants	had, I, can, see
27 - the letter o	o	on	
28 - the word is		bee, ant, bad, sad, cap, bat	is, good, a, has, see, the, can, bad, an, I, am
29 - the word on	on	zap, mat, sat, bee, ant	on, the, and, is, a, see, can, you, had, an
30 - the letter q	q	queen	I, am, a, an, at, can, see, the, you, and, in, had, is, on, good, bad
Reading Eggs Posters			
Reading Eggs Teaching Guide Book 2 Overview			
31 - the letter g	g	pig, bag	had, see, the, bad, on, is, good
32 - the letter l	l	lap, lad	
33 - the words he and she		cat, sat, tap, can, jam, van, man, Dan, zap, mat, fat, bee, see	he, she, on, had, the, can, see, is, you, and, in, a, I
34 - the letter k	k		
35 - the words as and has		cat, bat, mat, hat, can, map, rat, man, fan, ham	as, has, is, it, on, a, the, on
36 - the letter y	y	yoyo	had, has, can, is, she, he
37 - the words yes and you		hat, cat, ant, man, van, map, has, and, bat, Dan, can, fat, rat, bad, see, bee	yes, you, has, a, and, it, as, I, am, an, in, he, see, the, can
38 - the letter x	x	box, fox, wax, mix, six	yes, see
39 - the letter w	w	web, win, wig	
40 - Review	am, at, an, ap, ad	van, sad, dam, zap, hat, man, gap, ran, jam, bat, pad, ham, ram, cat, can, see, hid, in, tin, sits, pin, fin	he, she, as, has, yes, you, man, the, can, see, in, and, a
41 - the letter u	u	fun, sun, run	

Lesson	Phonic Letters and Sounds	Phonically Decodable Words	High Frequency Sight Words
42 - the alphabet	Alphabet	cat, mat, rat, ham, map, tap, hat, gap, zap, sat, bat, van, fan, can, man, ran, tan, pan, lap, cap, nap, jam, Sam, ant, fun, sun, fox, box, pin, fin, bee	words, it, the, see, you, yes
43 - the sound id	id	hid, lid, kid, Sid, did, bin, rid, hit, bat	has, a, the, can, see, I, am, yes, it, in, he
44 - the sounds ix and in	ix	six, fix, mix, tin, win, pin, fin, din, bin	in, him, I, can, see, you, yes, a
45 - the sound it	it	hit, sit, bit, fit, spin, lit, pit, wit	it, can, you, on, I, we, and
46 - the sound ig	ig	big, wig, dig, fig, gig, pig, rig	like, said, I, it, my, the, has
47 - the word this		wag, bin, kid, pig, big, wig, fig	this, is, yes, the, it, can, he
48 - the sound ip	ip	lip, zip, pip, rip, dip, hip, nip, sip, tip, wip	little, black, blue, big
49 - the sound il	ill	hill, will, sill, pill, bill, kill, till, mill, dill, fill, gill, jill	
50 - the sound ing	ing	king, ring, sing, wing	bird, two, cannot, has, the, can, this, and
51 - the word go		six	go, by, you, can, see, the
52 - the sound ot	ot	cot, dot, hot, pot, lot, got, jot, rot, not	look, got
53 - the sound og	og	dog, log, fog, cog, bog, hog, jog, rock, sock, shop	of, this, got, lots, the, had, to, go, at, and
54 - the sound op	op	cop, hop, mop, pop, top, shop, stop	play, got, can, the, we, all, in
55 - the sound o	o	lots, dog, hog, log, fog, jog, cog, bog, pop, mop, hop, top, sock, cot, put, dot, hot, not, nod	got, he, lots, of, the, on
56 - the word are		not	are, happy, said, not, this, you, yes, like, no, to
57 - the words his and her		dog	his, her, we, said, like, it, she, this, is, the, he, all
58 - the sound ock	od, ock, ox	fox, cod, rod, nod, god, pod, dock, lock, clock, boxes, sock, rock	
59 - the sound od, y at the end	ox, y at the end	puppy, muddy, bossy, messy, silly, sorry, pod, rod, cod, fox, box, rocks, socks, pot, cot, hot, dot, rot, got	very
60 - Review	ock, ot, og, od, op, ox	clock, dock, rock, sock, lock, pod, rod, cod, dog, cog, jog, hog, log, fog, dot, cot, hot, pot, rot, lot, top, mop, hop, pop, fox, box	
Reading Eggs Posters			
Reading Eggs Teaching Guide Book 3 Overview			
61 - the word me			me, be
62 - the sound up	ut, up	cup, pup, cut, up, but, gut, hut, jut, nut, put	three, green
63 - the sound ug	un, ug	bug, dug, hug, jug, mug, rug, tug, bun, sun, fun, gun, pun, run	
64 - the word to	uck	muck, duck, fluffy, luck, mud, bud	to
65 - the sound uck	uck	fluff, truck, puck, tuck, yuck, stuck	
66 - the word there		leaf, ant, green, duck, mud, sun	there, that, this, hello
67 - the word have		mug, log, cup, green, duck, bug, chin	have
68 - the word they		leg, dog, cat, sun, run	they
69 - the word do		jump, run	do, can, cannot
70 - Review	us	bus, bug, bun, cab, cup, cut, duck, hot, jog, muck, nun, not, pup, rug, run, slug, sun	
71 - the word come		band	come, my, here, goes, day, play
72 - the sound ed	ed, eg, ing	bed, red, leg, peg, beg, egg	baby, open, hello
73 - the sound et	ed, et	bed, fed, wed, red, led, ted, pet, net, jet, vet, wet, hen, ten, pen, leg, egg	
74 - the sound eg	en, et	pet, bet, get, jet, met, set, vet, wet, yet, den, pen, hen, ten, when, men, zen	where
75 - the word where		pen, ten, peg, men, hen, shop	where, when, down, up, go, now
76 - the sound en	eg	leg, beg, keg, peg, peck	
77 - the word who		peck, shell	who, lives, here, into
78 - the word what		wing, tail, log, bed, net, her	what
79 - the sound ell	ell	bell, tell, yell, fell, well, shell, sell, hell	who, what, where
80 - Review		egg, net, bed, red, jet, peg, ten, pen	seven

Lesson	Phonic Letters and Sounds	Phonically Decodable Words	High Frequency Sight Words
81 - the word with	short vowels	pen, pig, leg, log, mug, mop, hat, hug, bed, box	have, with, what, you
82 - the sound ie	ie, ile	pie, tie, lie, smile, crocodile	going, where, want
83 - the sound i-e	ie, ine, ike	lie, line, mine, like, hike	shoe, car, table
84 - the sound ine	ine, ide, ike	dine, pine, fine, spine, shrine	too, off, over, this
85 - the sound sh	sh	shell, shop, sheep, ship, shed	shop, bike
86 - the sound sh	sh	shelley, sheep, shop, shopping	buy, tried, these, new
87 - the sound ie	long i	kite, bite, bike, hike, hide, ride	white, nine, girl, boy
88 - the sound ch	ch	chat, chick, cheese, chin, chips, chest	says, ask, why
89 - the sound th	th	throw, thanks, thin, that, thud, thick, thorn, think	none, two, stayed, home
90 - the sound ch	ch	chimp, chicken, cheese, chilli	these, made, together
Reading Eggs Teaching Guide Book 4 Overview			
91 - the soft c sound	soft c	city, celery, cement, bicycle, park, shark, dark, bark	one, two, three, four, five
92 - the sound ice	ice	mice, rice, dice, slice, line, bike, nine, fine, lime, vine	fly, look, white, fine, nine
93 - the soft g sound	soft g	cage, page, sage, stage, rage	today, park, Saturday
94 - the sound ake	ake	cake, lake, rake, bake, take, snake, shake, make, wake	snake, giraffe, wheel, shark
95 - the sond a-e	long a, ane	cane, mane, lane, plane, cage, ape, game	flew, bowl, brother, everywhere, what, about, another
96 - the sound ace	ace	space, lace, face	clouds, sky, stars, above
97 - the vowels	vowels	life, space	hours, outside, white, purple, yellow, orange
98 - the vowel sounds	long vowel words	make, snake, five, ape	these, out, eight, blue
99 - the sound y	y on the end	itchy, hairy, floppy, rusty, party, creepy	sleep, party, work, easy, flew, plane, high
100 - Review		five, mice, cage	up, down, night, day, in, out, five, nine, eight
101 - the sound oo (short)	oo	cook, book, wool, foot, look, took	dressed, delicious, winner
102 - the sound oo (long)	oo	roof, zoo, noon, moon, cool, spoon, pool, hoop, wood, baboon, cockatoo, coop	moose, cocoon, kangaroo, raccoon, baboon
103 - the sound ole	ole	pole, sole, mole, hole, stole, woke, poke, joke, bone, stone, cone	wombat, ground, kangaroo, mole, phone, poke
104 - the sound o-e	long o, e sounds	rode, code, vote, rose, boat, coat, goat, float, tadpole, flagpole	tangled, seaweed, wavy, bubbly, foam
105 - blends	blends	frog, clam, slam, swam, grub, crab, plug, grab, slug, shell	phone
106 - more blends	blends	crab, clam, frog, fly, green, trunk, lunch, crash, tree	crash, butterfly, hungry
107 - the sound ea	ea	pea, seal, leaf, dream, peach, beach, beast, eat, peace	peace, sitting, scary
108 - the sound u-e	long u words	cube, flute, tune, duke, June, tube	worried, perfect, flute, choose, tongue,
109 - the sound er	er	helper, brother, sister, cleaner, badger, bigger, better, plumber, builder	garden, leaky
110 - adjectives	blends	strong, pretty, dry, crunchy, glossy, flower, ground, cloud, drank, crunchy, squishy	wept, weak, cloud, pretty, adjectives
111 - blends	blends	wanted, trip, crashed, stuck, three	happy, boat, leaf, clock
112 - syllables	syllables	exercise, somewhere, drink, growing, eaten	keeping, drinking, sunlight
113 - end blends	end blends	flamingo, rabbit, duckling, stamp, thump	stinky, wanted, running, wants, keeping
114 - the sound oa	oa	flowers, raincoat, house	picture
115 - the sound /er/	ir	sunlight, seedling, warm, leaf, fingernail	
116 - the sound igh	igh	moonlight, goodnight, sandpaper, icecube, caring	family, forest
117 - nouns	nouns	raincoat, coast, better, bathroom, friends	shirt, goat
118 - the sound or	or	boots, long pants, jumper, coat, cloudy	windy, snow, sunny, rainy, horse
119 - verbs	verbs	remember, imagine, insect, sideways, flap	whistle, squeal, swoop, scuttle, scared
120 - the sound ay	ay	their, apple, spelling, feet, crabs	library, cling, eight, walk

Lesson 31 the letter g

Learning objectives

Children will:

- identify the sound g.
- identify words that contain g.
- recognise and write g and G.

Australian Curriculum Content Descriptions

Sound and letter knowledge

ACELA1439 listen to the sounds a student hears in the word, and write letters to represent those sounds; identify and manipulate sounds (phonemes) in spoken words

ACELA1440 identify familiar and recurring letters and the use of upper and lower case in written texts

Creating texts

ACELY1653 follow clear demonstrations of how to construct each letter, learn to construct lower case letters

Expressing and developing ideas

ACELA1758 recognise the most common sound made by each letter of the alphabet, including consonants and short vowel sounds; know that spoken words are written down by listening to the sounds heard in the word and then writing letters to represent those sounds

Sight words

had, see, the, bad, on, is, good

Vocabulary words

girl, goat, ghost, guitar, garbage, glue, grape, goose, gift, glasses, glove, bag, pig

ESL/ELL

Students who speak Spanish and Hmong as a first language may have trouble pronouncing g, t, b, k, j or f as an end sound. This is not commonly done in these languages. Give them plenty of opportunity to practise with rhyming words, e.g. pig and gig, bag and sag, rat and cat, look and book.

Extra assistance

To students who have no experience with the Roman alphabet the idea of lower case and upper case letters may be new. Be sure to stress the differences between them, especially in cases where the capital letter is quite different to the lower case, as in g and G.

Classroom activities

Buzzy Bee

Sit in a circle. Everyone says, 'Buzzy Bee, Buzzy Bee, what have you got in your hive for me? Something beginning with g!' Then students take turns around the circle naming something that begins with the sound /g/.

Reading Eggs **Lesson sequence**	**TEACH** **Content and skills**	**PRACTISE** **Children will:**	**APPLY**
Hear: *Animated Lesson*	Introduce the sound /g/ through words and the song *Go Around the Globe.*	identify and read g sound in isolation and in words.	**Worksheet 1** Phonemic awareness
Write: *Dot-to-Dot*	Reinforce correct letter formation of lower case g.	write the letter g.	**Worksheet 2** Handwriting
Find: *Letter Grid, Mark Your Letter, Letter Lights, Golden Goose*	Recognise g in upper and lower case. Recognise a given word.	locate lower case g and capital G. Find the given word in a group.	**Worksheet 3** Initial sounds
Vocabulary: *Letter Book, Sound Streamers, Tiles, Label It, Rumble Jumble*	Build vocabulary skills: Recognise key vocabulary. Identify sounds in words. Blend and recognise words. Unjumble letters for a given word.	match pictures to words. Sound out and select letters to make words. Blend sounds to make the word. Write a word from jumbled letters.	**Worksheet 4** Check
Read: *Book*	Read aloud book.	listen, follow the reading and read along.	**Reading Eggs Alphabet book** g

Classroom activities

Say It Right!

Fill a bag with objects and pictures of things. Pass the bag around the class and each child picks an item out of the bag and says it incorrectly, using the wrong initial sound, eg tall for a ball. The students need to correct them by calling out the right word.

Related Reading Eggs Activities, Interactives, Songs and Books

Reading Eggs Playroom

Alphabet Activities

Book Shelf Song

Books:

Alphabet Song

Dress Up Corner:

Girl

Music Café

Go Around the Globe

Reading Eggs Puzzle Park

Alphabet match

Both ways

Read it

Reading Eggs Posters

Reading Eggs Library Books

My Program Books

Alphabet Flashcards

Game 1 – Letter shape with g.

Teacher Toolkit

Targeting Handwriting Interactively

Alphabet Activities

Reading Eggs Apps

Eggy Alphabet

Critter Card

Grumble goz

Lesson 31 • Worksheet 1

Name

Phonemic awareness

1 Match each letter to a picture.

g

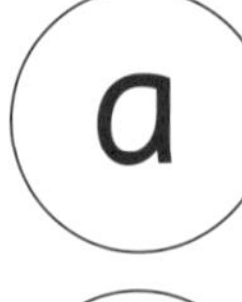

g

2 Join **g** things to Grumble goz.

3 Colour the **g** goldfish.

Name

Handwriting

Gg

Lesson 31 · Worksheet 2

1 Trace the wings of Grumble goz's friends.

2 Trace.

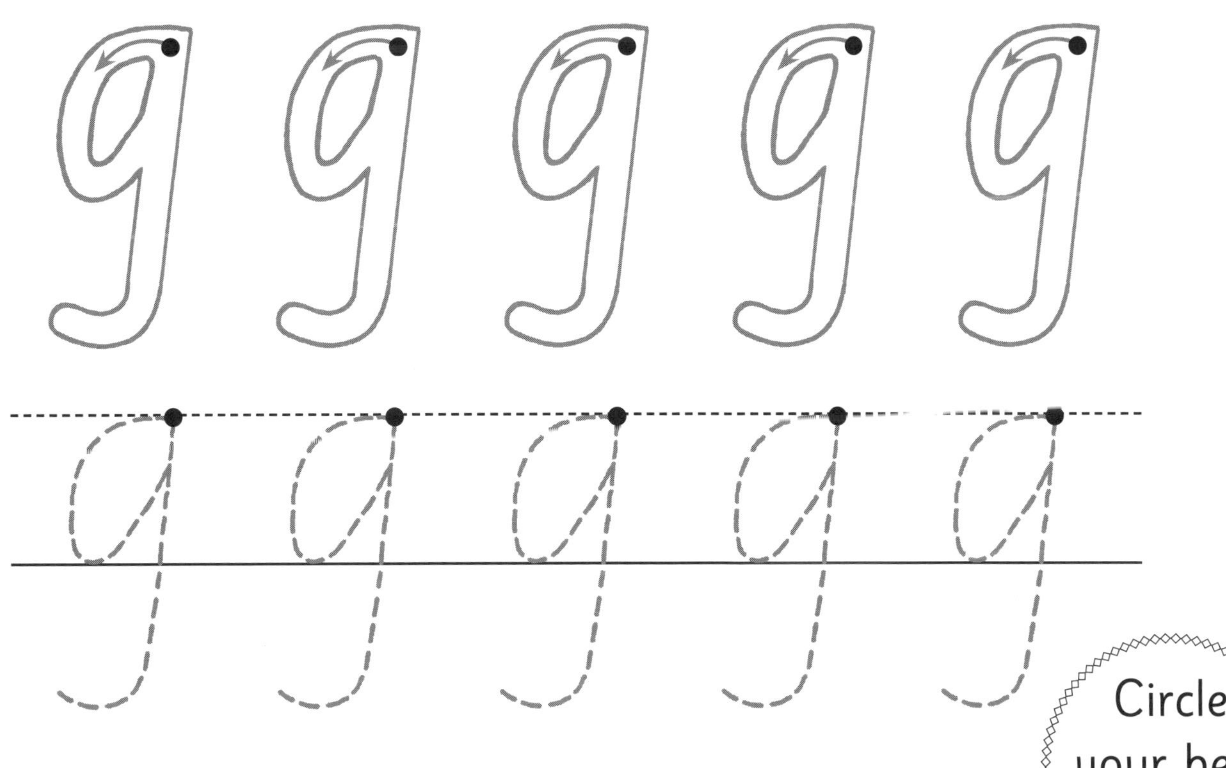

Circle your best letter.

Gg

Lesson 31 • Worksheet 3

Name

Initial sounds

1 Add **g** and then say the word.

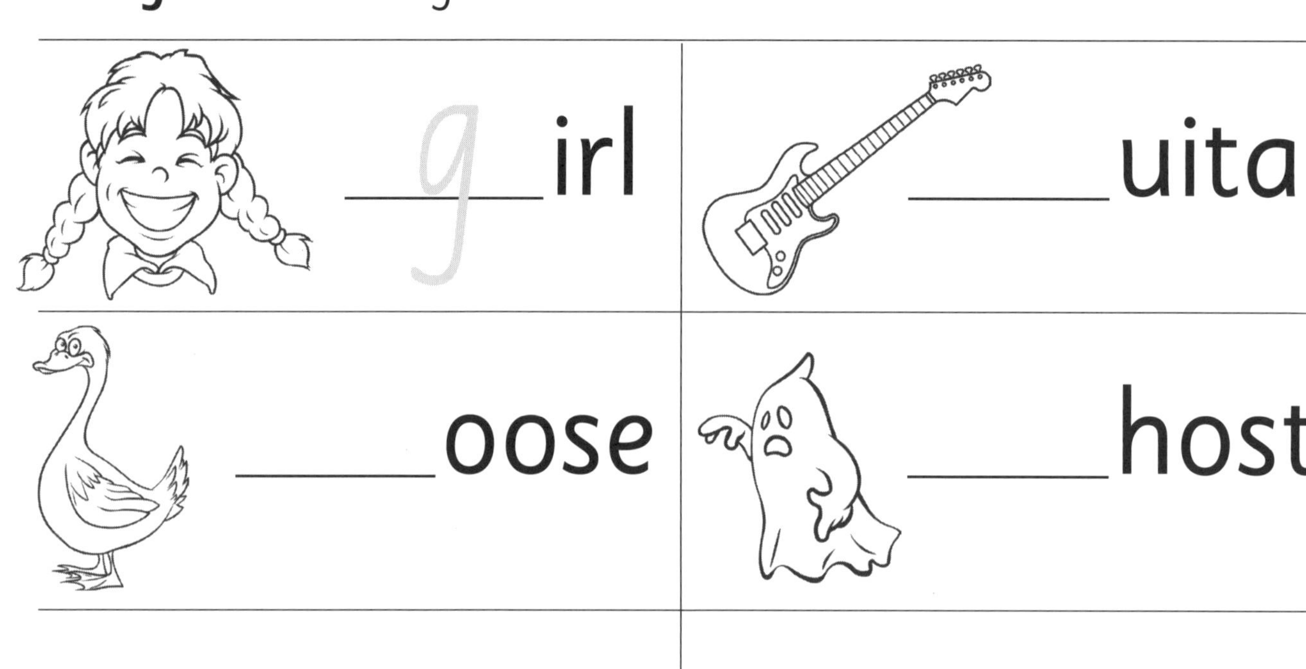

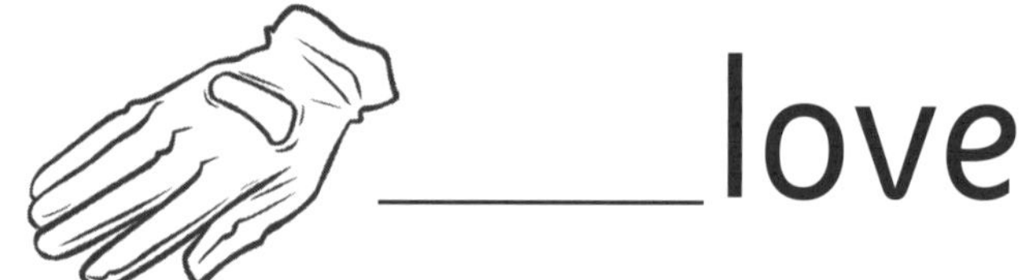

2 Colour Go go gizmo's garden.

Name

Check

Gg

Lesson 31 · Worksheet 4

1 Trace and write.

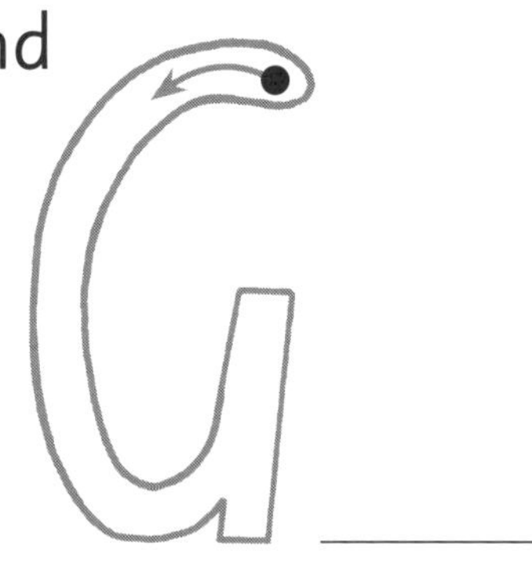

2 Circle every **G**.

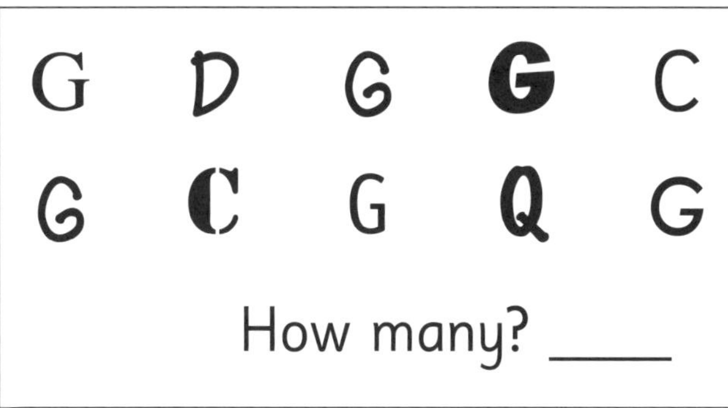

How many? ____

Circle every **g**.

g	g	g	y	g
j	b	g	a	g

How many? ____

3 Colour the pictures that start with **g**.

4 Add **g** and then say each word.

____oose

____ift

Lesson 32 the letter l

Learning objectives

Children will:

- identify the sound l.
- identify words that contain l.
- recognise and write l and L.

Australian Curriculum Content Descriptions

Sound and letter knowledge

ACELA1439 listen to the sounds a student hears in the word, and write letters to represent those sounds; identify and manipulate sounds (phonemes) in spoken words; identify onset and rime in one-syllable spoken words

ACELA1440 identify familiar and recurring letters and the use of upper and lower case in written texts

Creating texts

ACELY1653 follow clear demonstrations of how to construct each letter, learn to construct lower case letters

Expressing and developing ideas

ACELA1758 recognise the most common sound made by each letter of the alphabet, including consonants and short vowel sounds; know that spoken words are written down by listening to the sounds heard in the word and then writing letters to represent those sounds

Vocabulary words

lemon, leg, lizard, light, ladybird, ladybug, log, lock, ladder, lollipop

ESL/ELL

Many students from an Asian language background will have trouble distinguishing between /l/ and /r/. Practise listening to these sounds and separating them out by asking students which word is right.

My car goes on the road. / My car goes on the load.
I hurt my lip. / I hurt my rip.

Extra assistance

For the sound /l/, the tongue tip is on the part of the mouth behind the top teeth. For /r/ the tongue draws back from the teeth. Have students practise pronunciation using tongue twisters:

Lily Lizard looked for ladybugs.
Lincoln Lock licked a lemon lollipop.

Classroom activities

Letter Pictures

Provide the students with a piece of paper that has many different forms of the letter l on it – some dotted, some in bubble writing, some solid letters, a couple of capitals. Students turn each letter into a picture of something starting with l.

Find the Letter

Give each student 3 cards with the letters l, r and g. Say a word and ask students to listen to the initial sound. They should hold up the card which makes that initial sound. Use clear, recognisable words such as love, race, gate, lip, red, got.

Reading Eggs Lesson sequence	TEACH Content and skills	PRACTISE Children will:	APPLY
Hear: *Animated Lesson*	Introduce the sound /l/ through words and the song *Looking for Love*.	identify and read /l/ sound in isolation and in words.	**Worksheet 1** Phonemic awareness
Write: *Dot-to-Dot*	Reinforce correct letter formation of lower case l.	write the letter l.	**Worksheet 2** Handwriting
Find: *Letter Grid, Mark Your Letter, Missing Sound, Trains*	Recognise l in upper and lower case. Identify the correct onset letter to complete the word.	locate lower case l and capital L. Choose the correct initial letter to make the word.	**Worksheet 3** Initial sounds
Vocabulary: *Letter Book, Word Windows, Label It, Fishing Boats*	Build vocabulary skills: Recognise key vocabulary. Blend and recognise words.	match pictures to words. Blend sounds to read words.	**Worksheet 4** Check
Read: *Book*	Read aloud book.	listen, follow the reading and read along.	**Reading Eggs Alphabet book** l

Related Reading Eggs Activities, Interactives, Songs and Books

Reading Eggs Playroom

Alphabet Activities
Book Shelf Song
Books:
Alphabet Song,
Little Peter Rabbit,
Five Little Monkeys

Music Café

Looking for Love

Reading Eggs Puzzle Park

Alphabet Match
Both ways
Read it

Reading Eggs Posters

Reading Eggs Library Books

My Program Books

Alphabet Flashcards

Game 2 – Sound puzzles with l, r, g, c & q.

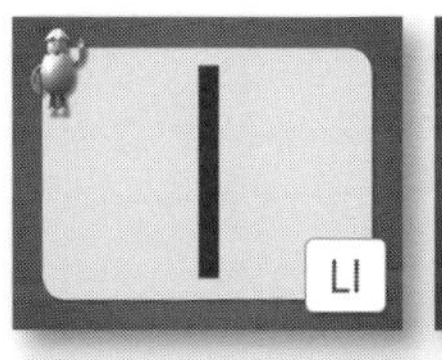

Teacher Toolkit

Targeting Handwriting Interactively

Alphabet Activities

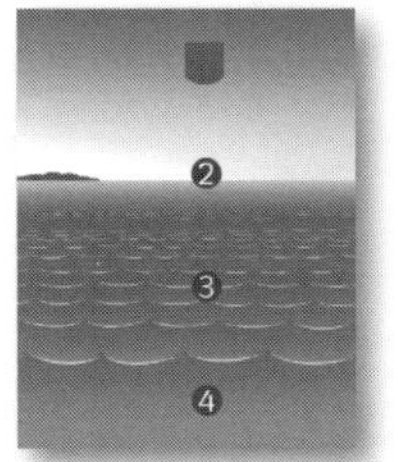

Reading Eggs Apps

Eggy Alphabet

Critter Card

Lemon lizard

Lesson 32 • Worksheet 1

Name

Phonemic awareness

Look out! It's Lemon lizard.

1 Match each letter to a picture.

2 Join **l** things to Lemon lizard.

3 Colour the **l** lemons.

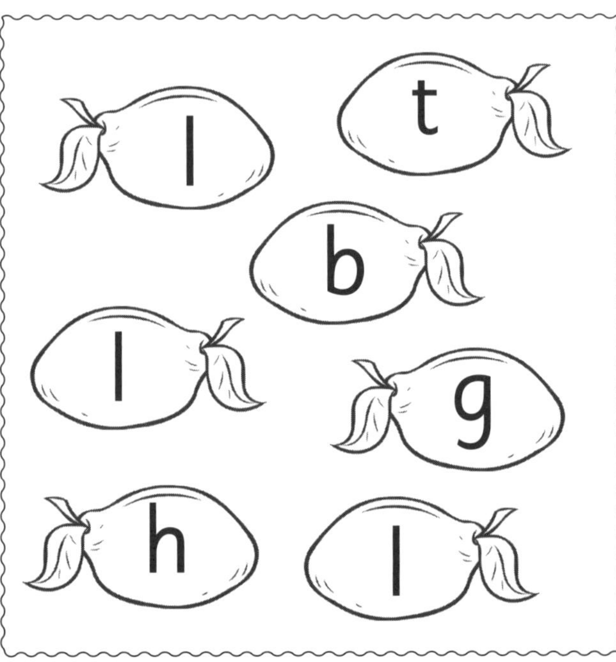

Name

Handwriting

Ll

Lesson 32 · Worksheet 2

1 Trace the dotted lines.

2 Trace.

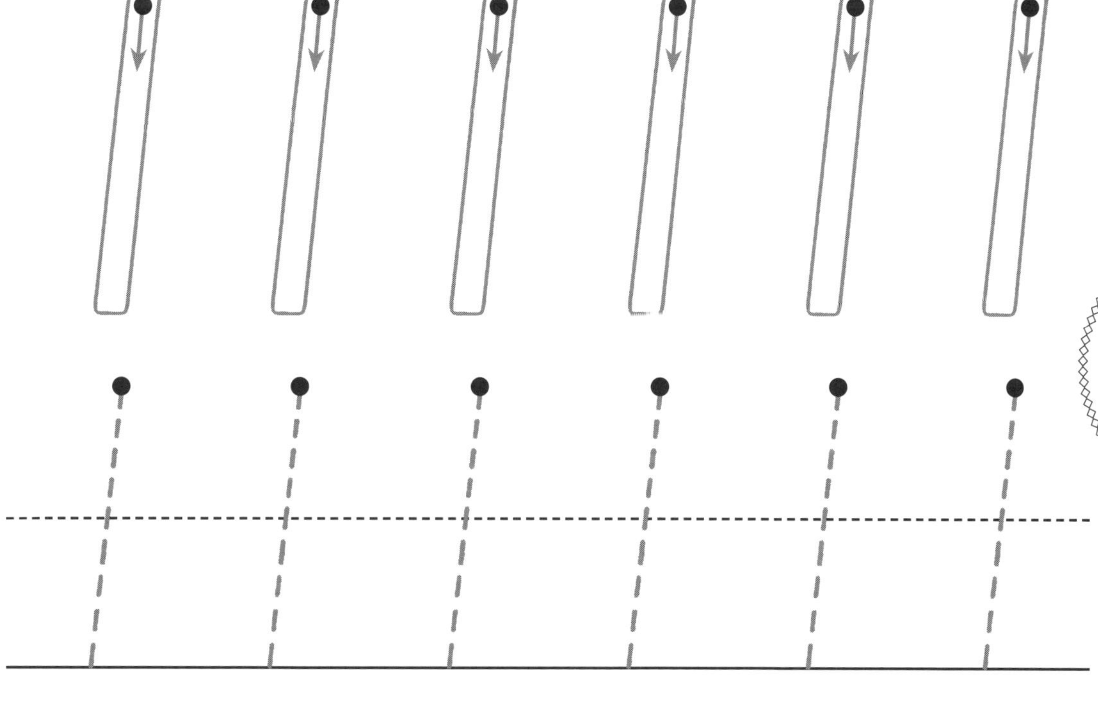

Circle your best letter.

Name

Initial sounds

1 Add **l** and then say the word.

l emon	 ____ izard
 ____ eg	 ____ adder
 ____ amp	 ____ ips

2 Draw 4 legs on the lion.

A lion has 4 legs.

Name

Check

1 Trace and write.

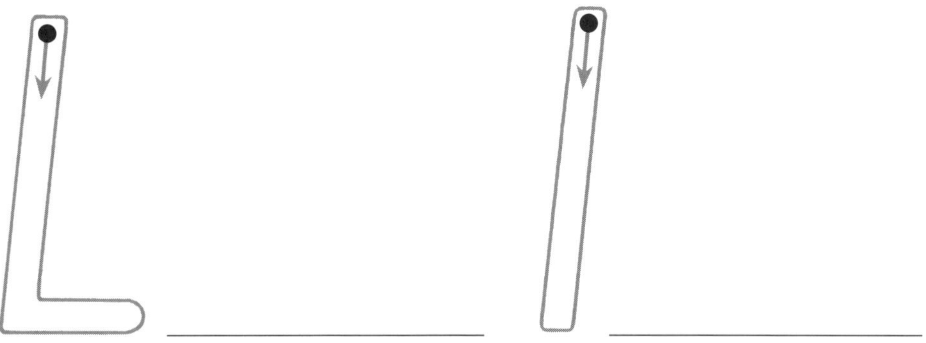

2 Colour the pictures that begin with **l**.

3 Add **l** to each word. Colour the picture.

_____adybug

_____eaf

Lesson 33 the words **he** and **she**

Learning objectives

Children will:

- identify the words he and she.
- read and write the words he and she.

Australian Curriculum Content Descriptions

Sound and letter knowledge

ACELA1439 listen to the sounds a student hears in the word, and write letters to represent those sounds; identify rhyme and syllables in spoken words; identify onset and rime in one-syllable spoken words

ACELA1440 identify familiar and recurring letters and the use of upper and lower case in written texts

Expressing and developing ideas

ACELA1758 write consonant-vowel-consonant words by writing letters to represent the sounds in the spoken words; know that spoken words are written down by listening to the sounds heard in the word and then writing letters to represent those sounds

Sight words

he, she, on, had, the, can, see, is, you, and, in, a, I

Word families

jam, can, van, man, Dan, zap, tap, sat, cat, mat, fat, bee, see

Vocabulary words

cans, taps, cats

ESL/ELL

Some languages do not have gender specific pronouns, such as Malay, Tagalog, Finnish, Chinese and Turkish. Some avoid pronouns altogether, for example Japanese and Korean. Students from these language backgrounds may need the idea of pronouns explained and gender specificity reinforced with practise.

Extra assistance

To practise using he and she, give the students a sentence which makes the gender of the subject clear and ask which pronoun could be used, for example:

Mary went to the shops and ____ bought a dress.
Bruce is a boy dog and ____ likes to chase balls.

Classroom activities

Which One?

Ask students to choose the pronoun for a list of names. Be sure to include some names that can be used as both boy and girl names, eg Kim and Alex, and discuss these with the class.

Mind the Gap!

Write some sentences on the board which are missing their pronouns but make the gender of the subject clear, for example: *The King sat on the mat and ____ had a nap.* Ask students to read the sentences by themselves, write them down and fill in the gap with he or she. Discuss their individual sentences as a group.

Reading Eggs Lesson sequence	TEACH Content and skills	PRACTISE Children will:	APPLY
Hear: *Animated Lesson*	Introduce the words he and she through words and the song *He and She*.	identify and read the words he and she in isolation and in a group.	**Worksheet 1** Sight words
Write: *Blend a Word, Rumble Jumble, Tiles*	Blend and recognise words. Unjumble letters for a given word.	blend sounds to read and make words. Write a word from jumbled letters.	**Worksheet 2** Read
Find: *Frog Hops, Time for 20*	Recognise a given word.	find the given word in a group.	**Worksheet 3** Word family
Vocabulary: *Wheel of Words, Rhyming Squares, Break it Up, Picture Picker*	Build vocabulary skills: Recognise key vocabulary. Identify rhyming words. Identify the number of phonemes in a word. Read and comprehend a sentence.	match pictures to words. Find images of rhyming words. Identify the number of sounds in a word. Read a sentence and match to a picture.	**Worksheet 4** Check
Read: *Book*	Read aloud book.	listen, follow the reading and read along.	**Reading Eggs Story book** Cans

Related Reading Eggs Activities, Interactives, Songs and Books

Reading Eggs Playroom

Book Shelf Song
Books:

Miss Polly,
The Grand Old Duke of York

My Wall:

Making Me,
Family Photos

Music Café

He and She

Reading Eggs Puzzle Park

More than one

Both ways

Read it

Reading Eggs Posters

Reading Eggs Library Books

My Program Books

Alphabet Flashcards

Game 6 – Critter concentration using known letters.

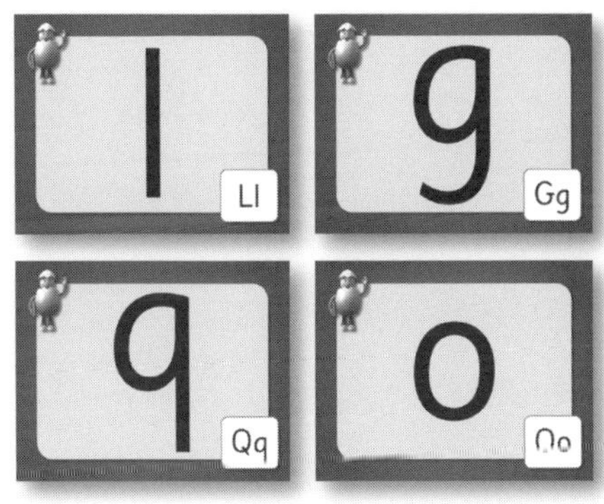

Teacher Toolkit

Targeting Handwriting Interactively

Spelling Activities

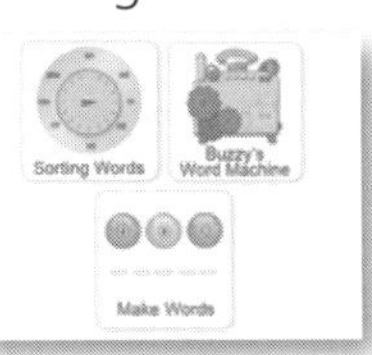

Reading Eggs Apps

Eggy sight words

Critter Card

Dan

he she

Lesson 33 · Worksheet 1

Name

Sight words

1 Trace the words.

2 Complete the words.

he she

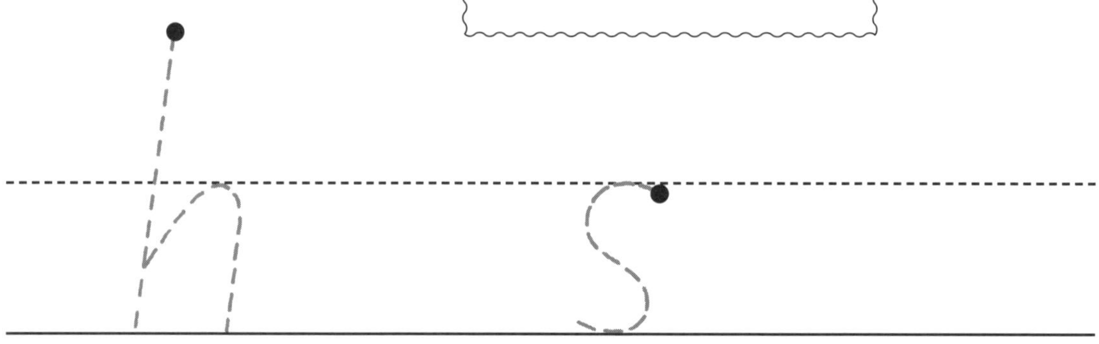

3 Match the word to its picture.

he

she

Name

Read

Lesson 33 · Worksheet 2

Look at the picture. Colour the right ending for the sentence. Read each sentence.

The cat can see

a cat on a can.

a man on a can.

The cat can see

jam in a can.

a tap on the can.

at

Name

Word family

Lesson 33 • Worksheet 3

Match the words to their pictures.

Name

Check

he she

Lesson 33 • Worksheet 4

1 Colour **he** = red, **she** = yellow.

2 Complete the sentence.

2 Read the sentence. Draw a picture.

He is a fat cat.

Lesson 34 the letter **k**

Learning objectives

Children will:

- identify the sound k.
- identify words that contain k.
- recognise and write k and K.

Australian Curriculum Content Descriptions

Sound and letter knowledge

ACELA1439 listen to the sounds a student hears in the word, and write letters to represent those sounds; identify and manipulate sounds (phonemes) in spoken words

ACELA1440 identify familiar and recurring letters and the use of upper and lower case in written texts

Creating texts

ACELY1653 follow clear demonstrations of how to construct each letter, learn to construct lower case letters

Expressing and developing ideas

ACELA1758 recognise the most common sound made by each letter of the alphabet, including consonants and short vowel sounds; know that spoken words are written down by listening to the sounds heard in the word and then writing letters to represent those sounds

Vocabulary words

kite, king, key, kangaroo, kiss, kitten, kennel, koala

ESL/ELL

The letter k is not commonly used in Spanish although the sound is used with c, que and qui. Model the letter more extensively for students with this language background as they may not recognise it and be sure to differentiate it from h and b, which have a very similar shape.

Extra assistance

When teaching students to form the Roman alphabet use two horizontal lines to divide the writing space into 3 sections (above, middle and below) and show how all letters have something in the middle, between the lines, and some letters have parts that go above or below.

Classroom activities

Decorate the Letters

Provide the students with a piece of paper that has many different forms of the letter k on it – some dotted, some in bubble writing, some solid letters, a couple of capitals. The students:

- trace over the dotted letters with different coloured pencils, textas or crayons.
- glue collage materials such as paper bits, leaves or wool to the solid letters.
- colour in the bubble letters with dots, stripes or shapes.

Reading Eggs Lesson sequence	TEACH Content and skills	PRACTISE Children will:	APPLY
Hear: *Animated Lesson*	Introduce the sound /k/ through words and the song *Sid's Key to K.*	identify and read /k/ sound in isolation and in words.	**Worksheet 1** Phonemic awareness
Write: *Dot-to-Dot*	Reinforce correct letter formation of lower case k.	write the letter k.	**Worksheet 2** Handwriting
Find: *Letter Grid, Mark Your Letter, Missing Sound, Letter Lights*	Recognise k in upper and lower case. Identify the correct letter to complete the word.	locate lower case k and capital K. Choose the correct letter to make the word.	**Worksheet 3** Initial sounds
Vocabulary: *Letter Book, Word Windows, Label It, Rumble Jumble*	Build vocabulary skills: Recognise key vocabulary. Blend and recognise words. Unjumble letters for a given word.	match pictures to words. Blend sounds to read words. Write a word from jumbled letters.	**Worksheet 4** Check
Read: *Book*	Read aloud book.	listen, follow the reading and read along.	**Reading Eggs Alphabet book** k

Classroom activities

Which Hat?

Place three hats on the floor with the labels k, c and q. Discuss the very similar sounds. Have a pile of objects or pictures of objects that start with k, c and q. Each student chooses one and works out which hat it must go in. Discuss their choice with the class.

Related Reading Eggs Activities, Interactives, Songs and Books

Reading Eggs Playroom

Alphabet Activities

Book Shelf Song

Books:
Alphabet Song,
1-2 Buckle My Shoe

Play Kitchen

Music Café

Sid's Key to K

Reading Eggs Puzzle Park

Alphabet match

Both ways

Read it

Reading Eggs Posters

Reading Eggs Library Books

My Program Books

Alphabet Flashcards

Game 3 – Sound hunt with the letter k.

Teacher Toolkit

Targeting Handwriting Interactively

Alphabet Activities

Reading Eggs Apps

Eggy Alphabet

Critter Card

Kangako

Name

Phonemic awareness

1 Match each letter to a picture.

2 Join **k** things to Kangako.

3 Colour the **k** keys.

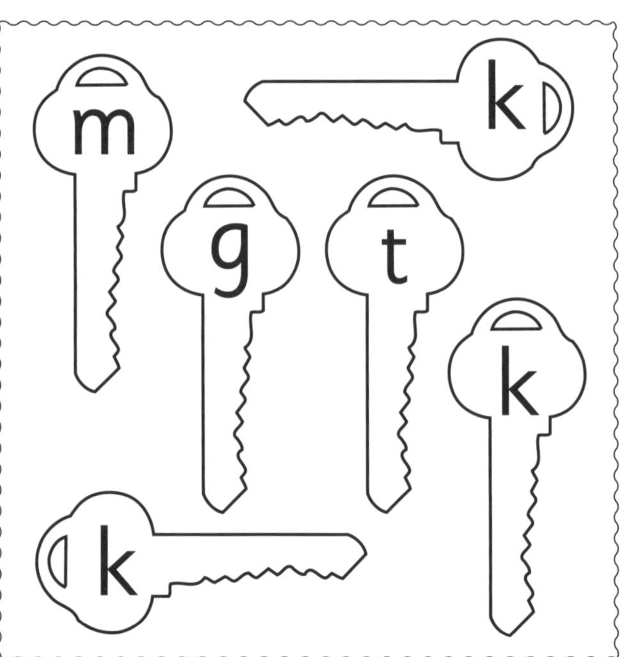

Name

Handwriting

Kk

Lesson 34 · Worksheet 2

1 Give each koala a kite.

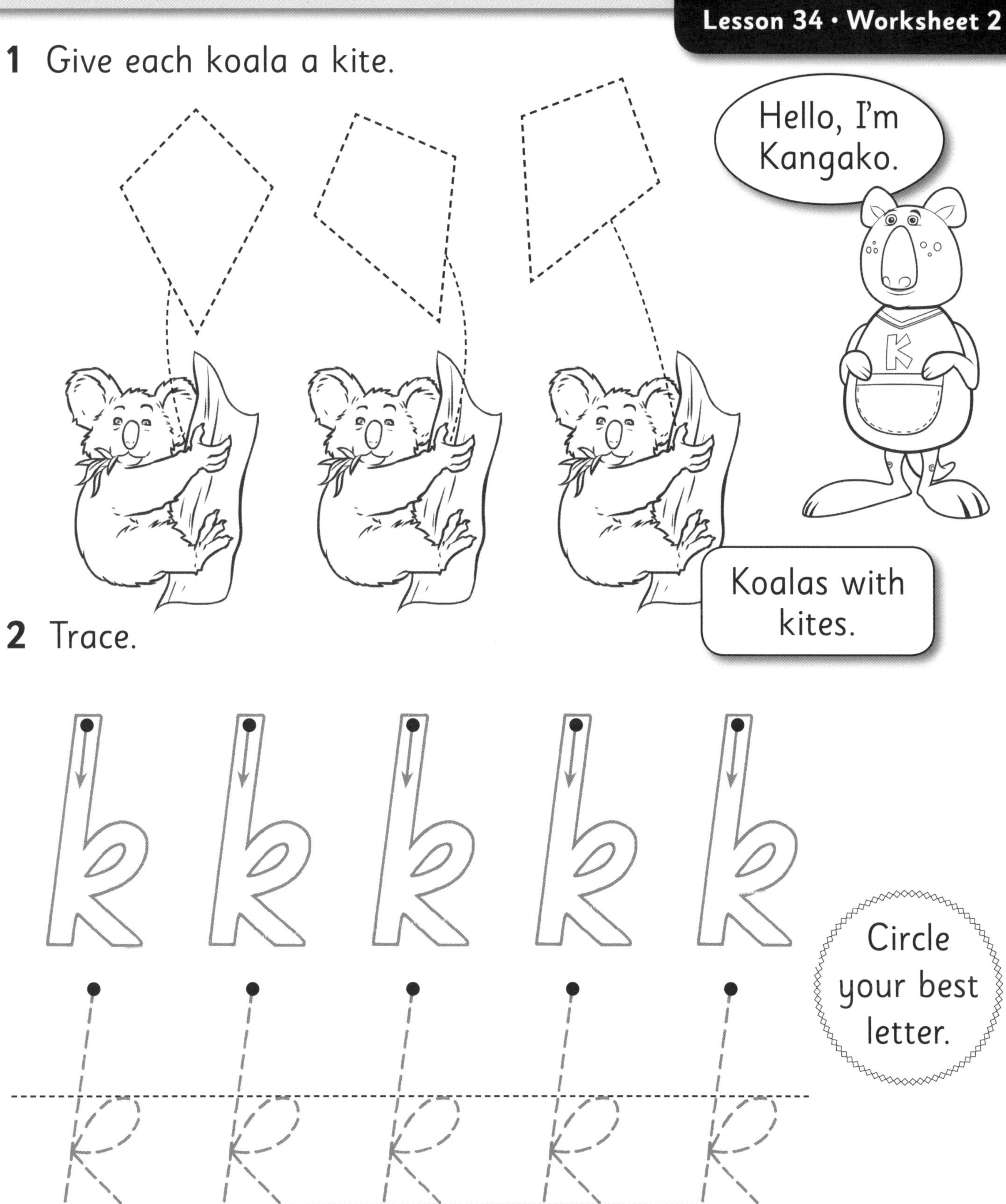

2 Trace.

Name

Initial sounds

1 Add **k** and then say the word.

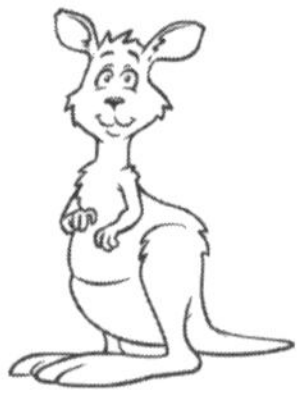

k angaroo	____oala
____ey	____iss
____ite	____itten

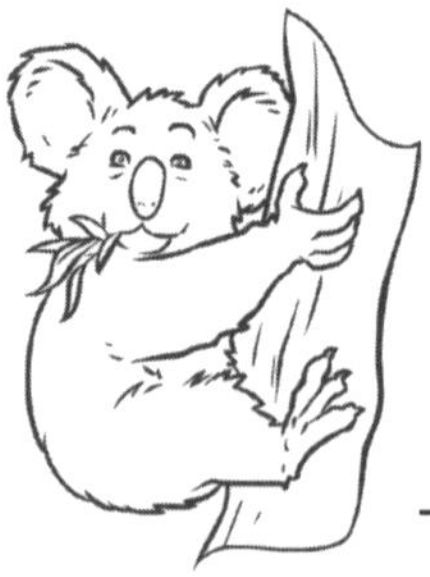

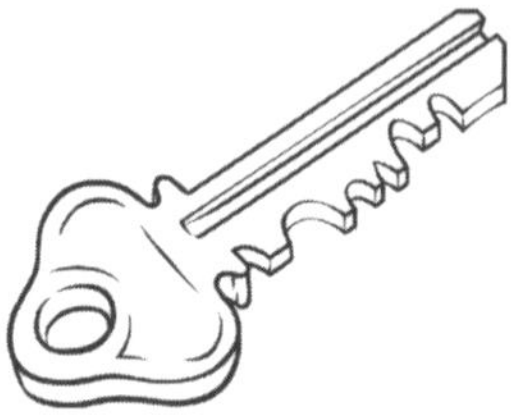

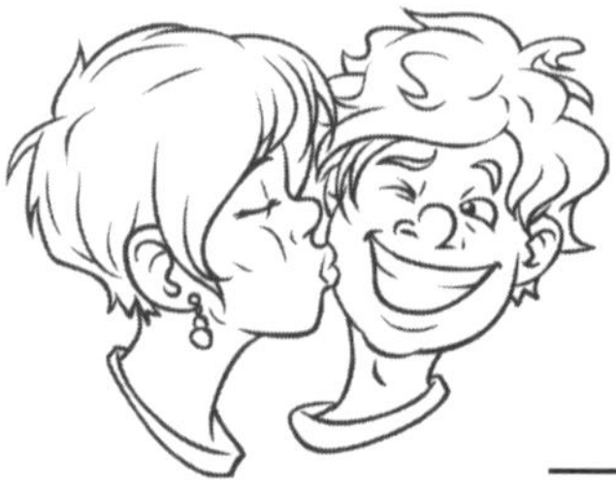

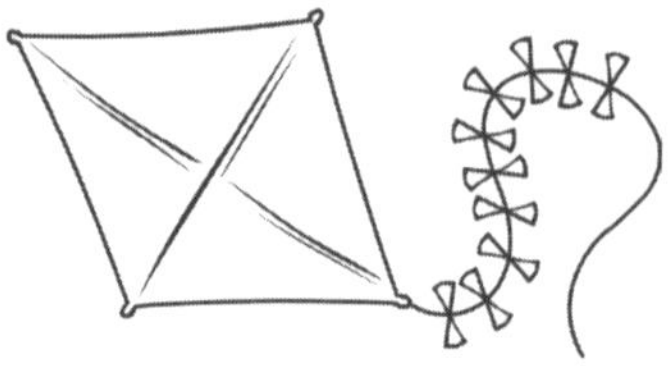

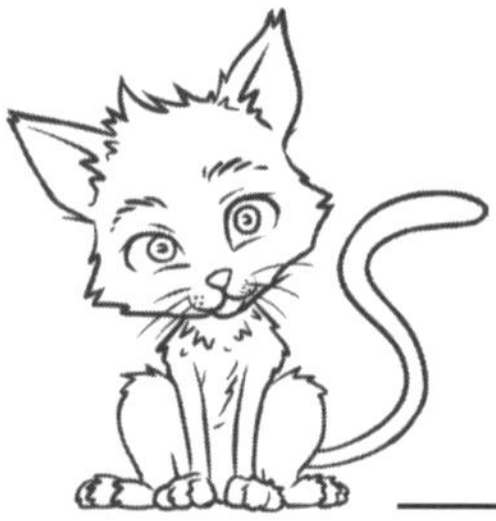

2 Colour Kangako's kite.

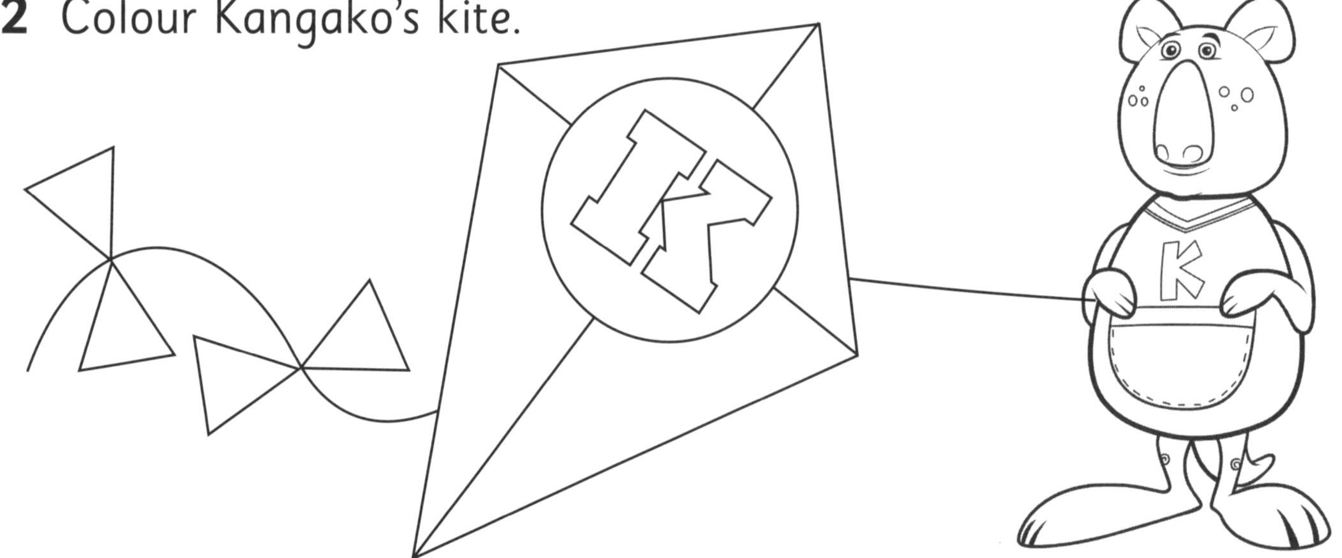

Name

Check

1 Colour the kites that begin with **k**.

2 Match each picture to its beginning sound.

Lesson 35 the words **as** and **has**

Learning objectives

Children will:

- identify the words as and has.
- read and write the words as and has.

Australian Curriculum Content Descriptions

Sound and letter knowledge

ACELA1439 listen to the sounds a student hears in the word, and write letters to represent those sounds; identify rhyme and syllables in spoken words; identify and manipulate sounds (phonemes) in spoken words; identify onset and rime in one-syllable spoken words

Expressing and developing ideas

ACELA1435 learn that word order in sentences is important for meaning

ACELA1438 build word families using onset and rime

ACELA1758 recognise the most common sound made by each letter of the alphabet, including consonants and short vowel sounds; write consonant-vowel-consonant words by writing letters to represent the sounds in the spoken words; know that spoken words are written down by listening to the sounds heard in the word and then writing letters to represent those sounds

Sight words

as, has, is, it, on, a, the, on

Word families

rat, cat, bat, hat, mat, man, fan, can, map, ham

ESL/ELL

Students who speak Spanish, Tagalog or Russian at home may mispronounce /a/ as /ar/, as in last. Give them opportunities to practise their pronunciation with matching pairs of words, like tap and tarp, fat and father, cap and car.

Extra assistance

Explain to students that the letter s can sometimes be used for a /z/ sound, like in as and has, and at the end of some words, e.g. eyes, days, shoes, as well as in other places. The English language is a very complex set of rules and exceptions.

Classroom activities

Flashcard Snap

Have at least two sets of flashcards for the short, known sight words: I, a, an, am, as, at, in, is, on, he, can, see, the, you, and, had, she, has. Shuffle and deal between two players. Keep cards face down. Players take turns to put a card from their pile onto a central pile, saying the word as they turn it over. If the two cards on top are the same, the players shout SNAP! The first to do so takes the central pile. Play continues until one player runs out of cards.

Make your own sentences

Students complete the sentences and discuss their answers:

He has _____. She has _____. It is as _____ as _____.

Reading Eggs Lesson sequence	TEACH Content and skills	PRACTISE Children will:	APPLY
Hear: *Animated Lesson*	Introduce the words as and has through words and the song *Little Words As and Has*.	identify and read the words as and has in isolation and in a group.	**Worksheet 1** Sight words
Write: *Pick Up Bricks*	Recognise correct word order for a sentence.	put the words in the correct order to make a sentence.	**Worksheet 2** Read
Find: *Word families, Missing Sound, Shooting Hoops*	Identify the correct onset or final letter to complete the word. Recognise a given word.	choose the correct initial or ending letter to make the word. Find the given word in a group.	**Worksheet 3** Word families
Vocabulary: *Tiles, Rhyming Squares, Sound Streamers, Break It Up*	Build vocabulary skills: Blend and recognise words. Identify rhyming words. Identify sounds in words. Identify the number of phonemes in a word.	blend sounds to make the word. Find images of rhyming words. Sound out and select letters to make words. Identify the number of sounds in a word.	**Worksheet 4** Check
Read: *Book*	Read aloud book.	listen, follow the reading and read along.	**Reading Eggs Story book** The map

Related Reading Eggs Activities, Interactives, Songs and Books

Reading Eggs Playroom

Book Shelf Song Books:

Little Peter Rabbit

Play Mat:

Words with blocks

Music Café

Little Words As and Has

Reading Eggs Puzzle Park

More than one

Both ways

Read it

Reading Eggs Posters

Reading Eggs Library Books

My Program Books

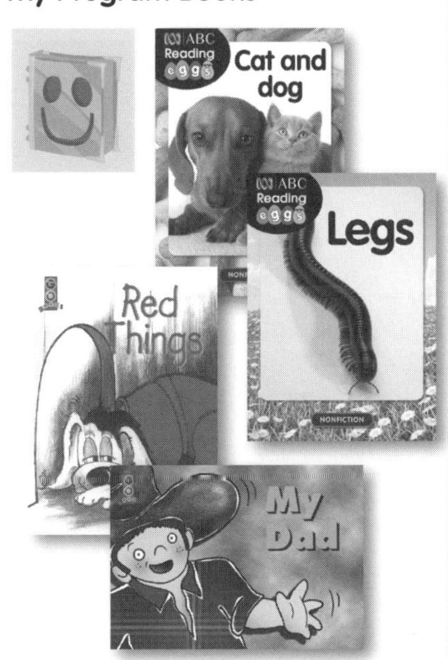

Alphabet Flashcards

Game 5 – From A to Z to revise all known letters.

Teacher Toolkit

Targeting Handwriting Interactively

Spelling Activities

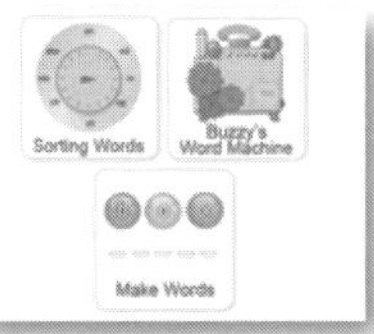

Reading Eggs Apps

Eggy Sight words

Critter Card

Fast as

Sight words

Lesson 35 · Worksheet 1

Name

1 Trace the words.

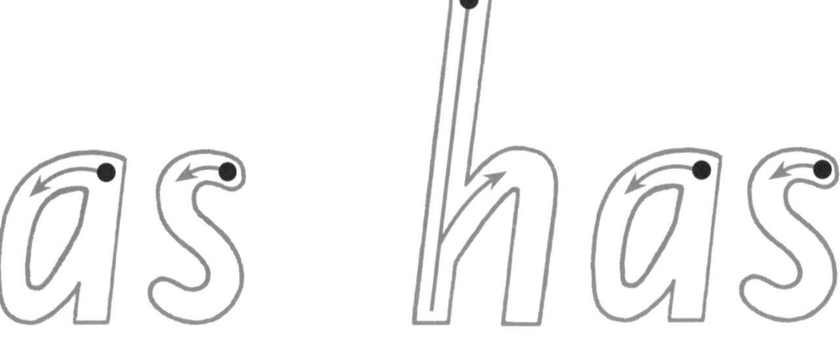

2 Colour **as** = blue **has** = yellow.

3 Guess the word by its shape. Write each word in the boxes.

Name

Read

Lesson 35 · Worksheet 2

Draw:

a fan on the cat.

a tap on the can.

a man on the map.

a rat on the mat.

Word families

Lesson 35 · Worksheet 3

Name

am, ap, at, an

1 Match the words to their pictures.

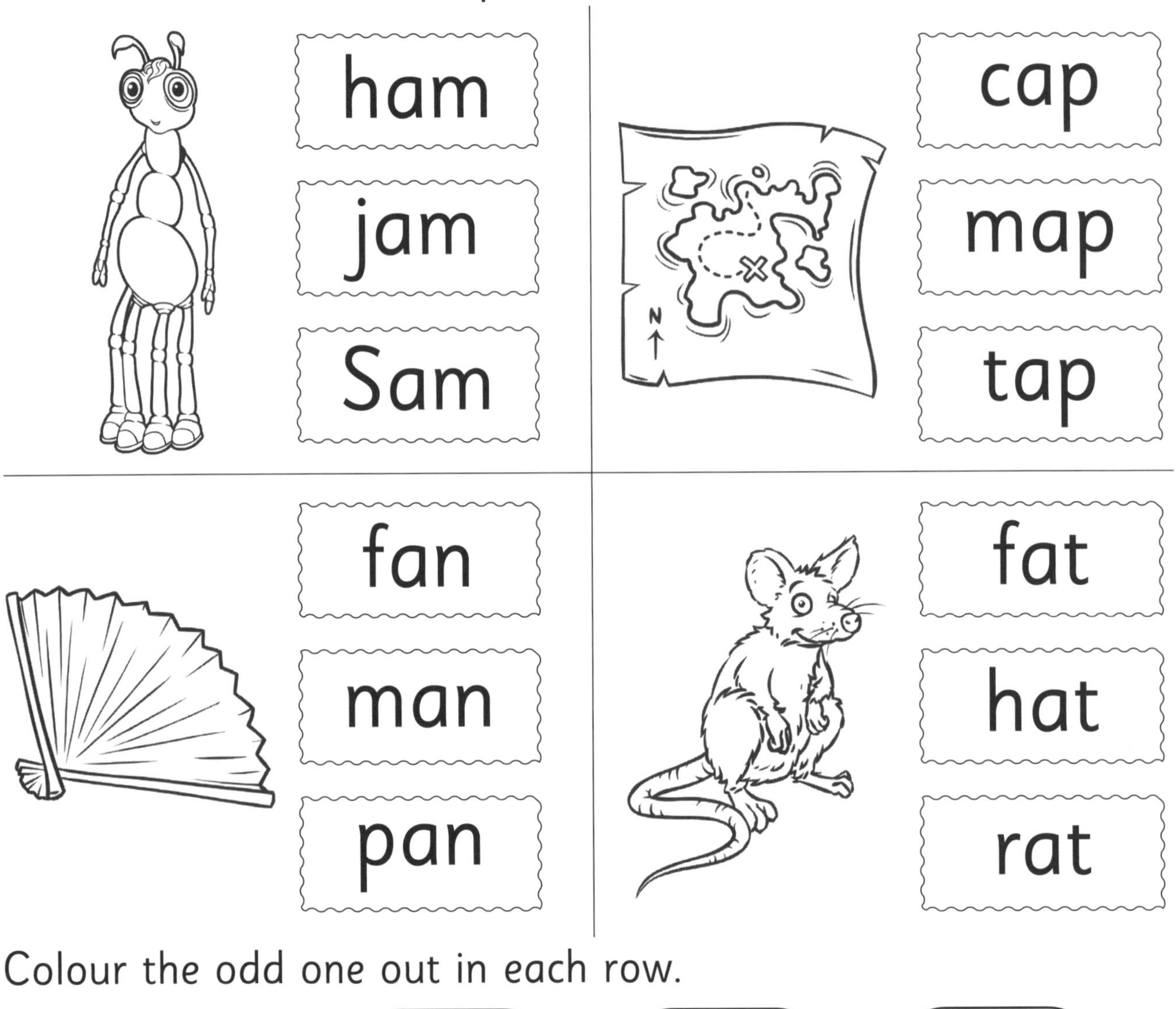

2 Colour the odd one out in each row.

fan	man	ran	cat
cap	tap	ham	map
pan	ham	Sam	jam
cat	can	mat	hat

Name

Check

Lesson 35 • Worksheet 4

1 Join the words that rhyme.

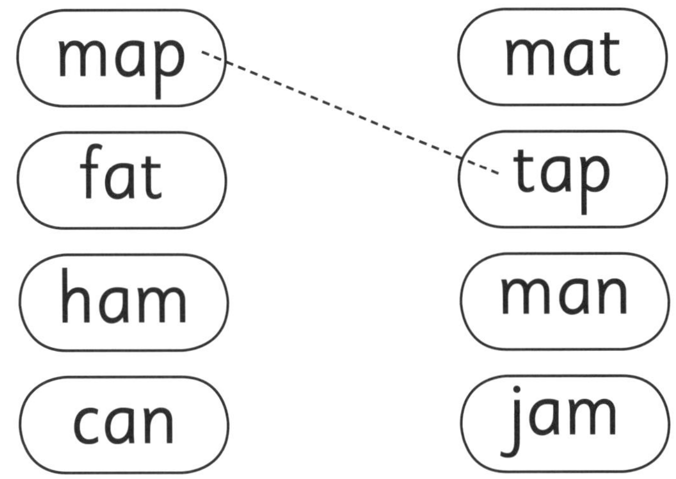

2 Colour the correct word. Cross out the wrong word.

She has as a map.

I am has as good as Sam.

3 Say the name of each picture. Colour its end sound.

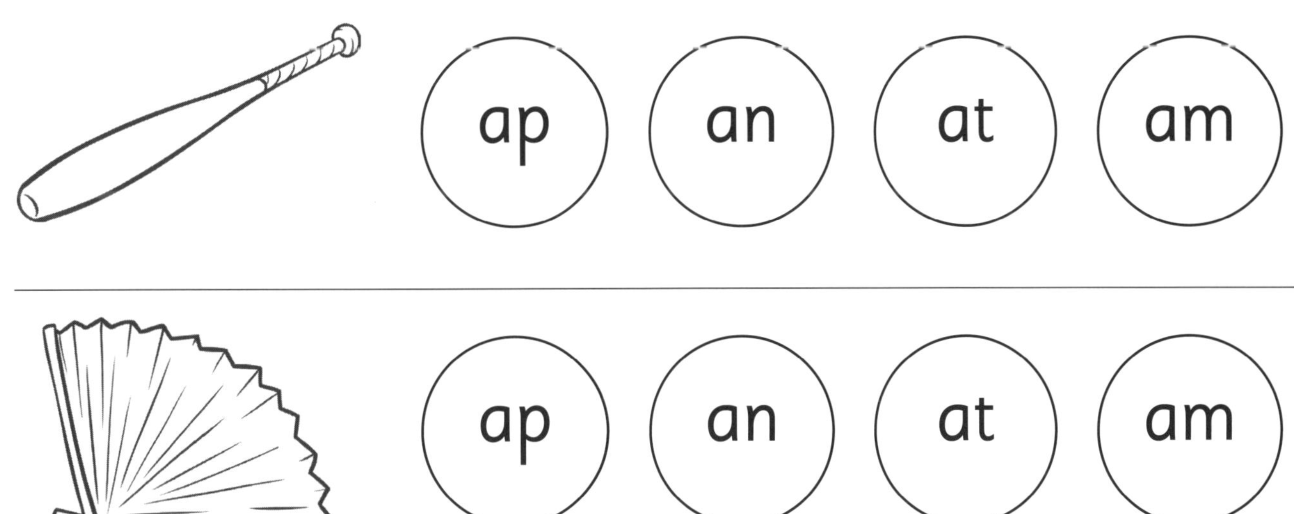

Lesson 36 the letter y

Learning objectives

Children will:

- identify the sound y.
- identify words that contain y.
- recognise and write y and Y.

Australian Curriculum Content Descriptions

Sound and letter knowledge

ACELA1439 listen to the sounds a student hears in the word, and write letters to represent those sounds; identify and manipulate sounds (phonemes) in spoken words

ACELA1440 identify familiar and recurring letters and the use of upper and lower case in written texts

Creating texts

ACELY1653 follow clear demonstrations of how to construct each letter, learn to construct lower case letters

Expressing and developing ideas

ACELA1758 recognise the most common sound made by each letter of the alphabet, including consonants and short vowel sounds; know that spoken words are written down by listening to the sounds heard in the word and then writing letters to represent those sounds

Sight words

has, can, is, she, he, had

Vocabulary words

yellow, yuck, yoyo, yell, year, yawn, yacht, yoghurt

ESL/ELL

Students who come from a Spanish or Tagalog language background may pronounce y with a /j/ sound as in joy or genre. Cambodian and Vietnamese students may say it like ny in canyon. Give these students lots of practise saying y words.

Extra assistance

A fun way to practise a sound repetitively is with tongue twisters. You should say it first, then ask the student to repeat it after you. Break the sentence into sections of 3 to 5 words if that is easier to start with.

The yucky yack yawned on a yellow yacht.
You yell at the yawning yabby in your yoghurt.

Classroom activities

Decorate the letters

Provide the students with a piece of paper that has many different forms of letter y on it – some dotted, some in bubble writing, some solid letters, a couple of capitals. The students:

- trace over the dotted letters with different coloured pencils, textas or crayons.
- glue collage materials such as paper bits, leaves or wool to the solid letters.
- colour in the bubble letters with dots, stripes or shapes.

Reading Eggs Lesson sequence	**TEACH Content and skills**	**PRACTISE Children will:**	**APPLY**
Hear: *Animated Lesson*	Introduce the sound /y/ through words and the song *Yes You Can*.	identify and read /y/ sound in isolation and in words.	**Worksheet 1** Phonemic awareness
Write: *Dot-to-Dot*	Reinforce correct letter formation of lower case y.	write the letter y.	**Worksheet 2** Handwriting
Find: *Letter Grid, Mark Your Letter, Trains, Golden Goose, Jumping Astronauts*	Recognise y in upper and lower case. Recognise a given word.	locate lower case y and capital Y. Find the given word in a group.	**Worksheet 3** Initial and end sounds
Vocabulary: *Letter Book, Tiles, Label It*	Build vocabulary skills: Recognise key vocabulary. Blend and recognise words.	match pictures to words. Blend sounds to make the word.	**Worksheet 4** Check
Read: *Book*	Read aloud book.	listen, follow the reading and read along.	**Reading Eggs Alphabet book** y

Classroom activities

Bingo!

Give students a laminated board with 10 squares on it. Ask them to write a letter in each square from the list y, k, l, g (use whiteboard markers). Hold up pictures of items starting with those letters and say the name of the item in the picture. Students put a cross on that initial letter on their board. First one to 10 calls out 'bingo' and wins!

Related Reading Eggs Activities, Interactives, Songs and Books

Reading Eggs Playroom

Alphabet Activities

Book Shelf Song Books:

Alphabet Song,

The Grand Old Duke of York

Music Café

Yes You Can

Reading Eggs Puzzle Park

Alphabet match

Both ways

Read it

Reading Eggs Posters

Reading Eggs Library Books

My Program Books

Alphabet Flashcards

Game 4 – Make the critters with known letters.

Teacher Toolkit

Targeting Handwriting Interactively

Alphabet Activities

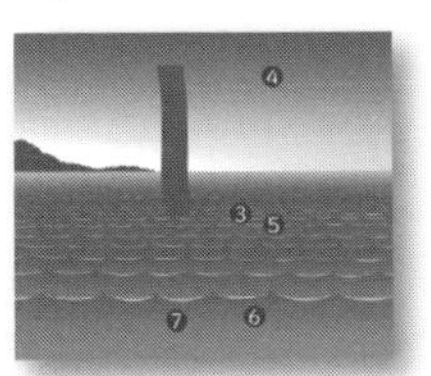

Reading Eggs Apps

Eggy Alphabet

Critter Card

Yetiyo

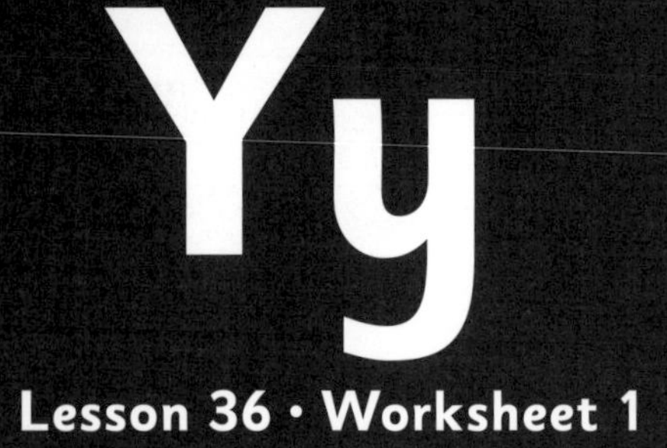

Name

Phonemic awareness

1 Match each letter to a picture.

2 Join **y** things to Yetiyo.

3 Colour the **y** yoyos.

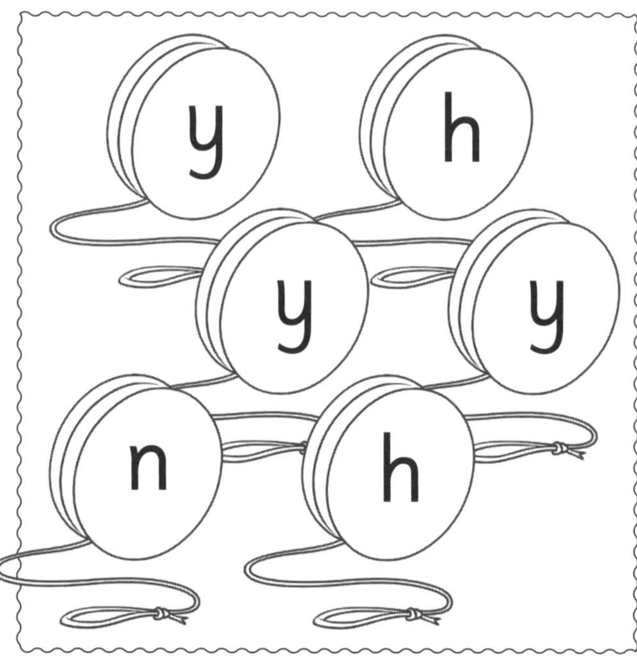

Name

Handwriting

Yy

Lesson 36 • Worksheet 2

1 Complete and colour Baby Face's bibs.

Yetiyo likes yoyos.

2 Trace.

Circle your best letter.

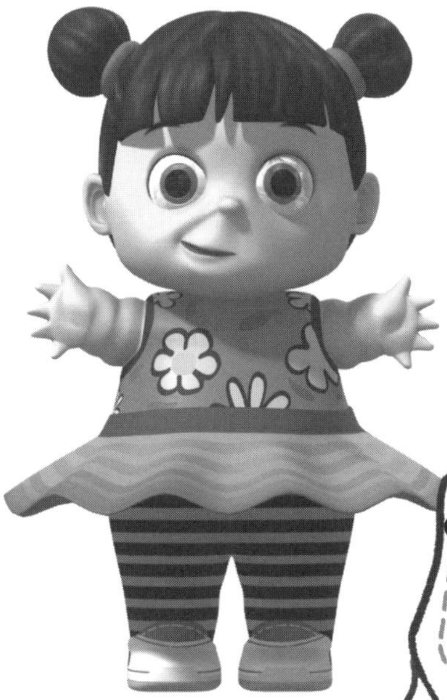

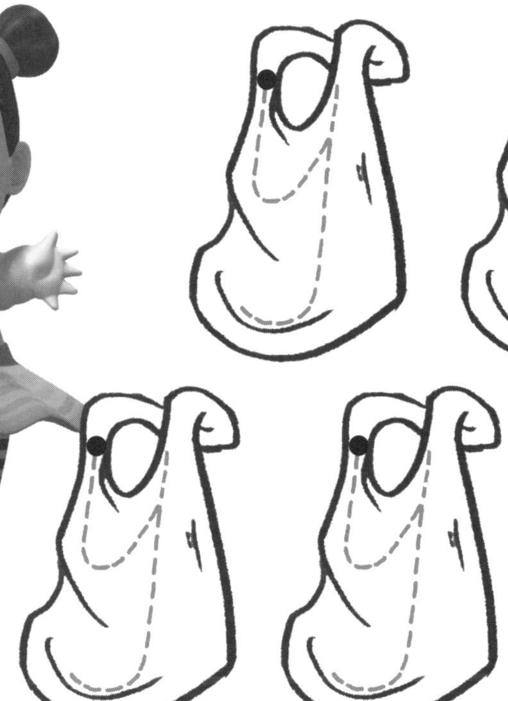

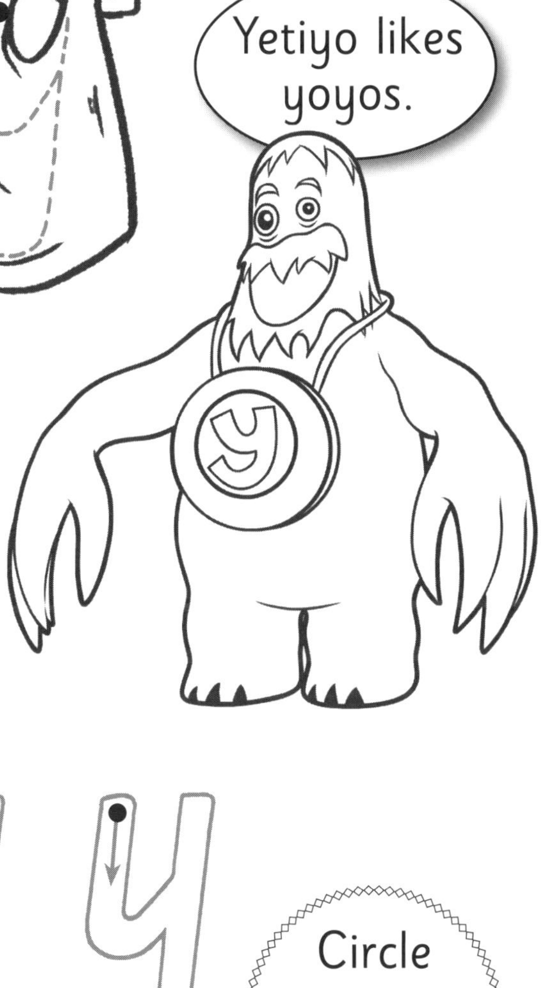

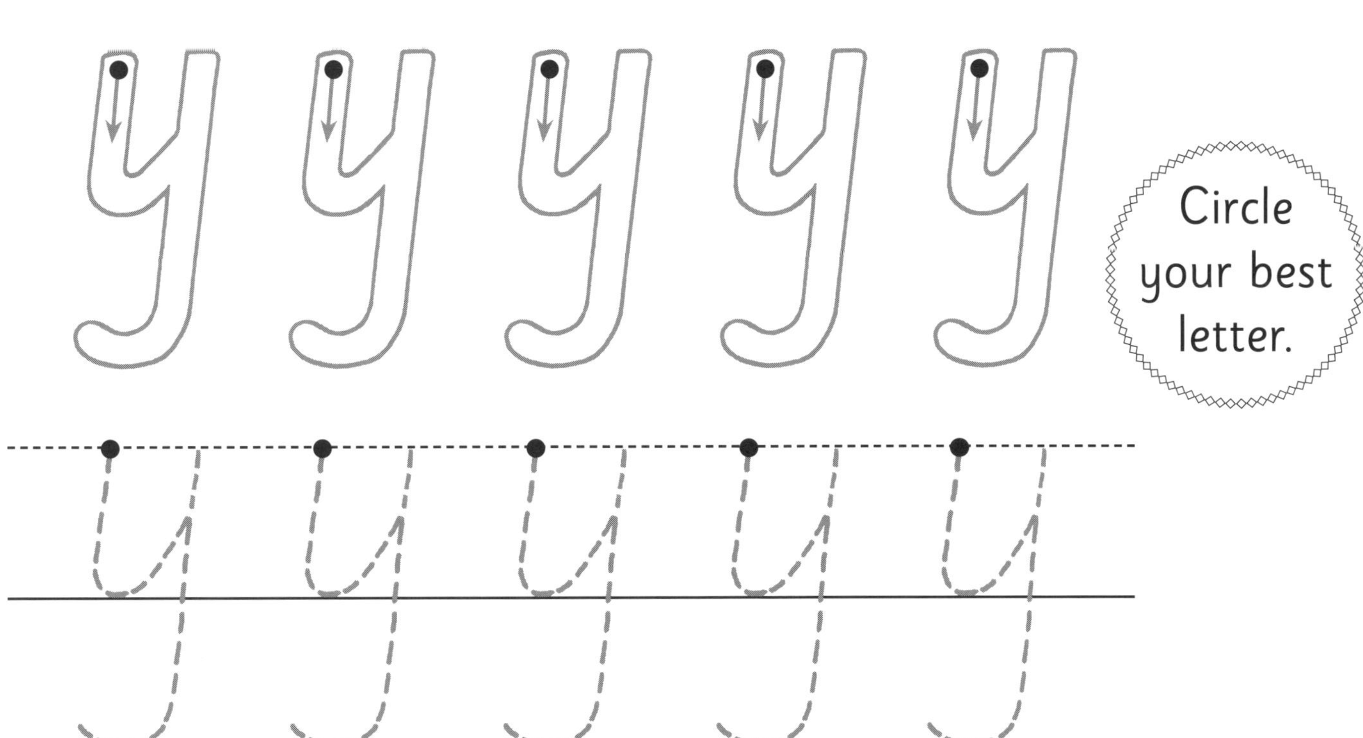

Yy

Lesson 36 • Worksheet 3

Name

Initial and end sounds

1 Add **y** to the beginning and then say the word.

2 Add **y** to the end and then say the word.

Name

Check

Yy

Lesson 36 • Worksheet 4

1 Trace and write.

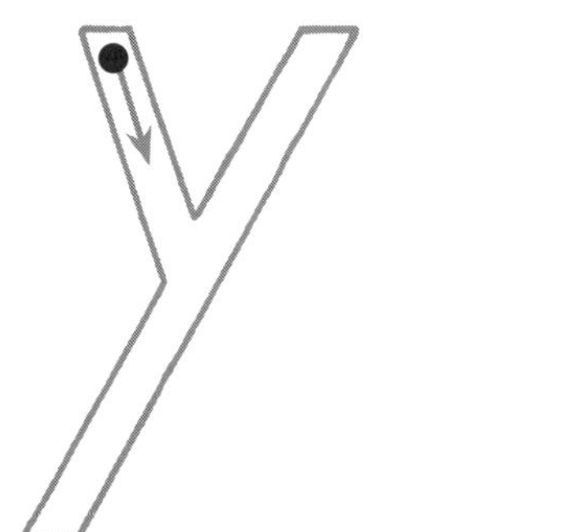

2 Circle every **Y**.

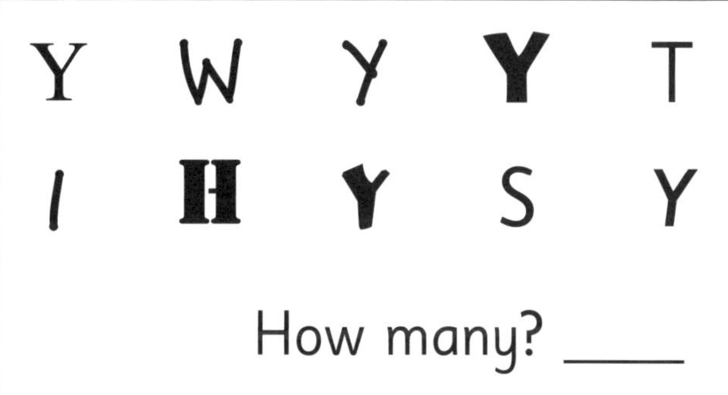

How many? ____

Circle every **y**.

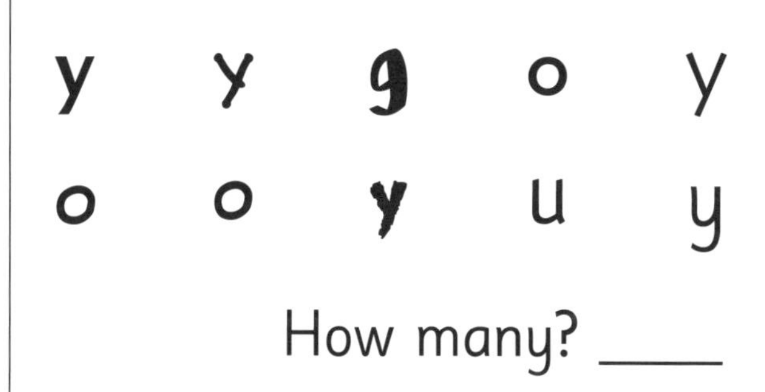

How many? ____

3 Say the name of each picture. Circle the beginning sound.

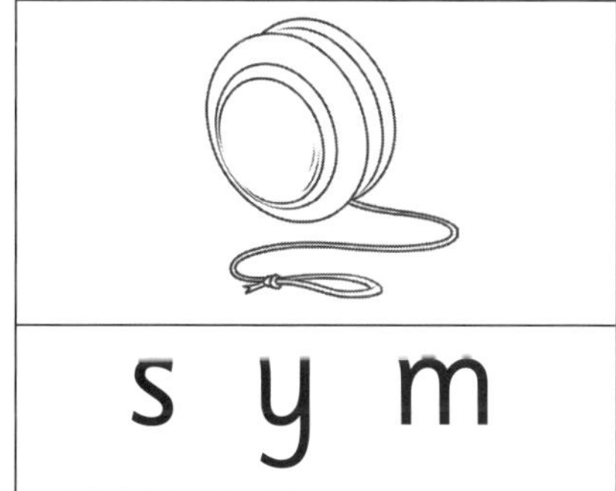

s y m

p b g

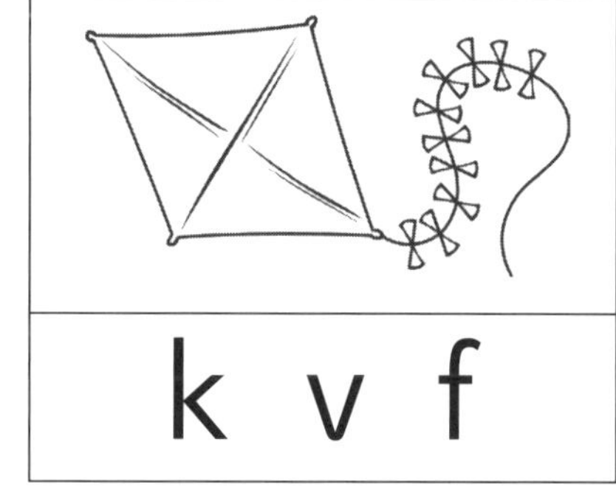

k v f

4 Say the name of each picture. Circle the end sound.

g t r

c z p

j n h

Lesson 37 the words **yes** and **you**

Learning objectives

Children will:

- identify the words yes and you.
- read and write the words yes and you.

Australian Curriculum Content Descriptions

Sound and letter knowledge

ACELA1439 listen to the sounds a student hears in the word, and write letters to represent those sounds; identify rhyme and syllables in spoken words; identify and manipulate sounds (phonemes) in spoken words; identify onset and rime in one-syllable spoken words

ACELA1440 identify familiar and recurring letters and the use of upper and lower case in written texts

Expressing and developing ideas

ACELA1435 learn that word order in sentences is important for meaning

ACELA1758 write consonant-vowel-consonant words by writing letters to represent the sounds in the spoken words; know that spoken words are written down by listening to the sounds heard in the word and then writing letters to represent those sounds

Sight words

yes, you, has, it, as, a, and, I, am, an, in, he, see, the, can

Word families

Dan, man, van, can, ant, hat, cat, bat, fat, rat, map, bad, see, bee

ESL/ELL

In English the second person pronoun 'you' covers both genders as well as singular and plural. Be aware that in other languages the second person may have multiple pronouns, including formal and informal forms, and students may want to narrow down the usage for 'you' or ask what the other second person pronouns are. Give them lots of examples using 'you' in a variety of contexts.

Extra assistance

Learning sight words is invaluable for all students, as these are words that occur frequently in all types of texts. They are often tricky words to sound out as they may not stick to the rules. Knowing sight words 'on sight' makes fluent reading easier.

Classroom activities

Make your own questions

Put the question *Can you see the sky?* on the board. Discuss when the answer is yes and when it is no. Ask students to write their own questions. Have them read and discuss the questions and answers in groups. Try to write a question as a class where the answer is always yes.

Reading Eggs Lesson sequence	**TEACH Content and skills**	**PRACTISE Children will:**	**APPLY**
Hear: *Animated Lesson*	Introduce the words yes and you.	identify and read the words yes and you in isolation and in a group.	**Worksheet 1** Sight words
Write: *Pick Up Bricks*	Recognise correct word order for a sentence.	put the words in the correct order to make a sentence.	**Worksheet 2** Read
Find: *Wheel of Words, Driving Trucks, Letter Lights*	Recognise key vocabulary. Identify a given word. Recognise letters in upper and lower case.	match pictures to words. Find the given word in a group. Locate lower case and capital letters.	**Worksheet 3** Word families
Vocabulary: *Blend a Word, Break it Up, Rhyming Squares, Missing Sound*	Build vocabulary skills: Blend and recognise words. Identify the number of phonemes in a word. Recognise rhyming words. Identify the correct onset letter to complete the word.	blend sounds to read words. Identify the number of sounds in a word. Find images of rhyming words. Choose the correct initial letter to make the word.	**Worksheet 4** Check
Read: *Book*	Read aloud book.	listen, follow the reading and read along.	**Reading Eggs Story book** Dan

Classroom activities

Bingo!

Give students a laminated board with 10 squares on it. Ask them to write a sight word in each square from the list yes, you, has, as, he and she (use whiteboard markers). Put flashcards for each word in a bag. Pull one out and say the word, then put it back in. Students put a cross on that word on their board. First one to 10 calls out 'bingo' and wins!

Related Reading Eggs Activities, Interactives, Songs and Books

Reading Eggs Playroom

Book Shelf Song

Books:

Baa Baa Black Sheep, Twinkle Twinkle Little Star

My Wall:

Make You

Music Café

Yes You Can!

Reading Eggs Puzzle Park

Both ways

Read it

Reading Eggs Posters

Reading Eggs Library Books

My Program Books

Alphabet Flashcards

Game 7 – Making known sight words.

Teacher Toolkit

Targeting Handwriting Interactively

Spelling Activities

Reading Eggs Apps

Eggy Sight words

Critter Card

Yessy

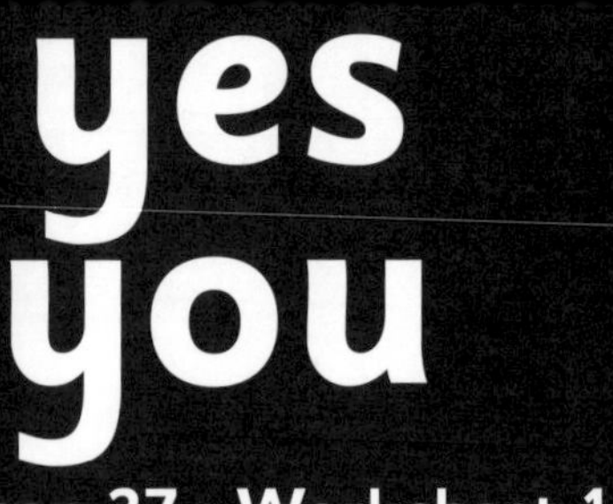

Lesson 37 • Worksheet 1

Name

Sight words

1 Trace the words.

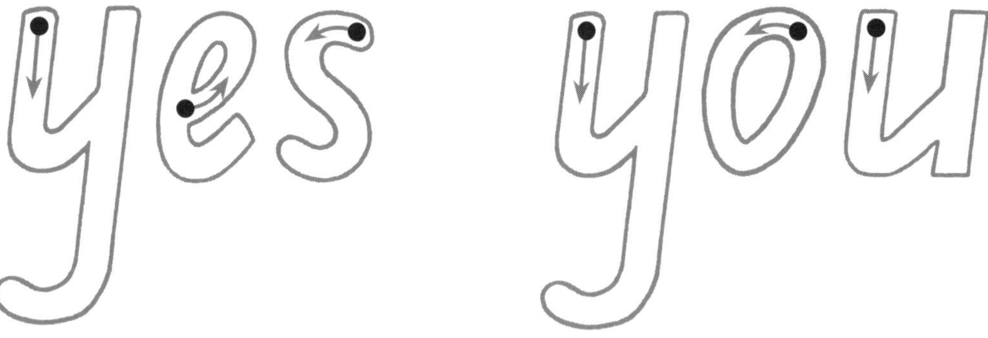

2 Complete the words **yes** and **you**.

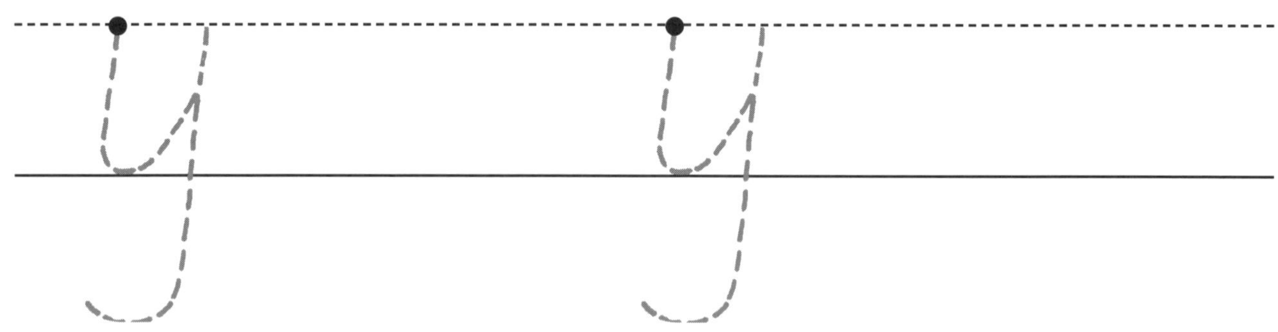

3 Colour **you** = red **yes** = yellow.

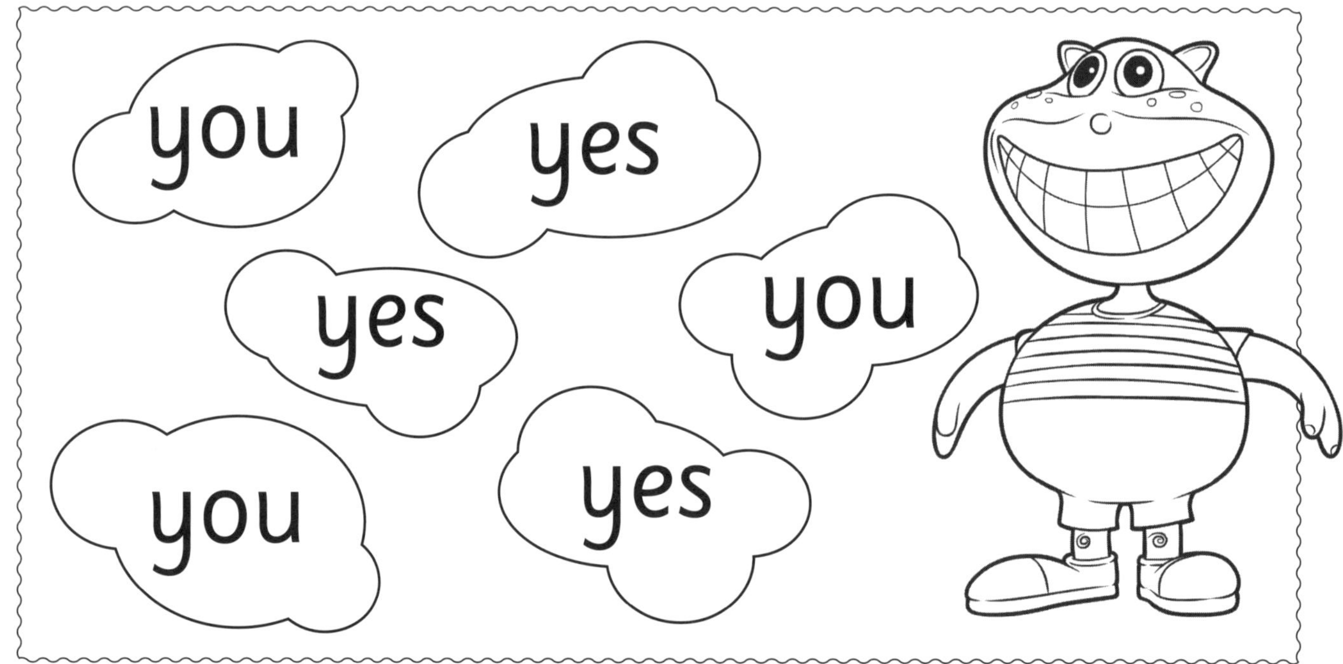

Name

Read

yes you

Lesson 37 • Worksheet 2

Finish each sentence with a word from the box. Read each sentence.

cat map van

Dan has a

______________________.

Dan has a

______________________.

Dan has a

______________________.

yes
you

Lesson 37 · Worksheet 3

Name

Word families

1 Colour the pairs that rhyme.

cat	rat

Dan	van

ant	bee

bat	hat

3 Use the wheels to make words. Write the words.

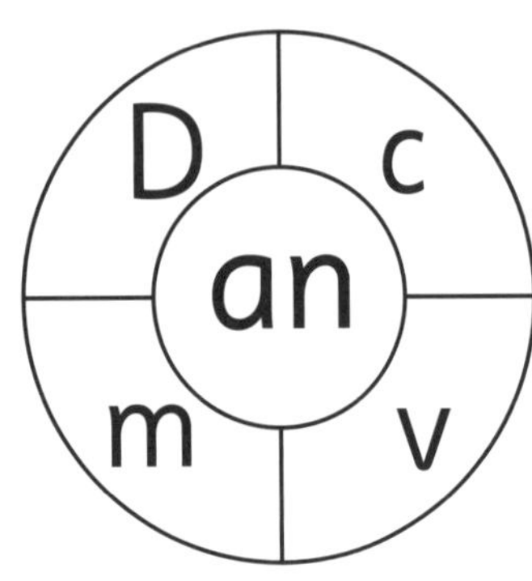

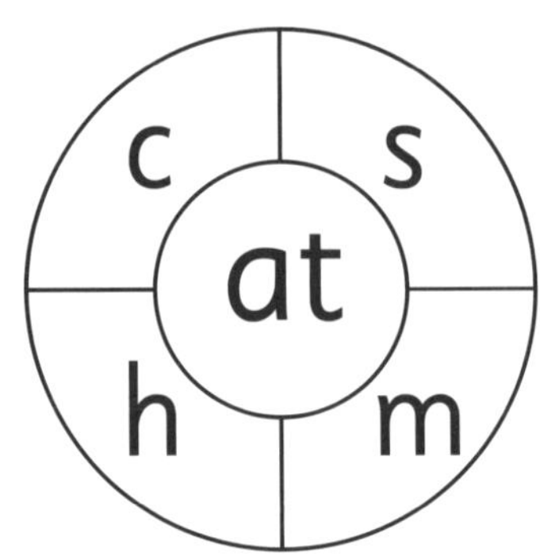

______________________ ______________________

______________________ ______________________

______________________ ______________________

______________________ ______________________

Name

Check

yes you

Lesson 37 · Worksheet 4

1 Write each word in the correct boxes.

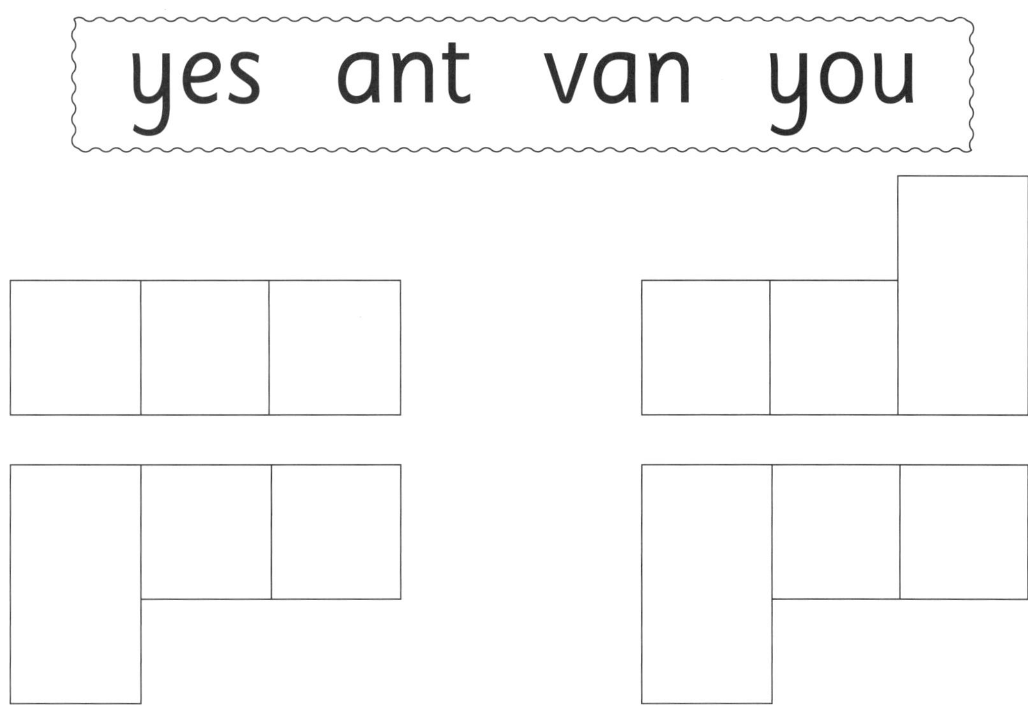

2 Join the jigsaw pieces. Write the word.

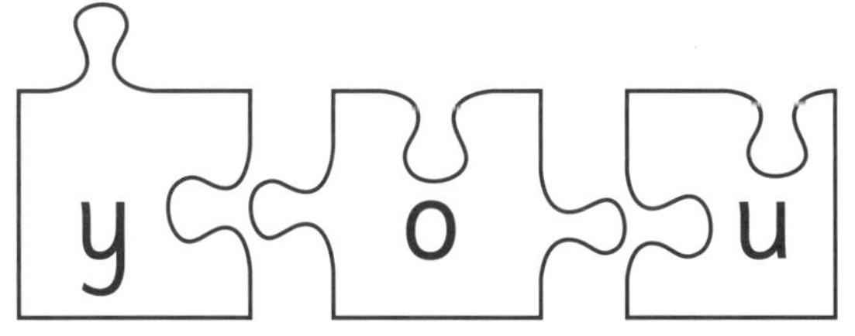

____

3 Complete the sentence.

Dan has an

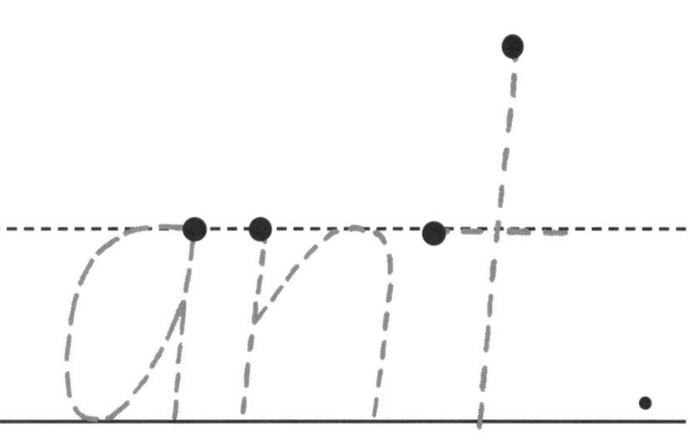

Lesson 38 the letter **x**

Learning objectives

Children will:

- identify the sound x.
- identify words that contain x.
- recognise and write x and X.

Australian Curriculum Content Descriptions

Sound and letter knowledge

ACELA1439 listen to the sounds a student hears in the word, and write letters to represent those sounds; identify and manipulate sounds (phonemes) in spoken words

ACELA1440 identify familiar and recurring letters and the use of upper and lower case in written texts

Creating texts

ACELY1653 follow clear demonstrations of how to construct each letter, learn to construct lower case letters

Expressing and developing ideas

ACELA1758 recognise the most common sound made by each letter of the alphabet, including consonants and short vowel sounds; know that spoken words are written down by listening to the sounds heard in the word and then writing letters to represent those sounds

Sight words

yes, see

Word families

box, fox, wax, mix, six, taxi, x-ray, mixer, exit

ESL/ELL

Students with a Spanish language background may have trouble pronouncing the x sound correctly – /ks/. Give them opportunities to practise with repetition and choral response activities.

Extra assistance

Students learning a second language need to practise. Choral responses, where groups of students recite the same word, phrase, sentence or sound, are an effective tool to build familiarity with new sounds and vocabulary. Have the students repeat /x/ words after you to practise pronunciation.

Classroom activities

Make the Letter

Use a variety of materials such as sticks, pencils, rulers, MAB blocks or the students' own bodies to create the letter x. Make a nature collage of the letter x with twigs, leaves and grass.

Say it Right!

Fill a bag with objects and pictures of things. Pull an item out of the bag and say it incorrectly, using the wrong end sound, eg bomb for a box. The students need to correct you by calling out the right word.

Reading Eggs **Lesson sequence**	**TEACH** **Content and skills**	**PRACTISE** **Children will:**	**APPLY**
Hear: *Animated Lesson*	Introduce the letter x.	identify x in isolation and in a group.	**Worksheet 1** Phonemic awareness
Write: *Dot-to-Dot*	Reinforce correct letter formation of lower case x.	write the letter x.	**Worksheet 2** Handwriting
Find: *Letter Grid, Island Hop, Make Your Mark, Time for 20*	Recognise x in upper and lower case. Recognise a given word.	locate lower case x and capital X. Find the given word in a group.	**Worksheet 3** Middle and end sounds
Vocabulary: *Blend a Word, Tiles, Label It, Break it Up*	Build vocabulary skills: Blend and recognise words. Recognise key vocabulary. Identify the number of phonemes in a word.	blend sounds to read and make words. Match pictures to words. Identify the number of sounds in a word.	**Worksheet 4** Check
Read: *Book*	Read aloud book.	listen, follow the reading and read along.	**Reading Eggs Alphabet book** x

Related Reading Eggs Activities, Interactives, Songs and Books

Reading Eggs Playroom

Alphabet Activities
Book Shelf Song
Books:
Alphabet Song,
1-2-3-4-5,
1-2 Buckle My Shoe

Music Café

Sam's Alphabet Song

Reading Eggs Puzzle Park

Alphabet match
Both ways
Read it

Reading Eggs Posters

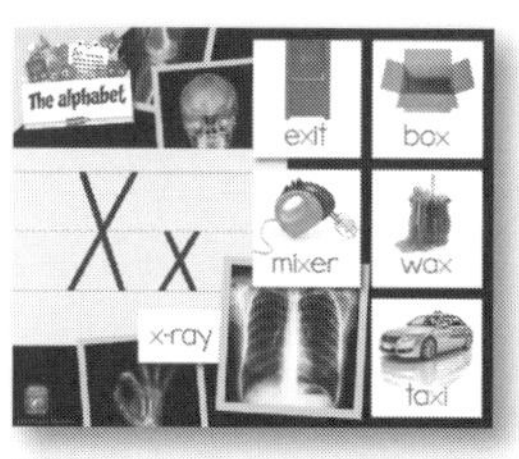

Reading Eggs Library Books

My Program Books

Alphabet Flashcards

Game 2 – Sound puzzles with x.

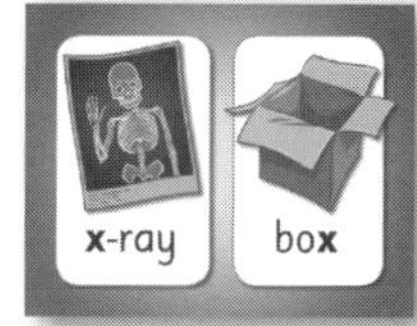

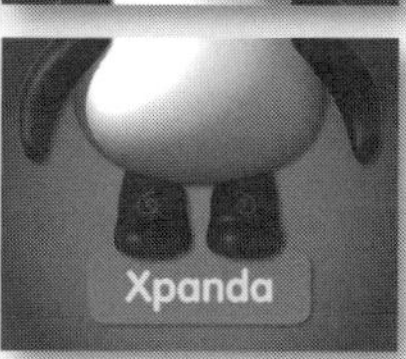

Teacher Toolkit

Targeting Handwriting Interactively

Alphabet Activities

Reading Eggs Apps

Eggy Alphabet

Critter Card

Xpanda

Lesson 38 • Worksheet 1

Name

Phonemic awareness

Say hello to Xpanda!

1 Match each letter to a picture.

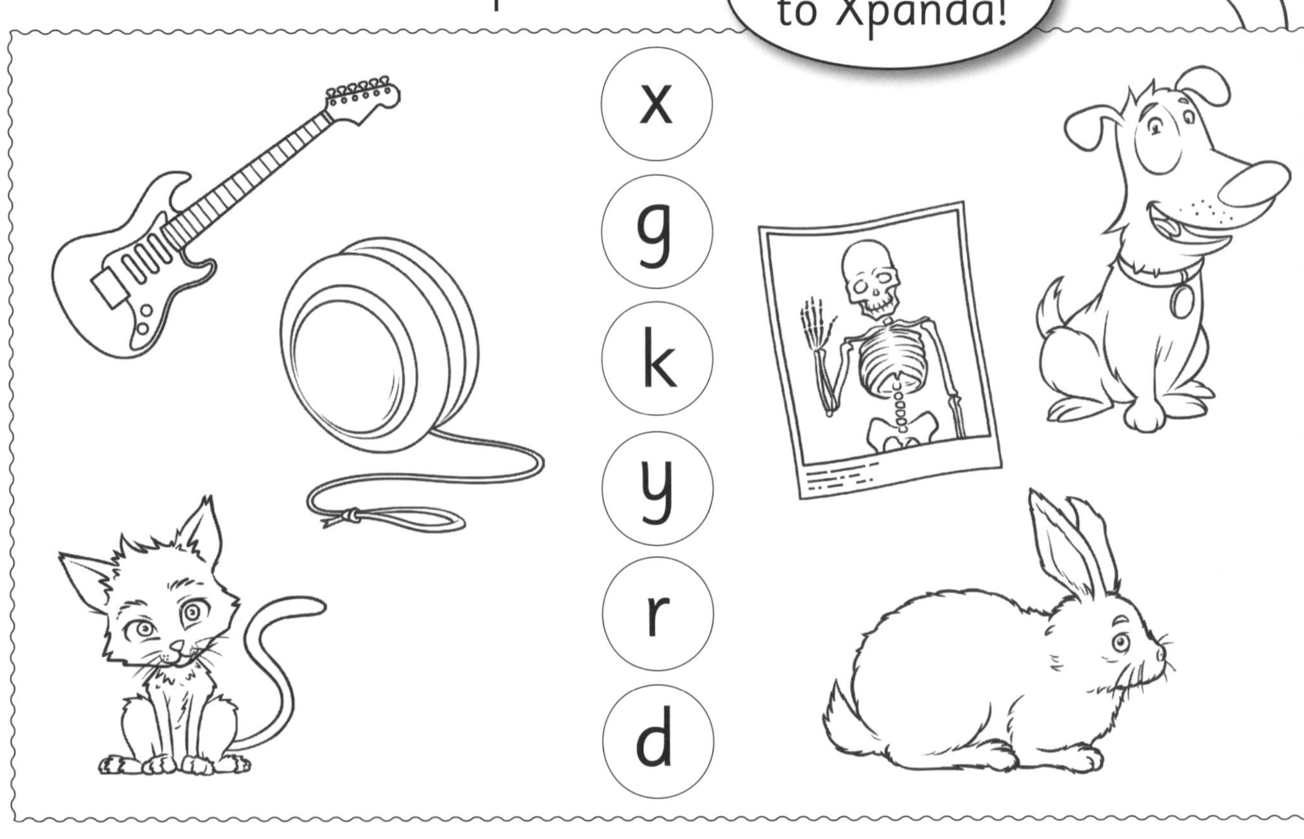

2 Which words end in **x**? Join to Xpanda.

3 Colour the **x** boxes.

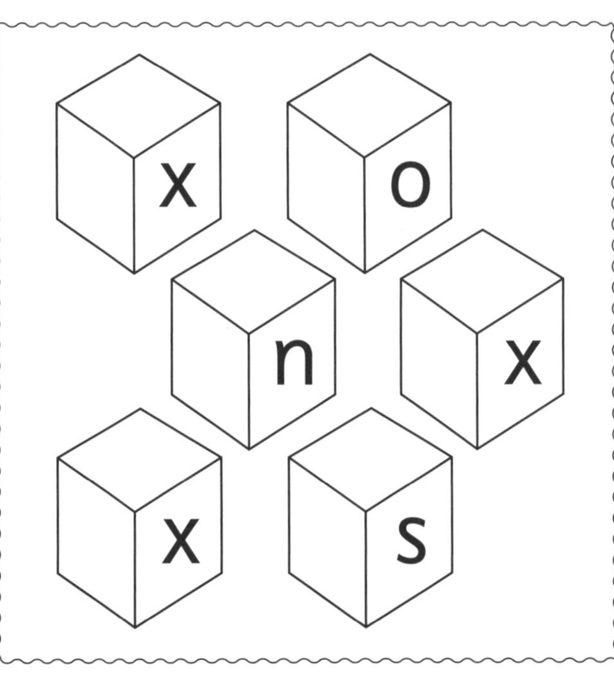

Name

Handwriting

Xx

Lesson 38 · Worksheet 2

1 Help Sixty six reach the finish line. Follow the track.

2 Slice the pizzas.

3 Trace and write.

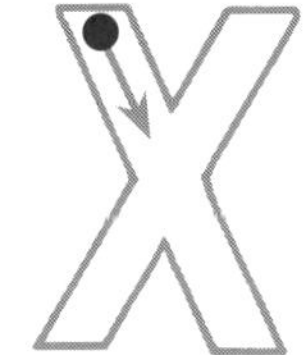
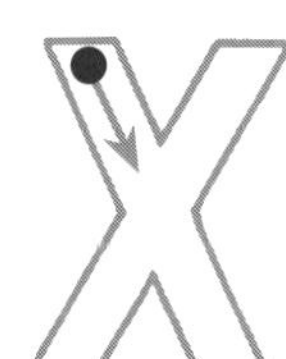
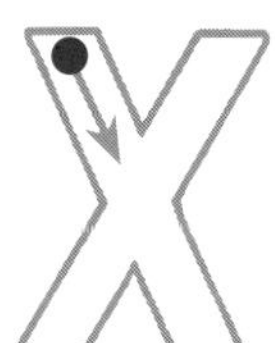
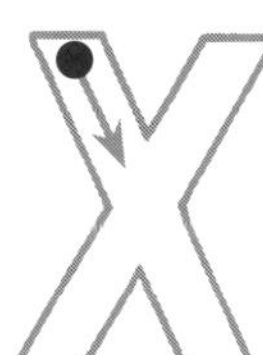
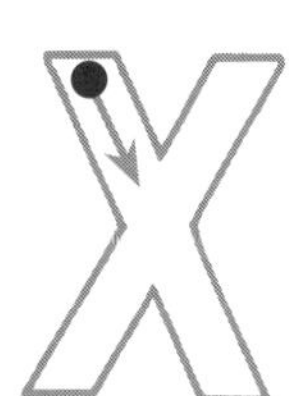

Circle your best letter.

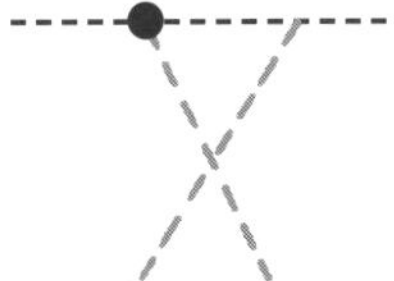
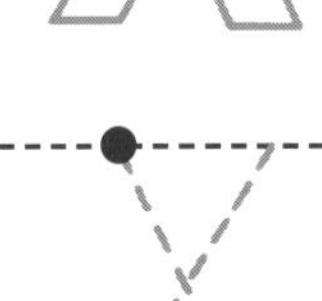
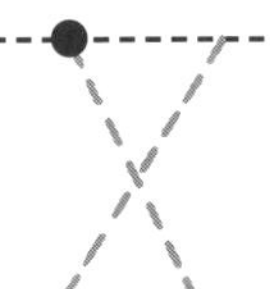
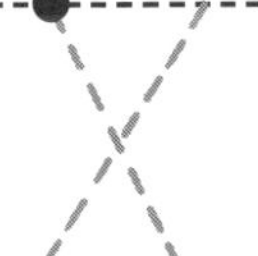
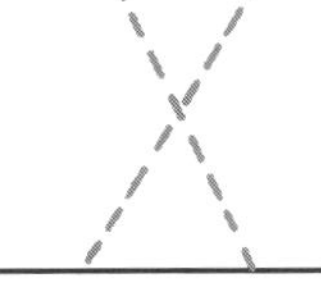

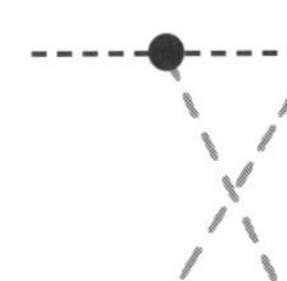
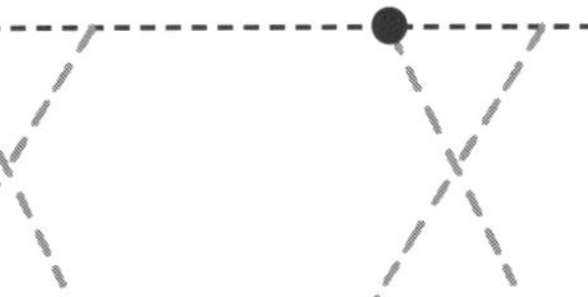
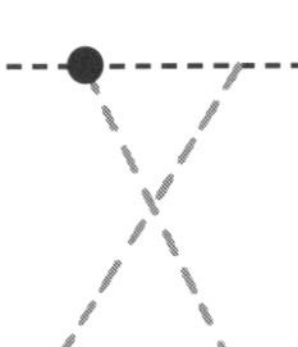
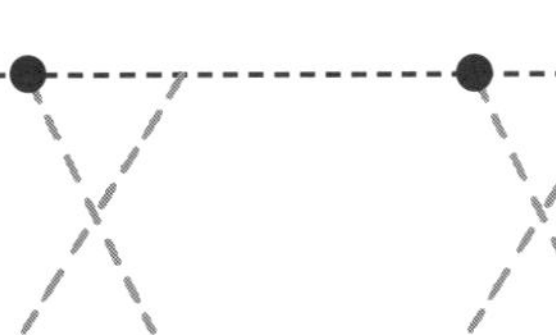
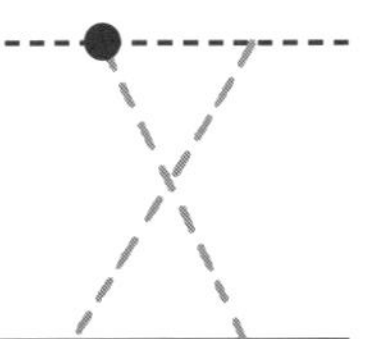

Xx

Lesson 38 • Worksheet 3

Name

Middle and end sounds

1 Finish each word with an **x**.

wa X	ta ____ i
mi ____ er	e ____ it
fo ____	bo ____

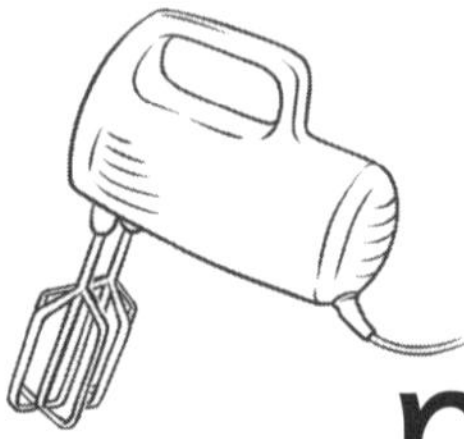

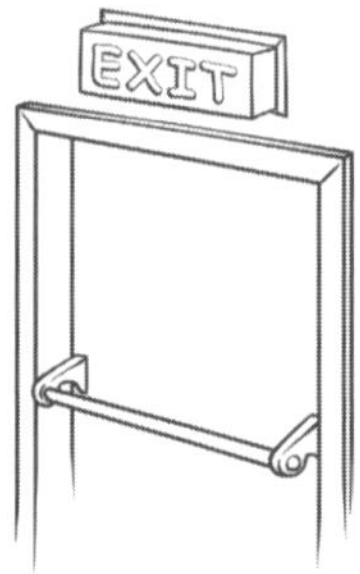

2 Put an **x** on every box.

Name

Check

1 Trace and write.

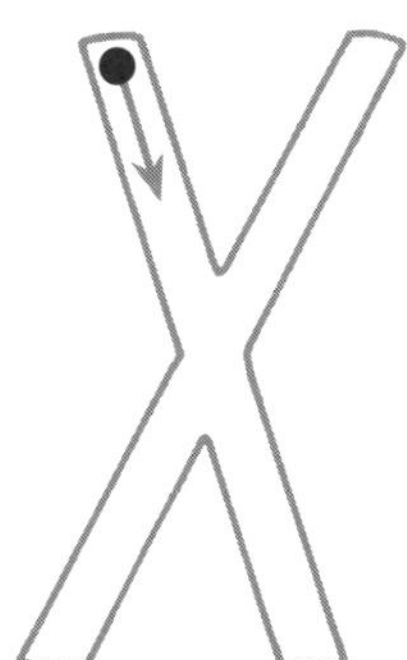

2 Circle every **X**.

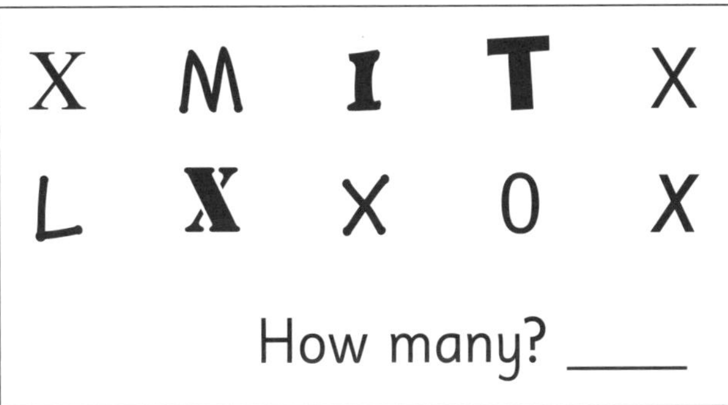

Circle every **x**.

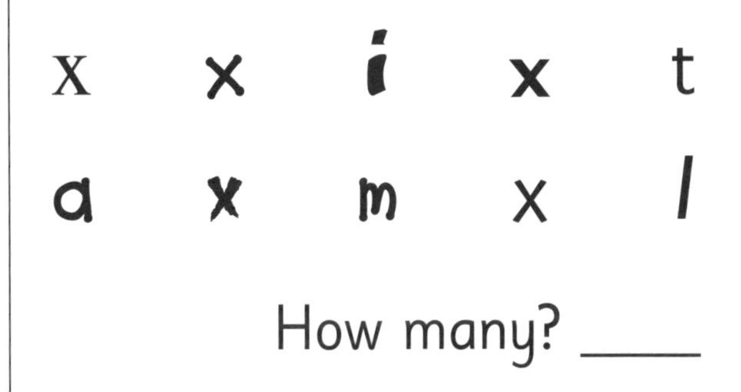

3 Add **x** and then say the word.

____-ray

si____

bo____

mi____

Lesson 39 the letter **w**

Learning objectives

Children will:

- identify the sound w.
- identify words that contain w.
- recognise and write w and W.

Australian Curriculum Content Descriptions

Sound and letter knowledge

ACELA1439 listen to the sounds a student hears in the word, and write letters to represent those sounds; identify rhyme and syllables in spoken words; identify and manipulate sounds (phonemes) in spoken words

ACELA1440 identify familiar and recurring letters and the use of upper and lower case in written texts

Creating texts

ACELY1653 follow clear demonstrations of how to construct each letter, learn to construct lower case letters

Expressing and developing ideas

ACELA1758 recognise the most common sound made by each letter of the alphabet, including consonants and short vowel sounds; write consonant-vowel-consonant words by writing letters to represent the sounds in the spoken words

Vocabulary words

wet, wing, web, whale, worm, water, windmill, wax, whistle, wand, woman

ESL/ELL

Many students who speak another language will confuse the sounds /w/ and /v/, as well as the graphemes w and v because w is uncommon in their home language. Give them lots of practise writing the letter, as well as identifying it in speech. Use pairs of words to differentiate: wet and vet, went and vent and so on.

Extra assistance

To help with pronunciation show students how to form the letters w and v. W is formed with lips rounded in a pout then relaxed. V is formed with top teeth resting on bottom lip then pulling away.

Classroom activities

Which Hat?

Place three hats on the floor with the labels w, v and f. Discuss the sounds. Have a pile of objects or pictures of objects that start with w, v and f. Each student chooses one and works out which hat it must go in. Discuss their choice with the class.

Flashcard Snap

Have two sets of cards for the letters of the alphabet. Shuffle and deal between two players. Keep cards face down. Players take turns to put a card from their pile onto a central pile, sounding out the letter they turn over. If the two cards on top are the same, the players shout SNAP! The first to do so takes the central pile. Play continues until one player runs out of cards.

Reading Eggs Lesson sequence	TEACH Content and skills	PRACTISE Children will:	APPLY
Hear: *Animated Lesson*	Introduce the sound /w/.	identify /w/ sound in isolation.	**Worksheet 1** Phonemic awareness
Write: *Dot-to-Dot*	Reinforce correct letter formation of lower case w.	write the letter w.	**Worksheet 2** Handwriting
Find: *Letter Grid, Mark Your Letter, Trains*	Recognise w in upper and lower case.	locate lower case w and capital W.	**Worksheet 3** Initial sounds
Vocabulary: *Blend a Word, Letter Book, Rhyming Squares, Label It, Rumble Jumble*	Build vocabulary skills: Blend and recognise words. Identify rhyming words. Unjumble letters for a given word.	blend sounds to read words. Match pictures to words. Find images of rhyming words. Write a word from jumbled letters.	**Worksheet 4** Check
Read: *Book*	Read aloud book.	listen, follow the reading and read along.	**Reading Eggs Alphabet book** w

Related Reading Eggs Activities, Interactives, Songs and Books

Reading Eggs Playroom

Alphabet Activities

Book Shelf Song Books:

Alphabet Song,

The Wheels on the Bus,

Incy Wincy Spider

Music Café

What you lookin' at?

Reading Eggs Puzzle Park

Alphabet match

Both ways

Read it

Reading Eggs Posters

Reading Eggs Library Books

My Program Books

Alphabet Flashcards

Game 3 – Sound hunt with w.

Teacher Toolkit

Targeting Handwriting Interactively

Alphabet Activities

Reading Eggs Apps

Eggy Alphabet

Critter Card

Wheely whale

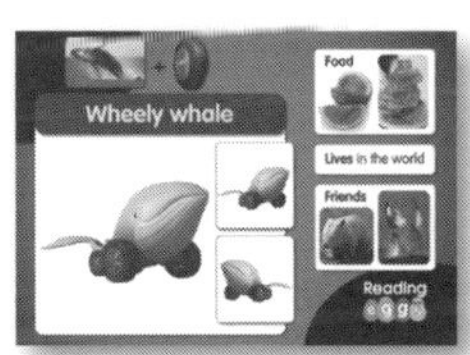

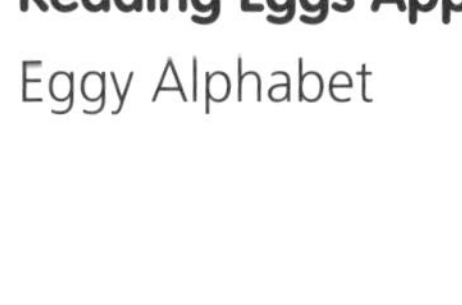

Lesson 39 • Worksheet 1

Name

Phonemic awareness

1 Match each letter to a picture.

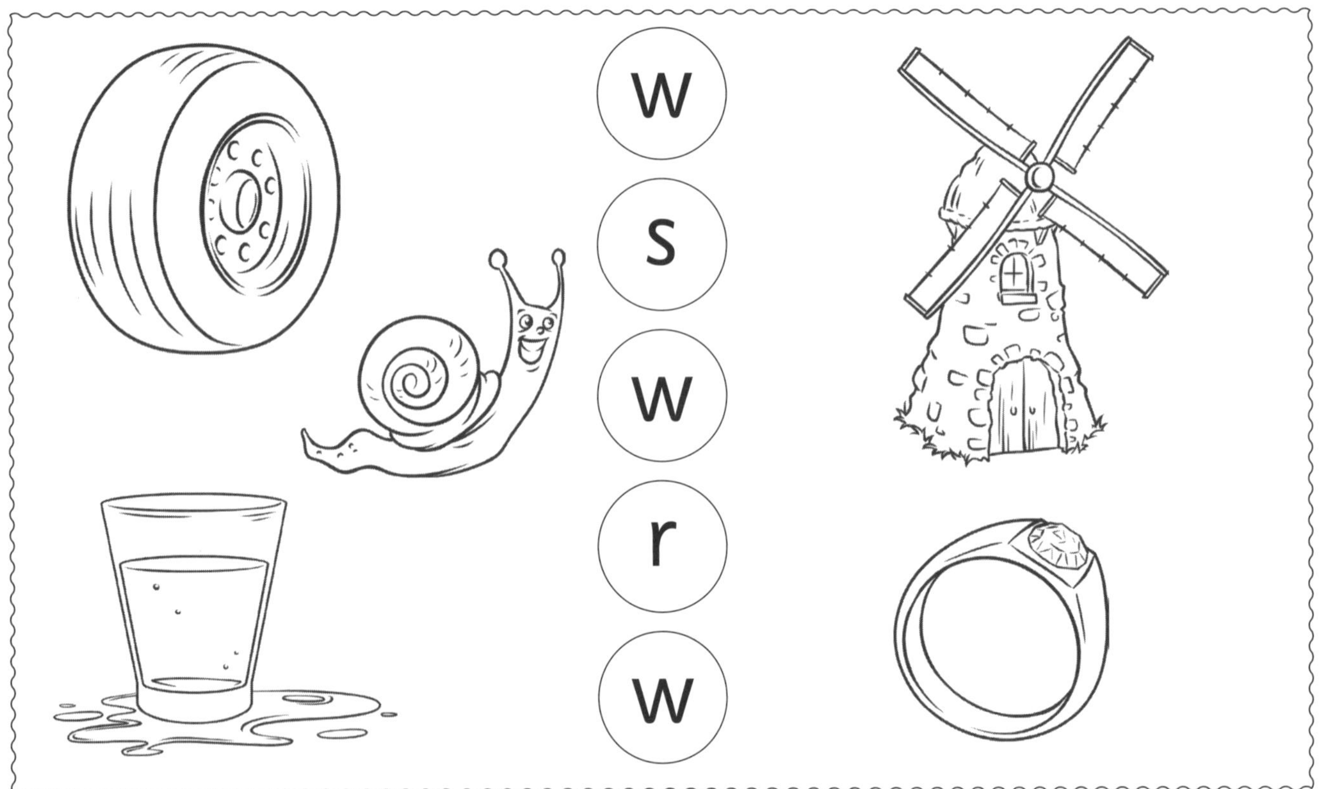

2 Join the **w** things to Wheely whale.

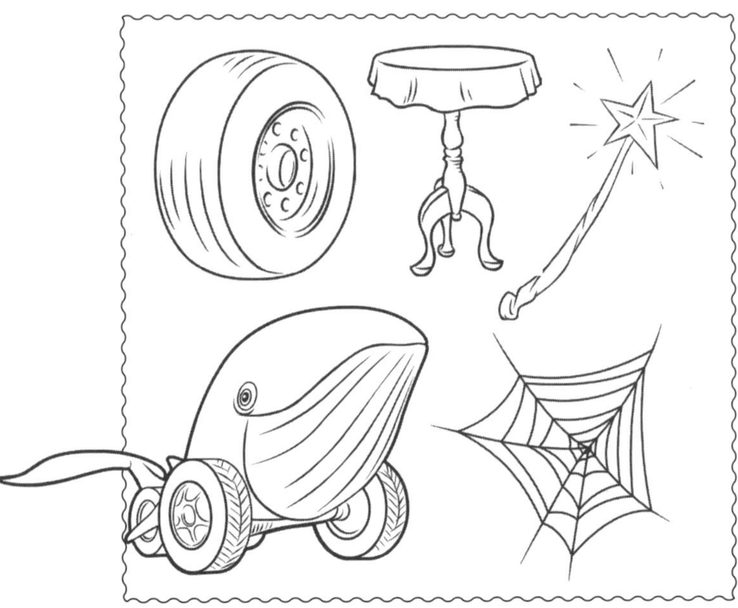

3 Colour the **w** whales.

Name

Handwriting

Ww

Lesson 39 · Worksheet 2

1 Draw waves for Wheely whale.

2 Trace.

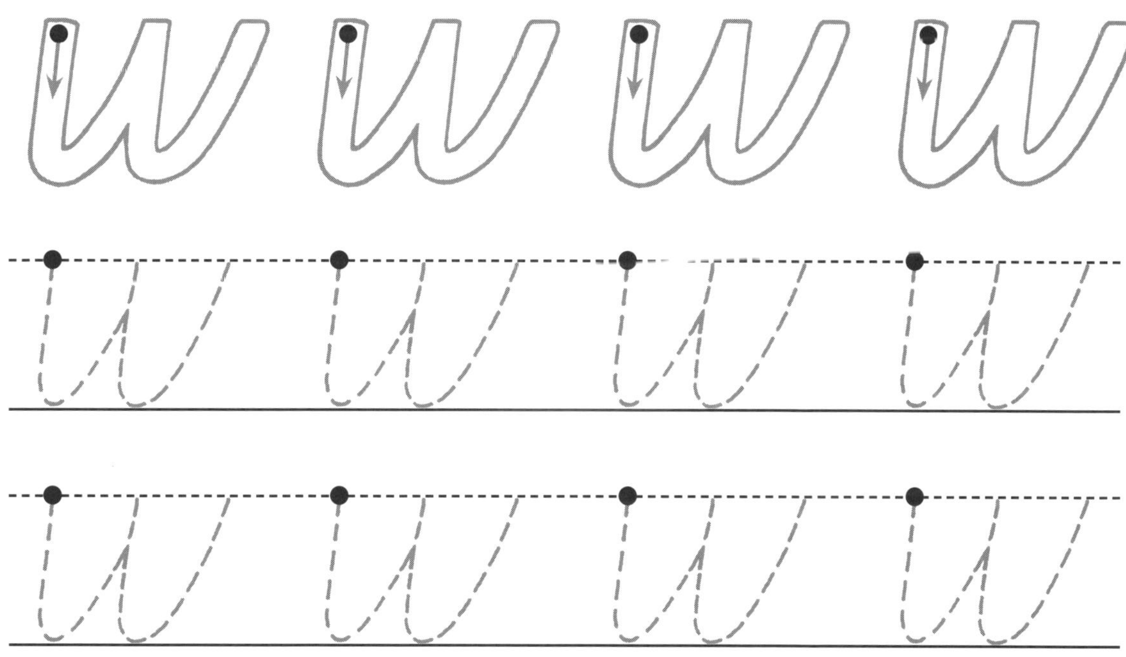

Circle your best letter.

Name ______________________

Initial sounds

1 Add **w** and then say the word.

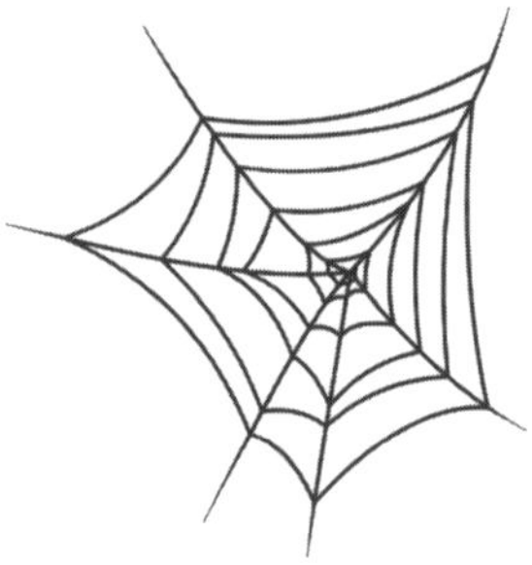

__w__eb	_____hale
_____in	_____orm
_____ell	_____ig

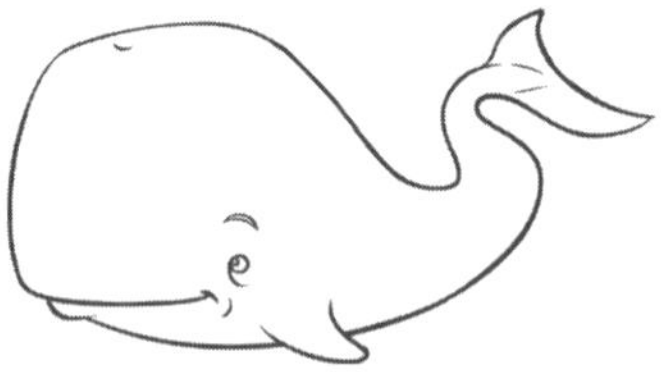

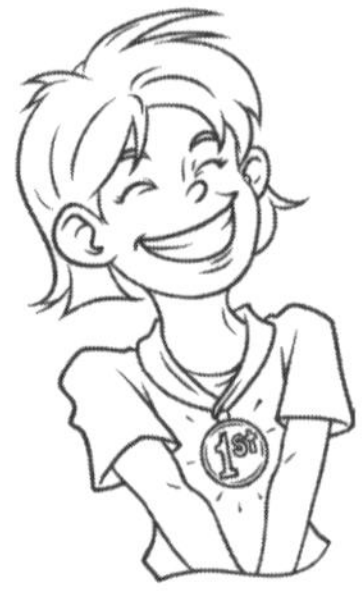

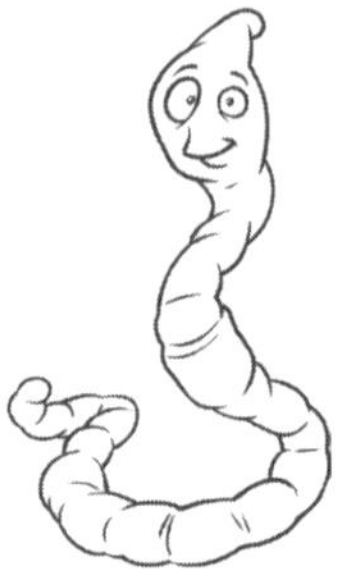

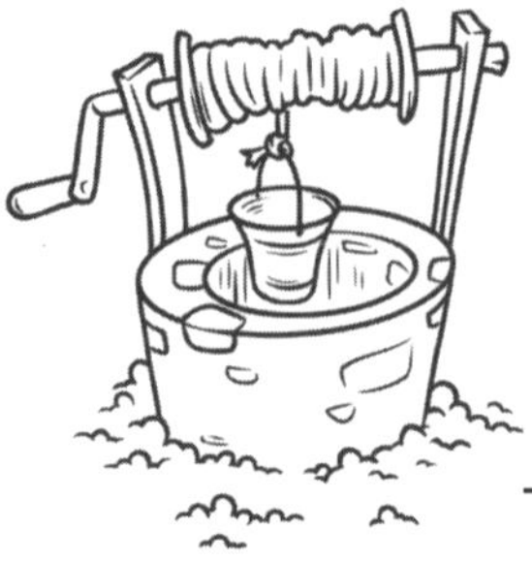

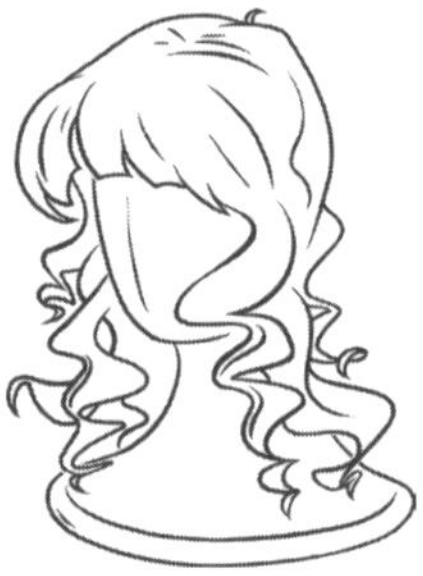

2 Draw some whiskers on the wolf.

Name

Check

Ww

Lesson 39 · Worksheet 4

1 Trace and write.

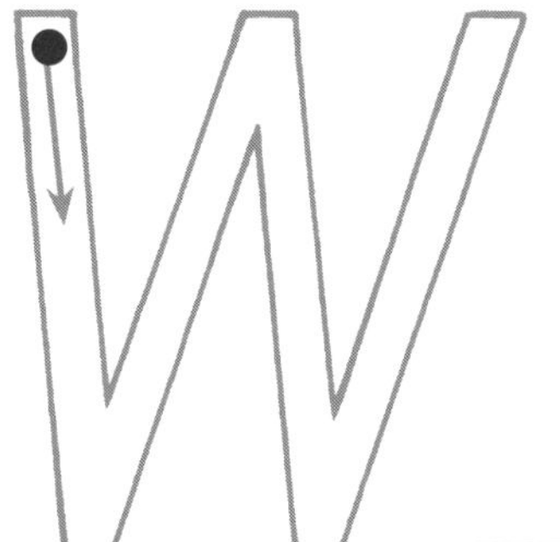

2 Circle every **W**.

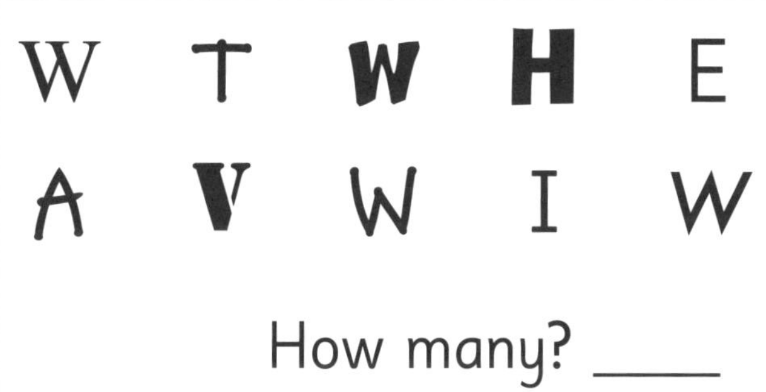

Circle every **w**.

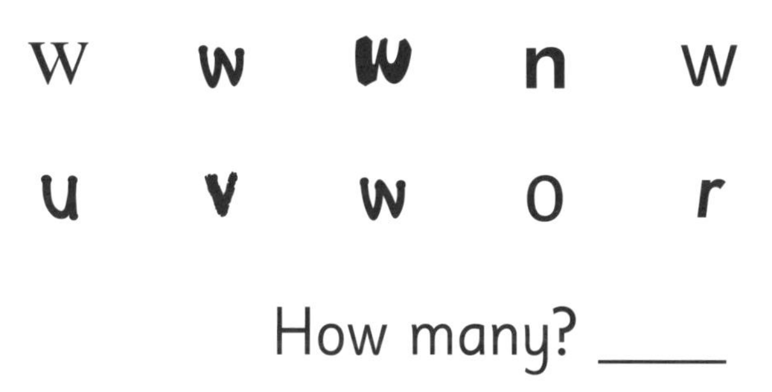

3 Colour the words in the web that begin with **w**.

Lesson 40 Review

Learning objectives

Children will:

- revise word families using /a/.
- recognise and write new word families using /i/.
- revise known letters and sight words.

Australian Curriculum Content Descriptions

Sound and letter knowledge

ACELA1439 listen to the sounds a student hears in the word, and write letters to represent those sounds; identify and manipulate sounds (phonemes) in spoken words; identify onset and rime in one-syllable spoken words

ACELA1440 identify familiar and recurring letters and the use of upper and lower case in written texts

Expressing and developing ideas

ACELA1435 learn that word order in sentences is important for meaning

ACELA1438 build word families using onset and rime

ACELA1758 write consonant-vowel-consonant words by writing letters to represent the sounds in the spoken words; know that spoken words are written down by listening to the sounds heard in the word and then writing letters to represent those sounds

Sight words

the, can, see, in, and, has, a

Word families

ad, am, at, ap, an

Vocabulary words

fish, dish, wish, pin, fin, tin, sit, hid

Extra assistance

Many languages do not distinguish between long and short vowel sounds. Give students opportunities to practise pronunciation with pairs of words, eg mad and made, din and dine, or tongue twisters.

Classroom activities

Bingo!

Give students a laminated board with 10 squares on it. Ask them to write a sight word in each square from the list yes, you, has, as, he and she (use whiteboard markers). Put flashcards for each word in a bag. Pull one out and say the word, then put it back in. Students put a cross on that word on their board. First one to 10 calls out 'bingo' and wins!

Mix and Match

Put the consonant letters of the alphabet on the board in writing or magnetic letters. Write the sounds ish, in, it and id on the board. Each student comes to the board and writes a word they can make using an /i/ ending and one of the other letters. Discuss their words with the class.

Reading Eggs **Lesson sequence**	**TEACH** **Content and skills**	**PRACTISE** **Children will:**	**APPLY**
Hear: *Animated Lesson*	Revise word families and blending.	choose the correct ending and initial letter to make the word.	**Worksheet 1** Word families
Write: *Pick Up Bricks*	Recognise correct word order for a sentence.	choose the correct words to make a sentence.	**Worksheet 2** Read
Find: *Word family, Catch the Fish, Letter Lights, Missing Sound*	Identify the correct onset letter to complete the word. Recognise a given word. Recognise letters in upper and lower case.	choose the correct initial letter to make the word. Find the given word in a group. Locate lower case and capital letters.	**Worksheet 3** Sight words
Vocabulary: *Blend a Word, Sound Streamers, Word Windows, Picture Picker*	Build vocabulary skills: Blend and recognise words. Identify sounds in words. Read and comprehend a sentence.	blend sounds to read words. Sound out and select letters to make words. Read a sentence and match to a picture.	**Worksheet 4** Check
Read: *Book*	Read aloud book.	listen, follow the reading and read along.	**Reading Eggs Story book** Cat and fish

Related Reading Eggs Activities, Interactives, Songs and Books

Spelling Bank

Level A - Ants

Lesson 1

Focus words:
sat, mat, cat, bat, fat, hat, rat

Sight words:
a, at, it

Challenge:
flat, that

Driving Tests

Letters and sounds:

Test 1:

b, h, n, v, c, j, p, w, q, d, k, r, y, f, l, z, g, m, t

Reading Eggs Posters

Reading Eggs Library Books

My Program Books

Music Café

Sam's alphabet song

Reading Eggs Puzzle Park

Alphabet match

More than one

Both ways

Read it

Critter Card

Flobby

Teacher Toolkit

Spelling Activities

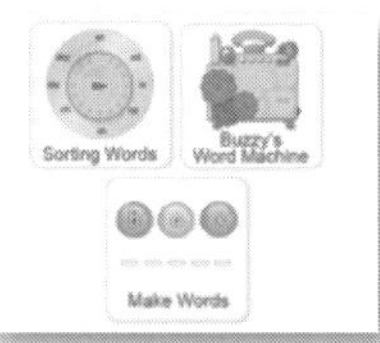

Targeting Handwriting Interactively

Reading Eggs Apps

Eggy Alphabet

Eggy Sight words

Eggy Phonics 1

Review

Lesson 40 • Worksheet 1

Name

Word families

1 Draw lines to match words that rhyme.

2 Colour the odd one out in each row.

ran	man	pat	can
mad	bad	had	van
zap	dam	jam	ham
hat	can	bat	sat
tap	map	rat	gap

Name

Read

Review

Lesson 40 · Worksheet 2

Match to a picture.

The fish has a tin.

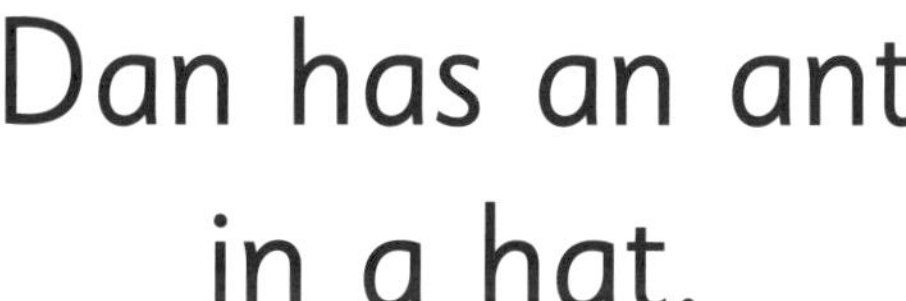

Dan has an ant in a hat.

A rat has a hat.

The cat can see a cat on a can.

Review

Lesson 40 • Worksheet 3

Name

Sight words

1 Trace and write the words.

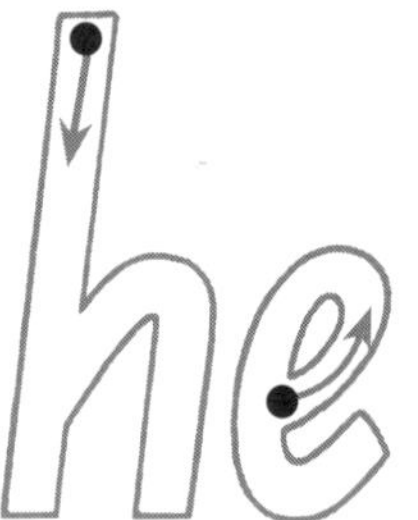

2 Join Sandy Can to the word **can**.

3 Write the words in the correct box.

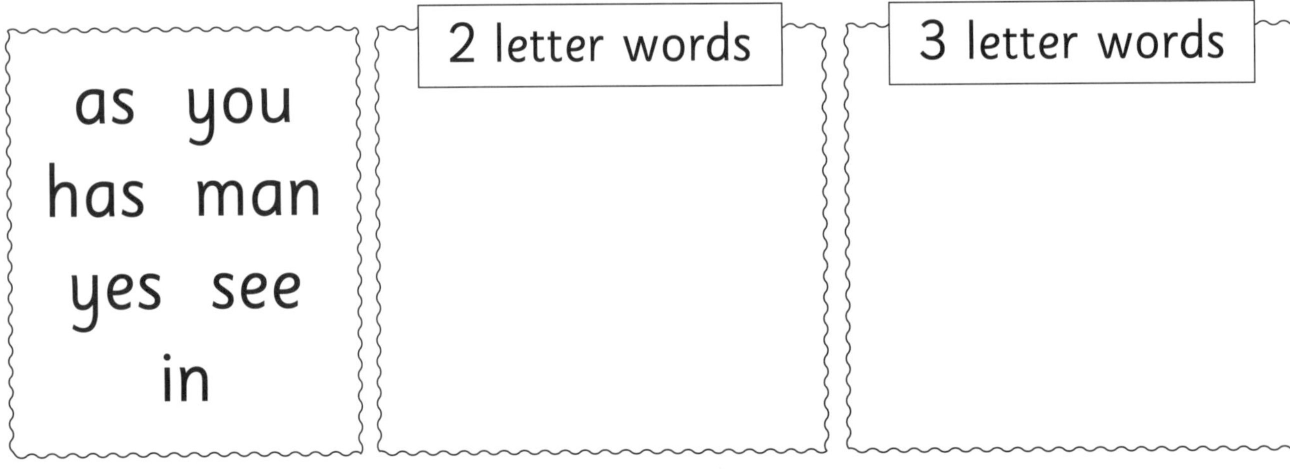

Name

Check

Review

Lesson 40 • Worksheet 4

1 Circle the pictures that start with the letter.

2 Write each word in a box.

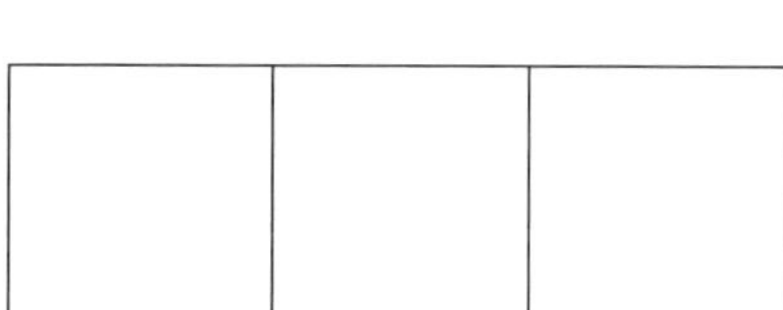

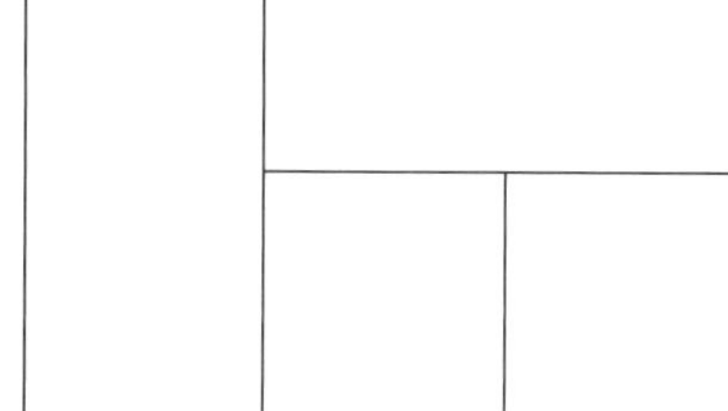

3 Draw a picture for each sentence.

The fish has a fin.	
The cat can see the fish.	

Lesson 41 the letter **u**

Learning objectives

Children will:

- identify the sound u.
- recognise and write u and U.
- identify reading rules.

Australian Curriculum Content Descriptions

Text structure and organisation

ACELA1432 point to the letters and the punctuation in a text

ACELA1433 learn about print: direction of print and return sweep, spaces between words

Expressing and developing ideas

ACELA1758 recognise the most common sound made by each letter of the alphabet, including consonants and short vowel sounds; know that spoken words are written down by listening to the sounds heard in the word and then writing letters to represent those sounds

Sound and letter knowledge

ACELA1440 identify familiar and recurring letters and the use of upper and lower case in written texts

Creating texts

ACELY1653 follow clear demonstrations of how to construct each letter, learn to construct lower case letters

Word families

fun, sun, run

Vocabulary words

umbrella, unlock, unhappy, unicorn, unwrap, underground, underwater, ugly

Extra assistance

The short /u/ sound may be mispronounced in a variety of ways depending on students' language backgrounds. Give them opportunities to practise saying /u/ words. Ask students to distinguish between vowel sounds in a pair of words by asking them a question and giving them two answers to choose from. For example:

Cut and cat. Which is a pet?

Cup and cop. Which do you drink from?

Classroom activities

Which Hat?

Place five hats on the floor with the labels a, e, i, o, u. Discuss the short vowel sounds. Have a pile of objects or pictures of objects that have a short vowel sound. Each student chooses one and works out which hat it must go in. Discuss their choice with the class.

Making Sentences

Write a sentence on the board with no capital letters, no spaces and no punctuation, for example: icanseethecat

Ask students to help you fix it. Take one suggestion at a time and rewrite the sentence using that suggestion, for example: Icanseethecat

Take more suggestions and rewrite the sentence again and again, until it is correct.

Reading Eggs Lesson sequence	**TEACH Content and skills**	**PRACTISE Children will:**	**APPLY**
Hear: *Animated Lesson*	Introduce reading rules: read across a line, gaps between words, capitals, full stops and question marks. Introduce the sound /u/.	make sentences and read them. Identify /u/ sound in isolation.	**Worksheet 1** Phonemic awareness
Write: *Dot-to-Dot*	Reinforce correct letter formation of lower case u.	write the letter u.	**Worksheet 2** Handwriting
Find: *Letter Grid, Know Your Alphabet, Frog Hops*	Recognise u in upper and lower case. Identify upper and lower case pairs of letters. Recognise a given word.	locate lower case u and capital U. Match lower case letters to their capital. Find the given word in a group.	**Worksheet 3** Beginning and middle sounds
Vocabulary: *Blend a Word, Letter Book, Rhyming Squares, Tiles, Label It*	Build vocabulary skills: Blend and recognise words. Recognise key vocabulary. Identify rhyming words.	blend sounds to read and make words. Match pictures to words. Find images of rhyming words.	**Worksheet 4** Check
Read: *Book*	Read aloud book.	listen, follow the reading and read along.	**Reading Eggs Alphabet book** u

Related Reading Eggs Activities, Interactives, Songs and Books

Reading Eggs Puzzle Park

Alphabet match

Both ways

Read it

Driving Tests

Test 2:

The Alphabet

Name upper and lower case letters of the alphabet.

Reading Eggs Posters

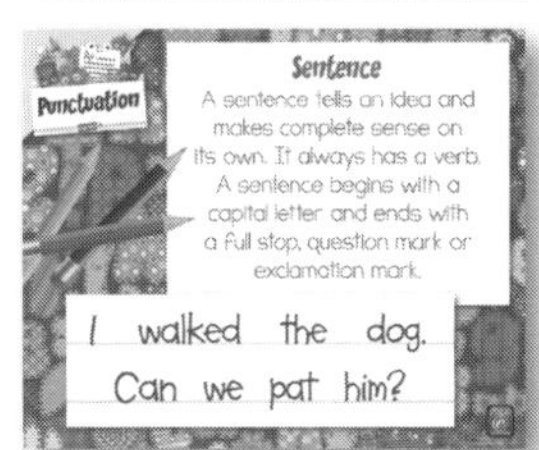

Reading Eggs Library Books

My Program Books

Teacher Toolkit

Spelling Activities

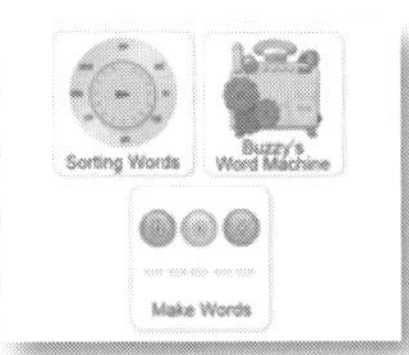

Alphabet Activities

Reading Eggs Apps

Eggy Alphabet

Eggy Sight words

Critter Card

Underting

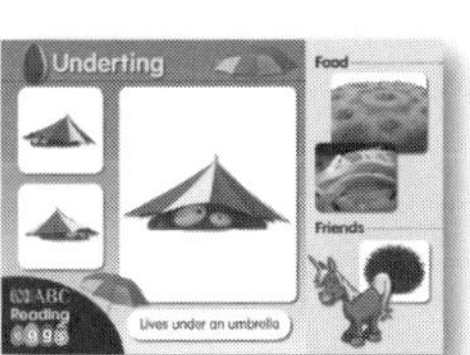

Name

Lesson 41 • Worksheet 1

Phonemic awareness

1 Match each letter to a picture.

2 Join **u** things to Underting.

3 Colour the **u** umbrellas.

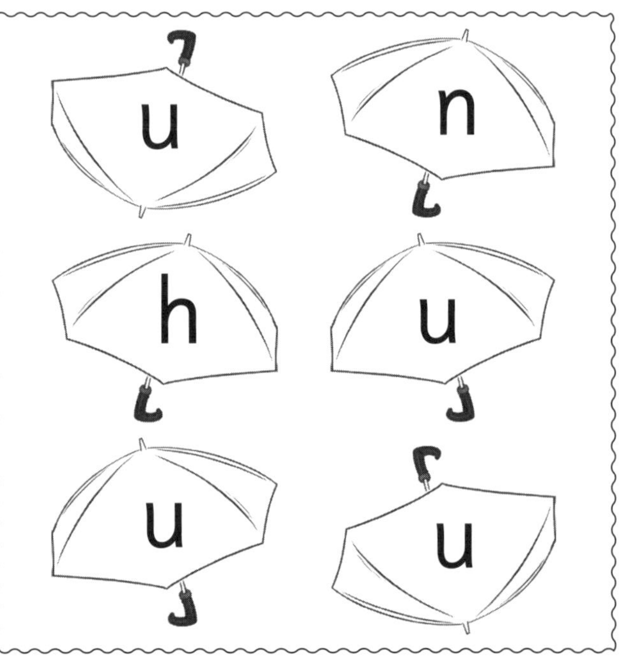

Name

Handwriting

U u

Lesson 41 · Worksheet 2

1 Trace the upside down umbrella.

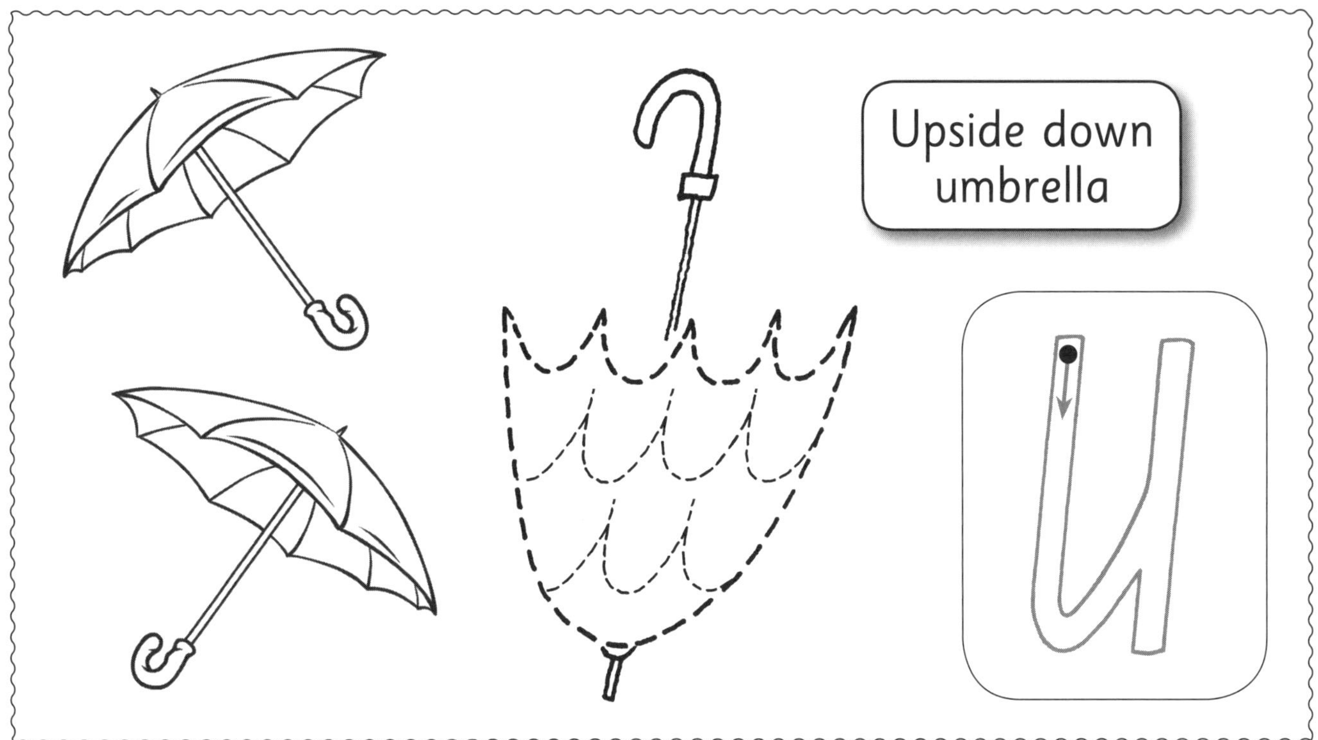

2 Trace.

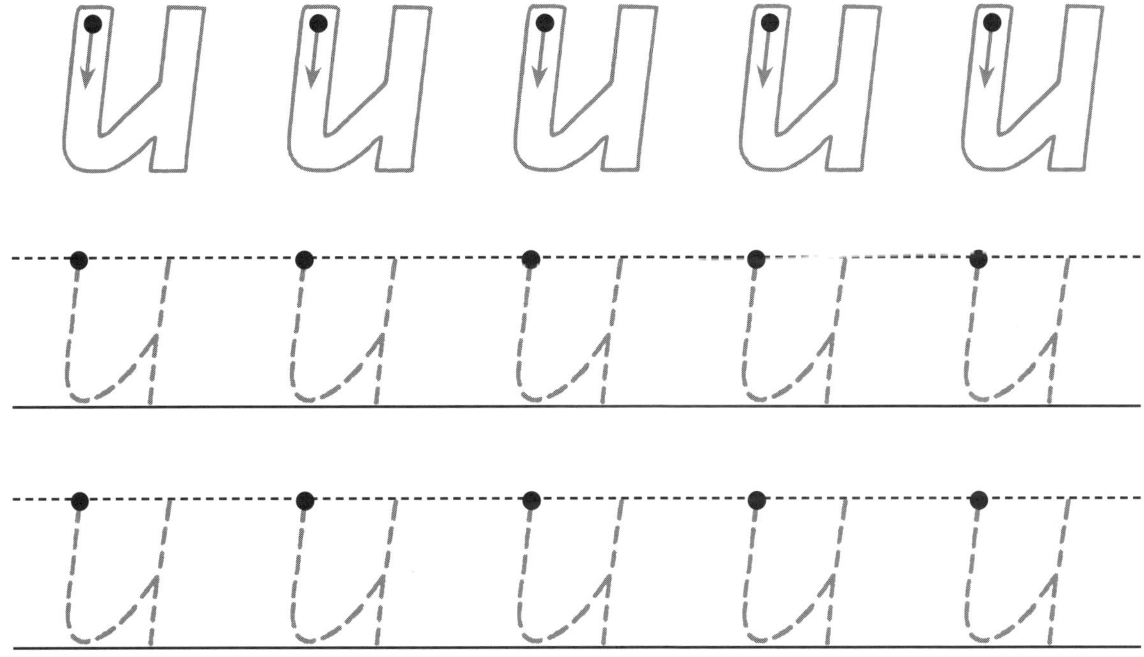

Underline your best letter.

U u

Lesson 41 • Worksheet 3

Name

Beginning and middle sounds

1 Add **u** and then say the word.

2 Add **u** and then say the word.

Name

Check

Lesson 41 • Worksheet 4

1 Trace and write.

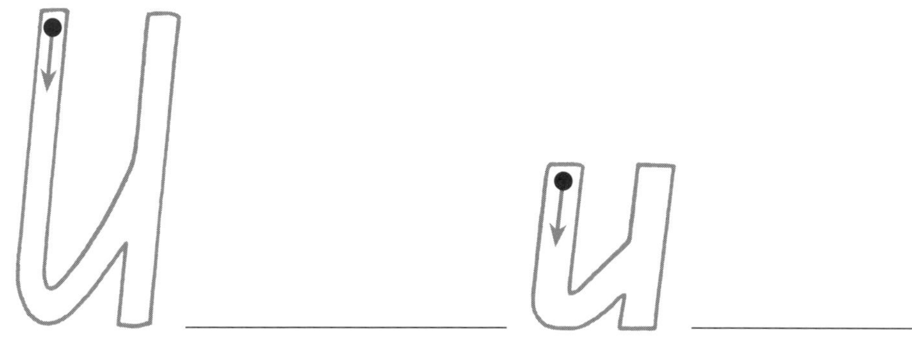

2 Circle all the **u** words.

3 Match each picture to a word.

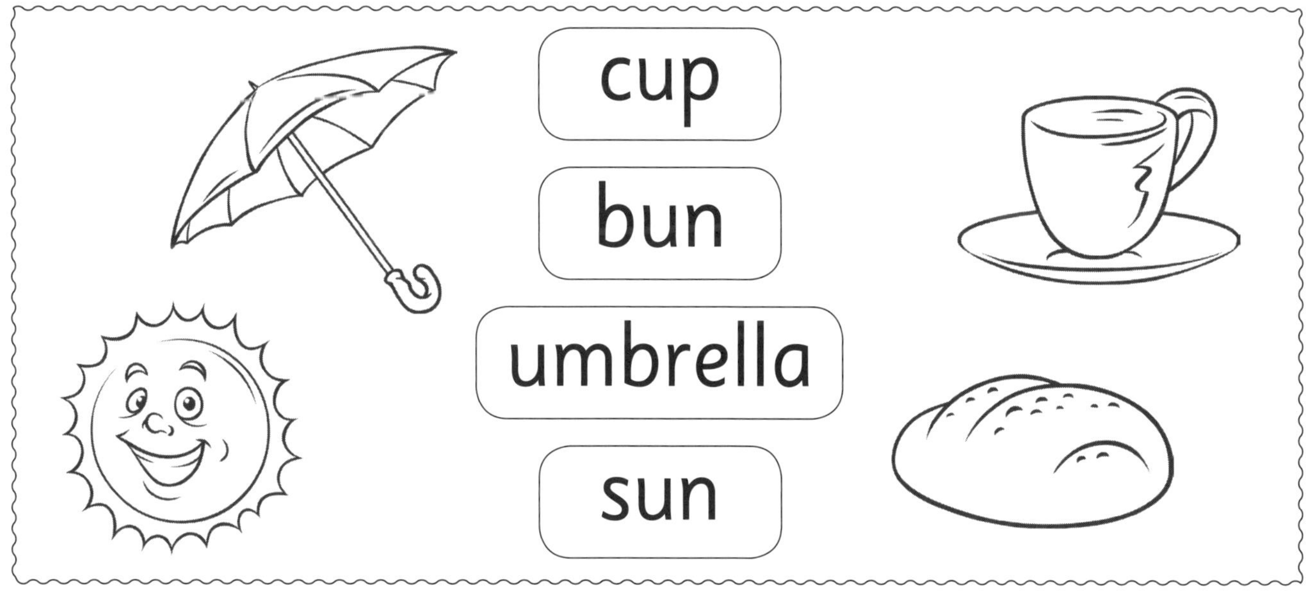

Lesson 42 the alphabet

Learning objectives

Children will:

- identify the phonemes, graphemes and names of the letters of the alphabet.
- identify the word 'words'.

Australian Curriculum Content Descriptions

Sound and letter knowledge

ACELA1439 listen to the sounds a student hears in the word, and write letters to represent those sounds; identify rhyme and syllables in spoken words; identify and manipulate sounds (phonemes) in spoken words; identify onset and rime in one-syllable spoken words

ACELA1440 identify familiar and recurring letters and the use of upper and lower case in written texts

Expressing and developing ideas

ACELA1438 build word families using onset and rime

ACELA1758 recognise the most common sound made by each letter of the alphabet, including consonants and short vowel sounds; write consonant-vowel-consonant words by writing letters to represent the sounds in the spoken words; know that spoken words are written down by listening to the sounds heard in the word and then writing letters to represent those sounds

Sight words

it, the, see, yes

Word families

cat, rat, hat, fat, sat, mat, bat, van, fan, can, man, ran, tan, pan, map, gap, lap, zap, tap, cap, nap, jam, ham, Sam

Vocabulary words

orange, zebra, words, carrot, tent, moon, pencil, apple, ant, fun, sun, fish, wish, fox, box, pin, fin, bee

Extra assistance

English language learners need to understand that in the English language there are 26 graphemes or written letters, but there are actually 44 sounds or phonemes. So far this program has covered the most common sounds for the consonants and the short vowel sounds, to give each student a sound to link to each letter. The letters also have names, which are often different to their sounds and should also be learnt by students.

Classroom activities

Decorate the letters

Provide the students with a piece of paper that has all the letters of the alphabet on it – some dotted, some in bubble writing, some solid letters. Trace over the dotted letters with different coloured pencils, textas or crayons. Glue collage materials such as paper bits, leaves or wool to the solid letters. Colour in the bubble letters with dots, stripes or shapes.

Reading Eggs Lesson sequence	TEACH Content and skills	PRACTISE Children will:	APPLY
Hear: *Animated Lesson*	Introduce the alphabet using letters, sounds and names and *Sam's Alphabet Song.*	identify lower case letters by their sounds and capital letters by their name.	**Worksheet 1** The alphabet
Write: *Rumble Jumble, Sound Streamers*	Unjumble letters for a given word. Identify sounds in words.	write a word from jumbled letters. Sound out and select letters to make words.	**Worksheet 2** Word families
Find: *Honey Bees, Fishing Boats, Word family, Letter Lights, Make a Word, Golden Goose*	Recognise a given word. Identify the correct onset letter to complete the word. Recognise letters in upper and lower case. Identify initial letters by sound and read written words.	find the given word in a group. Choose the correct initial letter to make the word. Locate lower case and capital letters. Match pictures to their initial letter. Match a word to its picture.	**Worksheet 3** Read and write
Vocabulary: *Wheel of Words, Rhyming Squares*	Build vocabulary skills: Recognise key vocabulary. Identify rhyming words.	match pictures to words. Find images of rhyming words.	**Worksheet 4** Check
Read: *Book*	Read aloud book.	listen, follow the reading and read along.	**Reading Eggs book** Word families for at, an, ap, am

Classroom activities

Bingo!

Give students a laminated board with ten squares on it. Ask them to write a different letter in each square (use whiteboard markers). Hold up pictures of items and say the name of the item in the picture. Students put a cross on that initial letter on their board. First one to 10 calls out 'bingo' and wins!

Related Reading Eggs Activities, Interactives, Songs and Books

Spelling Bank

Level A - Ants

Lesson 2

Focus words:
tap, map, cap, nap, ram, jam, ham

Sight words:
am, as, has

Challenge:
clap, swam

Driving Tests

Test 2:

The Alphabet

Name upper and lower case letters of the alphabet.

Reading Eggs Posters

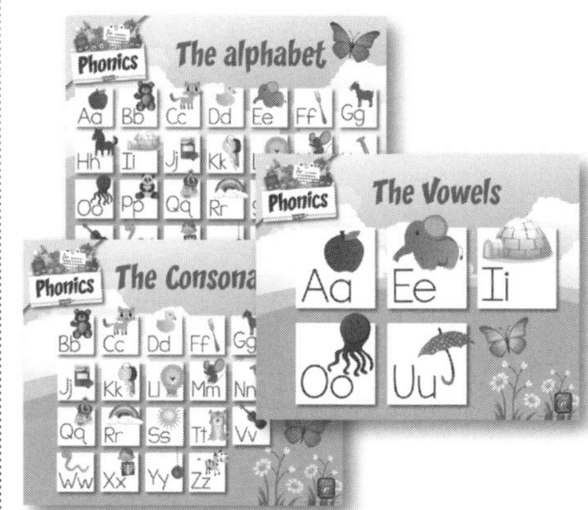

Reading Eggs Library Books

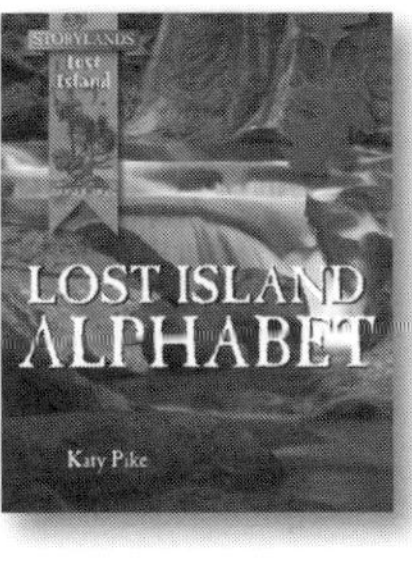

My Program Books

Music Café

Sam's Alphabet Song

Reading Eggs Puzzle Park

Alphabet match

More than one

Both ways

Read it

Teacher Toolkit

Spelling Activities

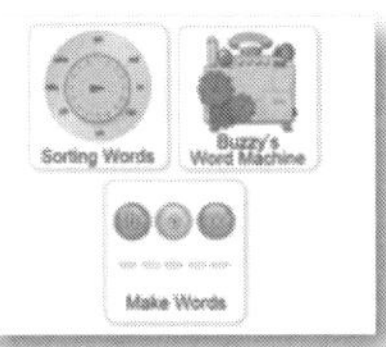

Alphabet Activities

Reading Eggs Apps

Eggy Alphabet

Eggy Sight words

Eggy Phonics 1

Critter Card

Alpha Beetle

a-z

Lesson 42 • Worksheet 1

Name

The alphabet

1 Complete the alphabet snakes.

a b d e

g h j k

m o q s

t u w y

2 Draw lines to match.

Name

Word families

1 Join each letter to the **at** machine.
Write each word you make.

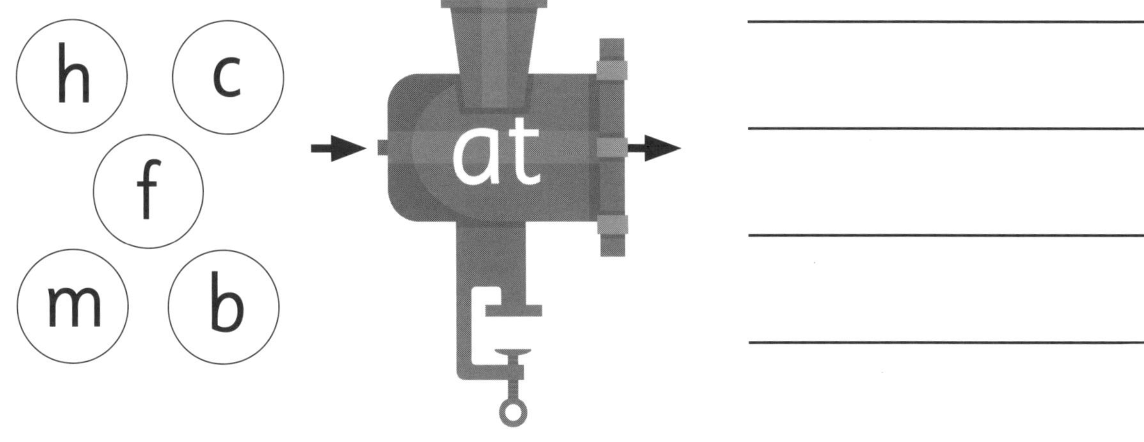

2 Colour the pairs that rhyme.

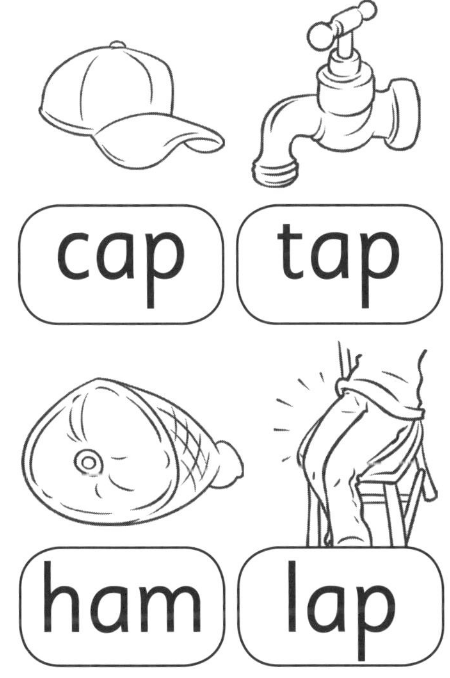

3 Colour the **ap** words.

tan

Name

Read and write

1 Complete each sentence. Draw a picture.

Sam has a hat.

I can see a rat.

2 Colour the correct word. Cross out the wrong word.

The man had a ran / nap.

She sat / map in the van.

Name

Check

a-z

Lesson 42 · Worksheet 4

1 Draw lines to match.

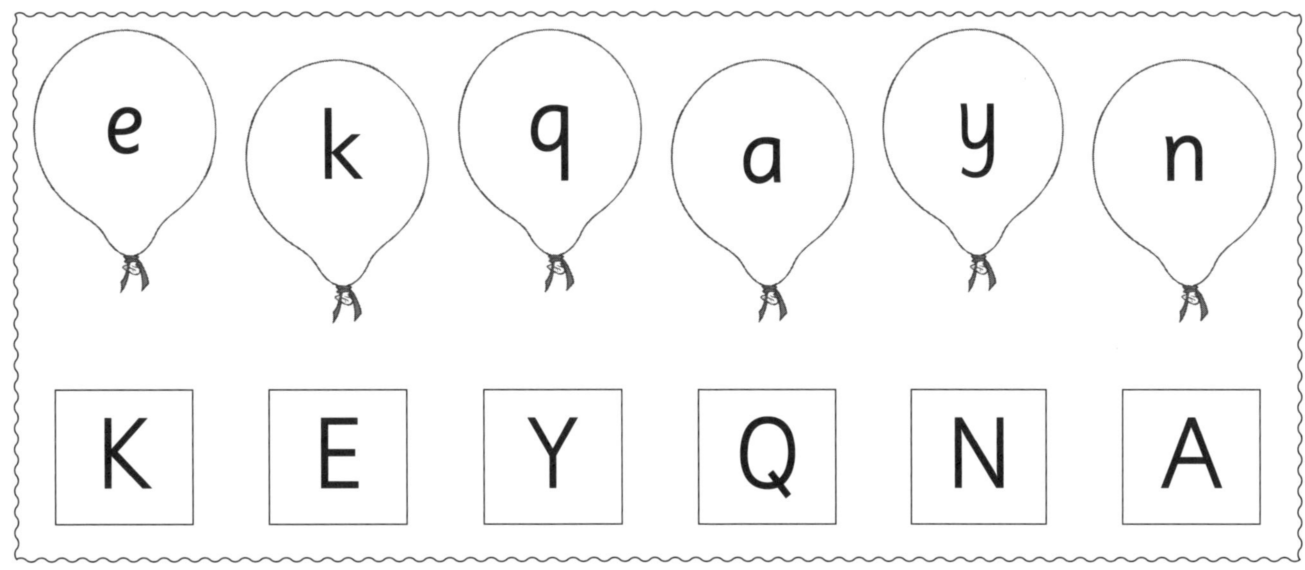

2 Colour **at** words = red **an** words = blue.

cat hat man fan

van rat pan tan

3 Complete the sentences.

hat fat can

I ________ see Sam.

She has a ________ .

The rat is ________ .

Lesson 43 the sound **id**

Learning objectives

Children will:

- identify the rime /id/.
- read and write words using id.

Australian Curriculum Content Descriptions

Sound and letter knowledge

ACELA1439 listen to the sounds a student hears in the word, and write letters to represent those sounds; identify onset and rime in one-syllable spoken words

Expressing and developing ideas

ACELA1434 explore spoken, written and multimodal texts and identify elements, for example words and images

ACELA1435 learn that word order in sentences is important for meaning

ACELA1438 build word families using onset and rime

ACELA1758 write consonant-vowel-consonant words by writing letters to represent the sounds in the spoken words

Interpreting, analysing and evaluating

ACELY1649 navigate a text correctly, starting at the right place and reading in the right direction, returning to the next line as needed, matching one spoken word to one written word

Sight words

has, a, the, can, see, I, am, yes, it, in, he

Word families

did, kid, hid, lid, rid, Sid

Vocabulary words

hit, bat, bin

Extra assistance

To teach consonant-vowel-consonant words use cut-outs of animal heads, bodies and tails. Each part should have a letter printed on it – remember the body parts will always be vowels. Ask children to make up words from the different body parts. Body parts do not have to be from the same animal, children will find this amusing. For kinaesthetic learners you could include nodding for the first letter, wriggling for the second letter and stamping for the third letter.

Classroom activities

For Starters

Put the sound id on the board in magnetic letters. Put all the letters of the alphabet around it. Students take turns to make id words by simply changing the initial phoneme. Can anyone use more than one letter to start an id word?

Find the Start

Give students a list of words with the first letter missing. Ask them to figure out which letter could be the starter for all the given words, for example:
_id _ap _et _og _uck
Discuss the answers as a class. Was there more than one possible answer?

Reading Eggs Lesson sequence	TEACH Content and skills	PRACTISE Children will:	APPLY
Hear: *Animated Lesson*	Introduce the rime id through words and the song *Sid the Kid does id.*	identify id in isolation and make words using onset letters and the rime id.	**Worksheet 1** Ending sound
Write: *Make a Sentence, Pick Up Bricks*	Recognise correct word order for a sentence.	choose the correct words to make a sentence.	**Worksheet 2** Read and write
Find: *Word family, Island Hop, Sequence*	Identify the correct onset letter to complete the word. Recognise a given word. Identify the order of a sequence of events.	choose the correct initial letter to make the word. Find the given word in a group. Put pictures in order to show a sequence of events.	**Worksheet 3** Word families
Vocabulary: *Jigsaw, Word Windows, Rhyming Squares, Sound Streamers, Tiles*	Build vocabulary skills: Recognise key vocabulary. Blend and recognise words. Identify rhyming words. Identify sounds in words.	match pictures to words. Blend sounds to read and make words. Find images of rhyming words. Sound out and select letters to make words.	**Worksheet 4** Check
Read: *Book*	Read aloud book.	listen, follow the reading and read along.	**Reading Eggs Story book** Sid the kid

Related Reading Eggs Activities, Interactives, Songs and Books

Music Café

Sid the Kid does id

Reading Eggs Puzzle Park

Alphabet match
Both ways
Read it

Reading Eggs Posters

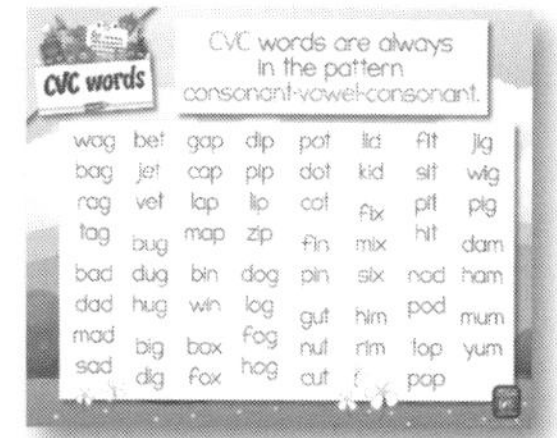

Reading Eggs Library Books

My Program Books

Interactives

Driving Tests

Spelling Bank

Critter Card

Sid the Kid

Teacher Toolkit

Spelling Activities

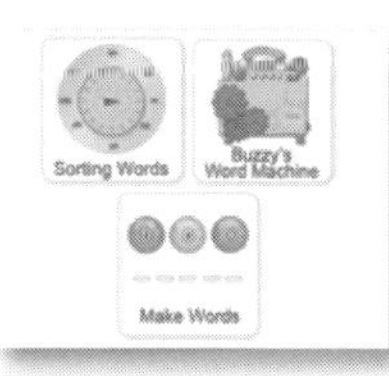

Reading Eggs Apps

Eggy Alphabet

Eggy Sight words

id

Lesson 43 • Worksheet 1

Name

Ending sound

1 Trace.

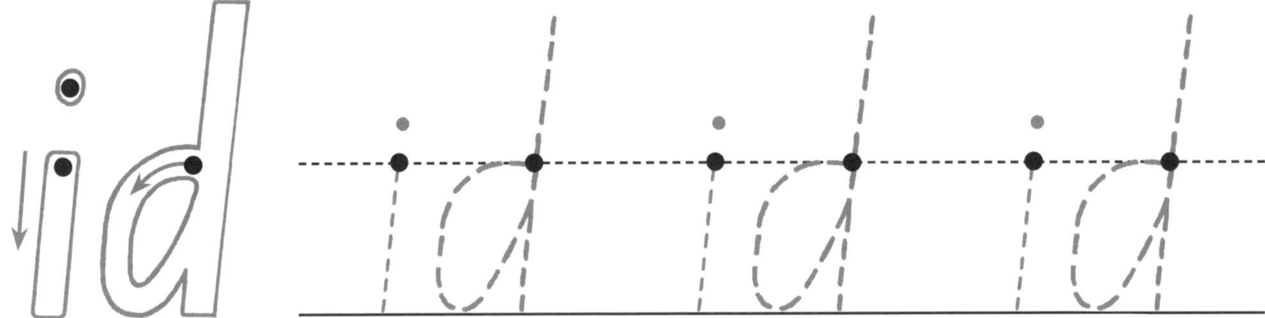

2 Colour **id** words.

did	Sid	fat	cup	hid
sat	lid	man	kid	van

3 Match each picture to a word.

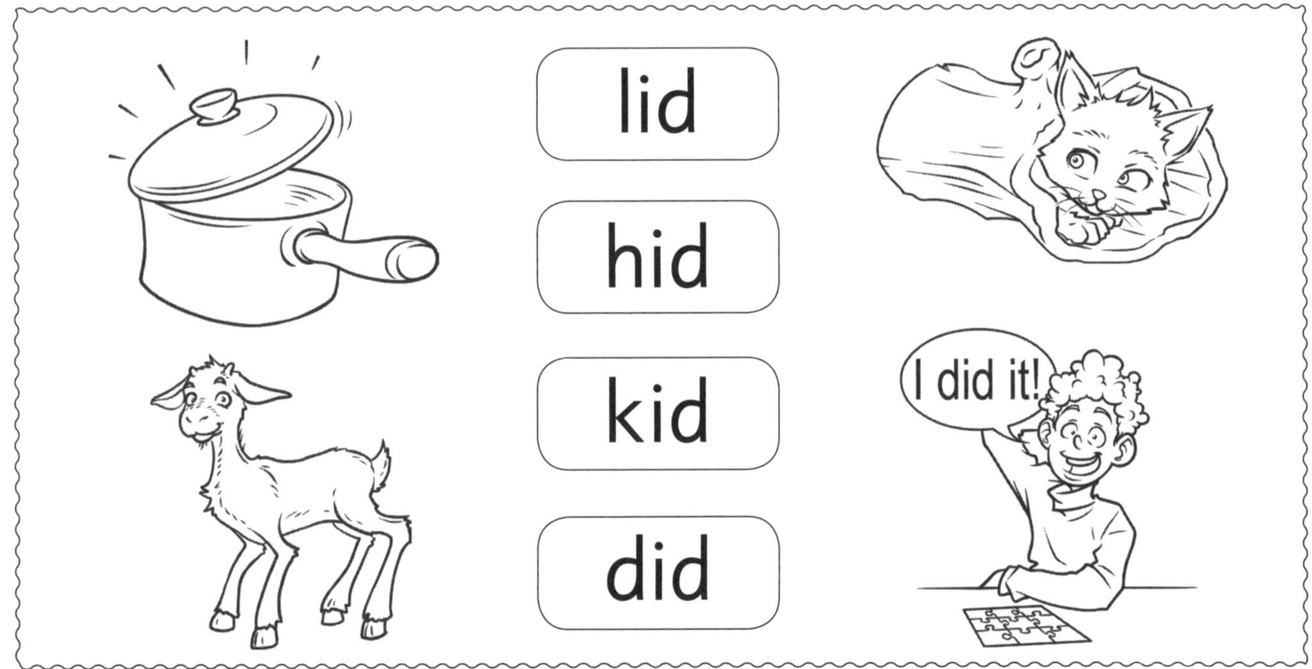

Name

id

Lesson 43 · Worksheet 2

Read and write

1 Complete the sentence.

I am Sid the

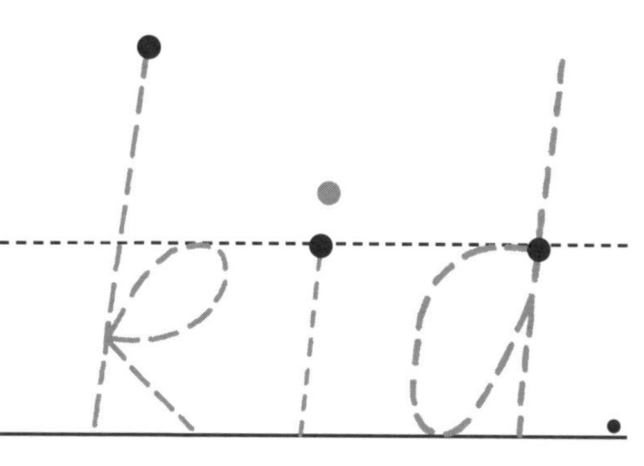

2 Complete the sentences.

did Sid lid

________ has a bat.

Can Sid hit the ________ ?

Yes! Sid ________ hit the lid.

id

Name

Word families

Lesson 43 • Worksheet 3

1 Complete the words. Use Sid the Kid's letters.

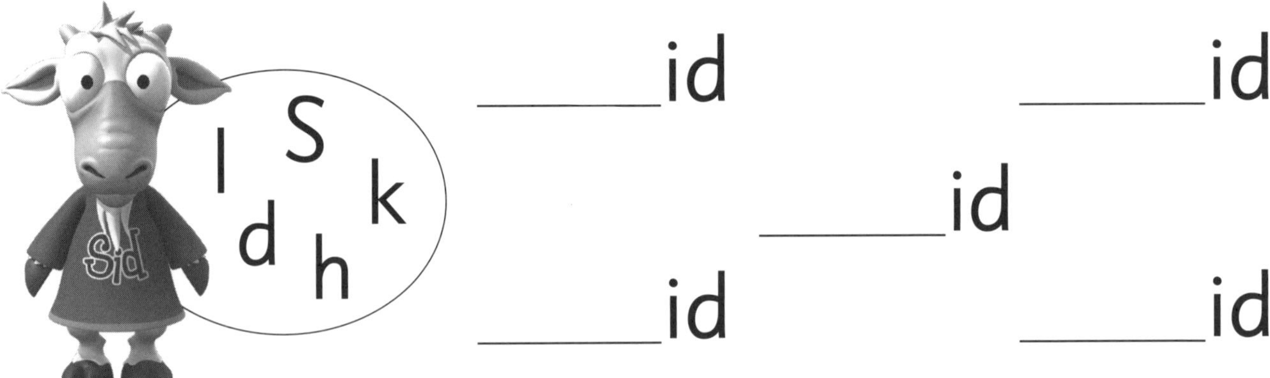

2 Colour the lids if they have the sound **id**.

3 Draw:

Name

Check

id

Lesson 43 • Worksheet 4

1 Use the wheel to make words.
Write the words.

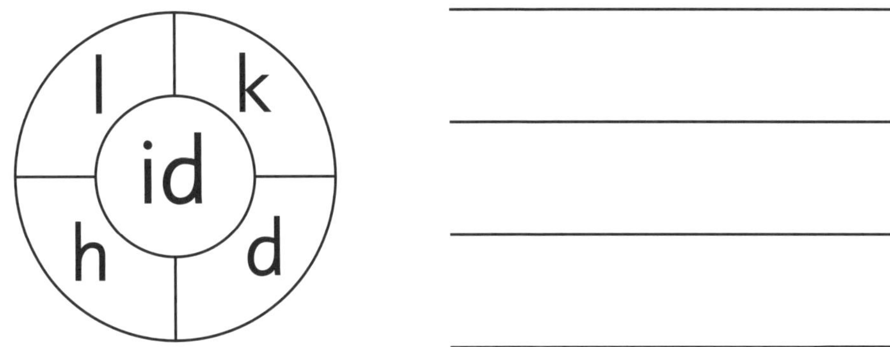

2 Colour the odd one out in each row.

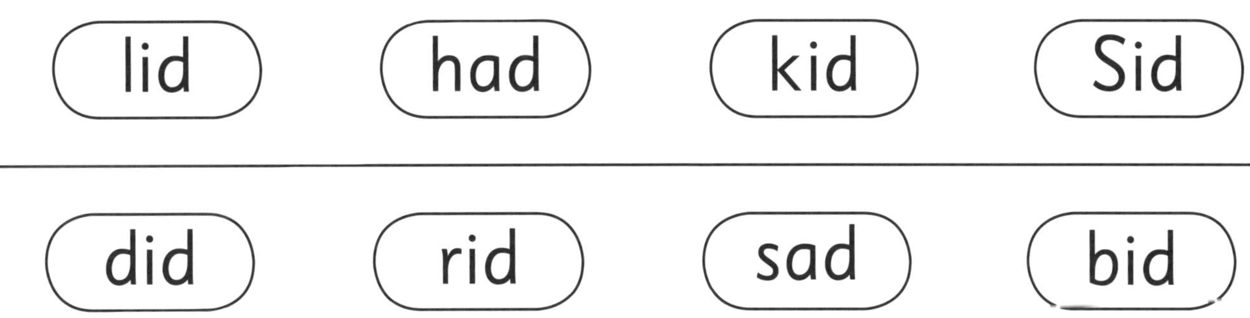

3 Complete the sentence.

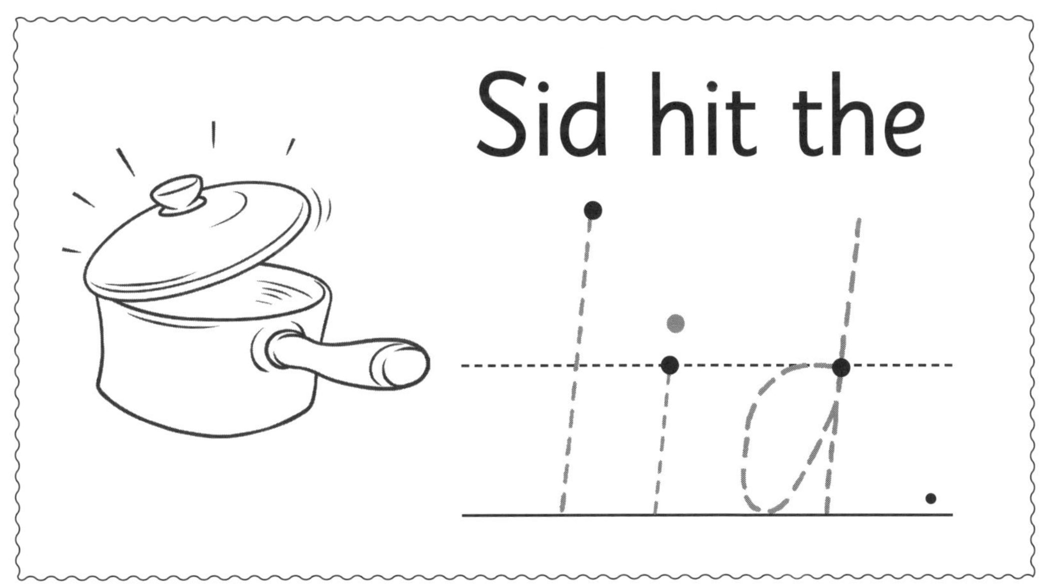

Lesson 44 the sounds **ix** and **in**

Learning objectives

Children will:

- identify the rimes ix and in.
- read and write words using ix and in.

Australian Curriculum Content Descriptions

Sound and letter knowledge

ACELA1439 identify and manipulate sounds (phonemes) in spoken words

Creating texts

ACELY1653 follow clear demonstrations of how to construct each letter

Expressing and developing ideas

ACELA1435 learn that word order in sentences is important for meaning

ACELA1438 build word families using onset and rime

ACELA1758 recognise the most common sound made by each letter of the alphabet, including consonants and short vowel sounds; write consonant-vowel-consonant words by writing letters to represent the sounds in the spoken words; know that spoken words are written down by listening to the sounds heard in the word and then writing letters to represent those sounds

Sight words

him, in, I, can, see, you, yes, a

Word families

six, mix, fix, tin, win, pin, bin, fin, din

Vocabulary words

rabbits, birds, pigs, red, blue, big

Extra assistance

Teach onset and rime for visual learners by using animal bodies for rimes and a variety of animal heads for the onsets. Students can have fun making crazy creatures while learning to blend and recognise words they know, reinforcing the idea of the onset and the rime.

Classroom activities

How does it end?

Give the students a letter each (b, d, f, k, m, p, s, t, w), either written on a card or a magnetic letter. Write the sounds ix and in on the top of the board. Each student comes to the board and writes the words they can make using their initial letter and one or both endings. Discuss their words with the class.

Which Hat?

Place three hats on the floor with the labels ix, in and id. Discuss the sounds. Have a pile of objects or pictures of objects that end with ix, in and id. Each student chooses one and works out which hat it must go in. Discuss their choice with the class.

Reading Eggs Lesson sequence	TEACH Content and skills	PRACTISE Children will:	APPLY
Hear: *Animated Lesson*	Introduce the rime ix and the word him using the song *In The Mix*. Introduce the rime in using the song *In Time with Sam and Sid*.	identify, read and make ix words. Read and make him. Identify, read and make in words.	**Worksheet 1** Word families
Write: *Dot-to-Dot, Pick Up Bricks*	Reinforce correct letter formation of lower case x. Recognise correct word order for a sentence.	write the letter x. Choose the correct words to make a sentence.	**Worksheet 2** Read and write
Find: *Fishing Boats, Missing Sound, Word family*	Recognise a given word. Identify the correct onset letter to complete the word.	find the given word in a group. Choose the correct initial letter to make the word.	**Worksheet 3** Sight words
Vocabulary: *Blend a Word, Break it Up, Wheel of Words, Tiles*	Build vocabulary skills: Blend and recognise words. Identify the number of phonemes in a word. Recognise key vocabulary.	blend sounds to read and make words. Identify the number of sounds in a word. Match pictures to words.	**Worksheet 4** Check
Read: *Book*	Read aloud book.	listen, follow the reading and read along.	**Reading Eggs Story book** I can see six

Related Reading Eggs Activities, Interactives, Songs and Books

Music Café

In The Mix

In Time with Sam and Sid

Reading Eggs Puzzle Park

More than One

Hidden Words

Song Lines

Animal Colours

Colour Code

Reading Eggs Posters

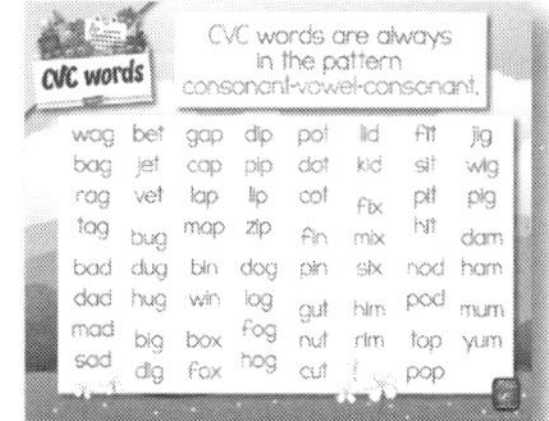

Reading Eggs Library Books

My Program Books

Interactives

Driving Tests

Spelling Bank

Critter Card

Insillyect

Teacher Toolkit

Spelling Activities

Reading Eggs Apps

Eggy Sight words

ix in

Lesson 44 · Worksheet 1

Name

Word families

1 Match each picture to a word.

2 Write the words on the correct tin.

fix win
bin six
mix pin

3 Complete each word family.

six	pin
f______	b______
m______	t______

Name

Read and write

Lesson 44 • Worksheet 2

1 Draw a picture for each sentence.

I can see six blue birds.	
I can see six red rabbits.	

2 Complete the sentences.

see can six

I ________ see six pigs.

You can ________ six bats.

He can see ________ fish.

ix in

Lesson 44 • Worksheet 3

Name

Sight words

1 Trace and write the words.

2 Help Itsy Bitsy see the blue birds. Colour the path of **see** words.

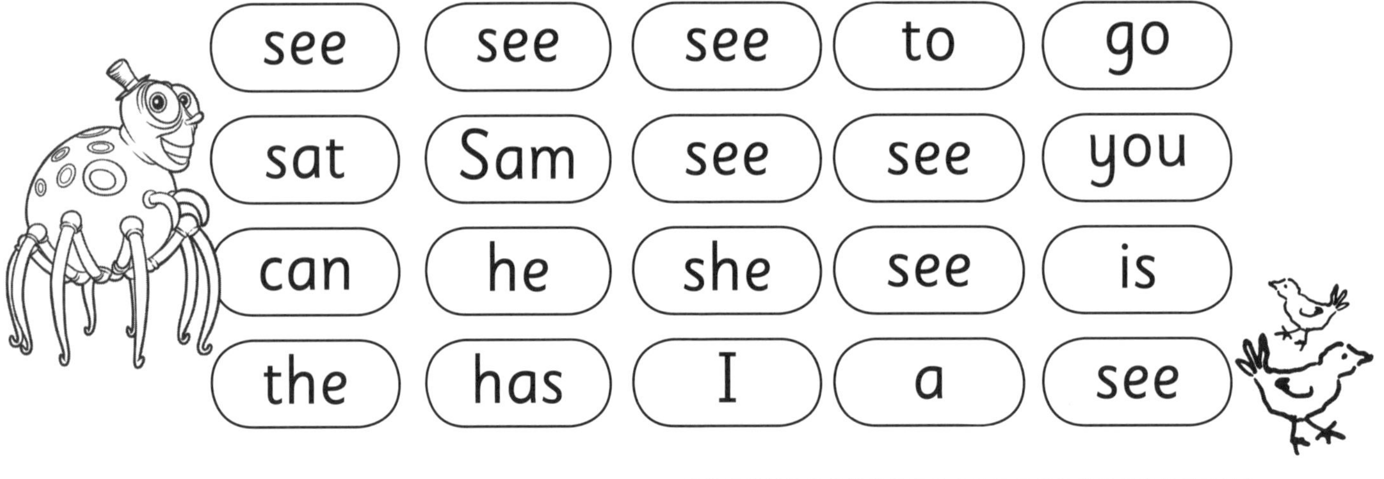

3 Write each word in a box.

you can see

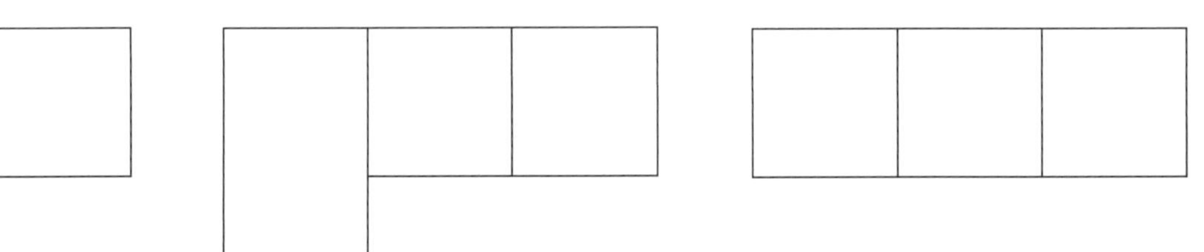

Name

Check

1 Find the words. Colour **you** = blue, **can** = red, **see** = green.

y	o	u	s	e	e	c	a	n
s	e	e	c	a	n	y	o	u
c	a	n	y	o	u	s	e	e
s	e	e	c	a	n	y	o	u

2 Make a word with the letters on the fridge.

______ix ______in

______in ______ix

3 Draw a picture for this sentence.

I can see six pink pigs.

Lesson 45 the sound **it**

Learning objectives

Children will:

- identify the rime it.
- read and write words using it.
- read the word it.

Australian Curriculum Content Descriptions

Sound and letter knowledge

ACELA1439 identify and manipulate sounds (phonemes) in spoken words

ACELA1440 identify familiar and recurring letters and the use of upper and lower case in written texts

Creating texts

ACELY1653 follow clear demonstrations of how to construct each letter, learn to construct lower case letters

Expressing and developing ideas

ACELA1435 learn that word order in sentences is important for meaning

ACELA1758 write consonant-vowel-consonant words by writing letters to represent the sounds in the spoken words; know that spoken words are written down by listening to the sounds heard in the word and then writing letters to represent those sounds

Sight words

it, can, you, on, I, we, and

Word families

hit, sit, bit, fit

Vocabulary words

spin, swing, stand

Extra assistance

Students who speak another language may find the short /i/ sound difficult and pronounce it as /ee/. Give them opportunities to practise the sound using games. For example, use pairs of word cards like is, it, in, hit, sit, bin, lid, six and so on to play Memory. The students only get to keep the cards if they can pronounce the word properly.

Classroom activities

Make It!

Give each student some playdough or plasticine or clay to make the rime /it/. Then ask them to shape an onset letter to make a word. How many /it/ words can they make out of their materials? They could also collect natural items such as leaves and twigs to combine with their modelling material to make /it/ words.

Find the Letter

Give each student 3 cards with the sounds /it/, /in/ and /ix/. Say a word and ask students to listen to the end sound. They should hold up the card which makes that final sound. Use clear, recognisable words such as: fit thin six kit chin mix

Reading Eggs Lesson sequence	TEACH Content and skills	PRACTISE Children will:	APPLY
Hear: *Animated Lesson*	Introduce the rime it using the song *The it Bit*.	identify and read it words.	**Worksheet 1** Word families
Write: *Dot-to-Dot, Make a Sentence*	Reinforce correct letter formation. Recognise correct word order for a sentence.	write the word it. Choose the correct words to make a sentence.	**Worksheet 2** Read and write
Find: *Driving Trucks, Catch the Fish, Time for 20*	Recognise a given word.	find the given word in a group.	**Worksheet 3** Sight words
Vocabulary: *Blend a Word, Jigsaw, Tiles, Book Ends*	Build vocabulary skills: Blend and recognise words. Recognise key vocabulary. Read basic vocabulary and identify key words.	blend sounds to read and make words. Match pictures to words. Choose from a list of words to finish the sentence.	**Worksheet 4** Check
Read: *Book*	Read aloud book.	listen, follow the reading and read along.	**Reading Eggs Story book** Sit

Related Reading Eggs Activities, Interactives, Songs and Books

Music Café

The it Bit

Reading Eggs Puzzle Park

Hidden Words

Song Lines

Reading Eggs Posters

Reading Eggs Library Books

My Program Books

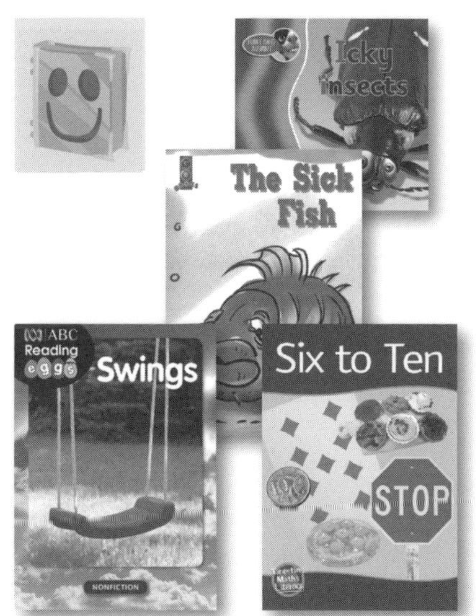

Interactives

Driving Tests

Spelling Bank

Critter Card

Itsy bitsy

Teacher Toolkit

Spelling Activities

Reading Eggs Apps

Eggy Sight words

Lesson 45 • Worksheet 1

Name

Word families

1 Match each picture to a word.

2 Colour the **it** words blue. Colour the **in** words red.

pin	spin	it	tin	sit
bit	fit	bin	hit	fin

3 Join each sound to the **it** machine.
Write each word you make.

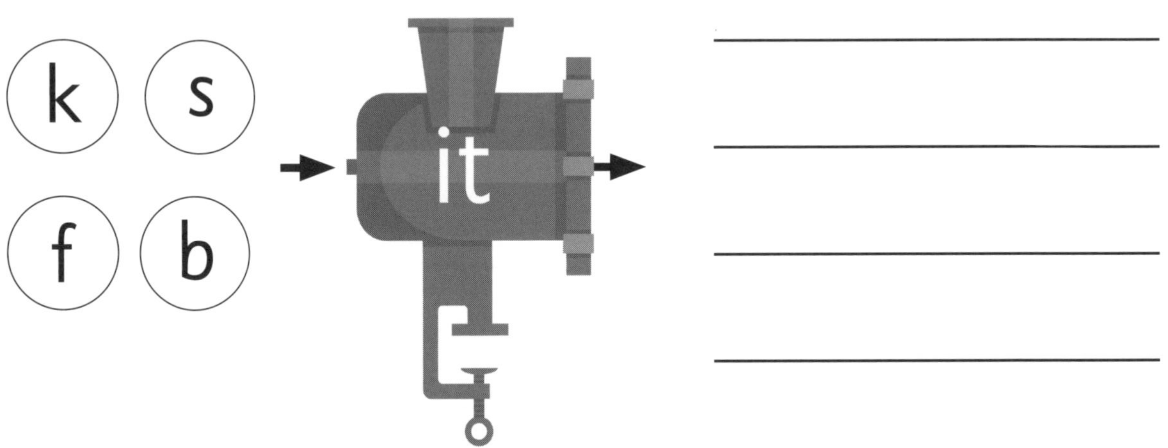

Name

Read and write

Write each word. Read it and match to a picture.

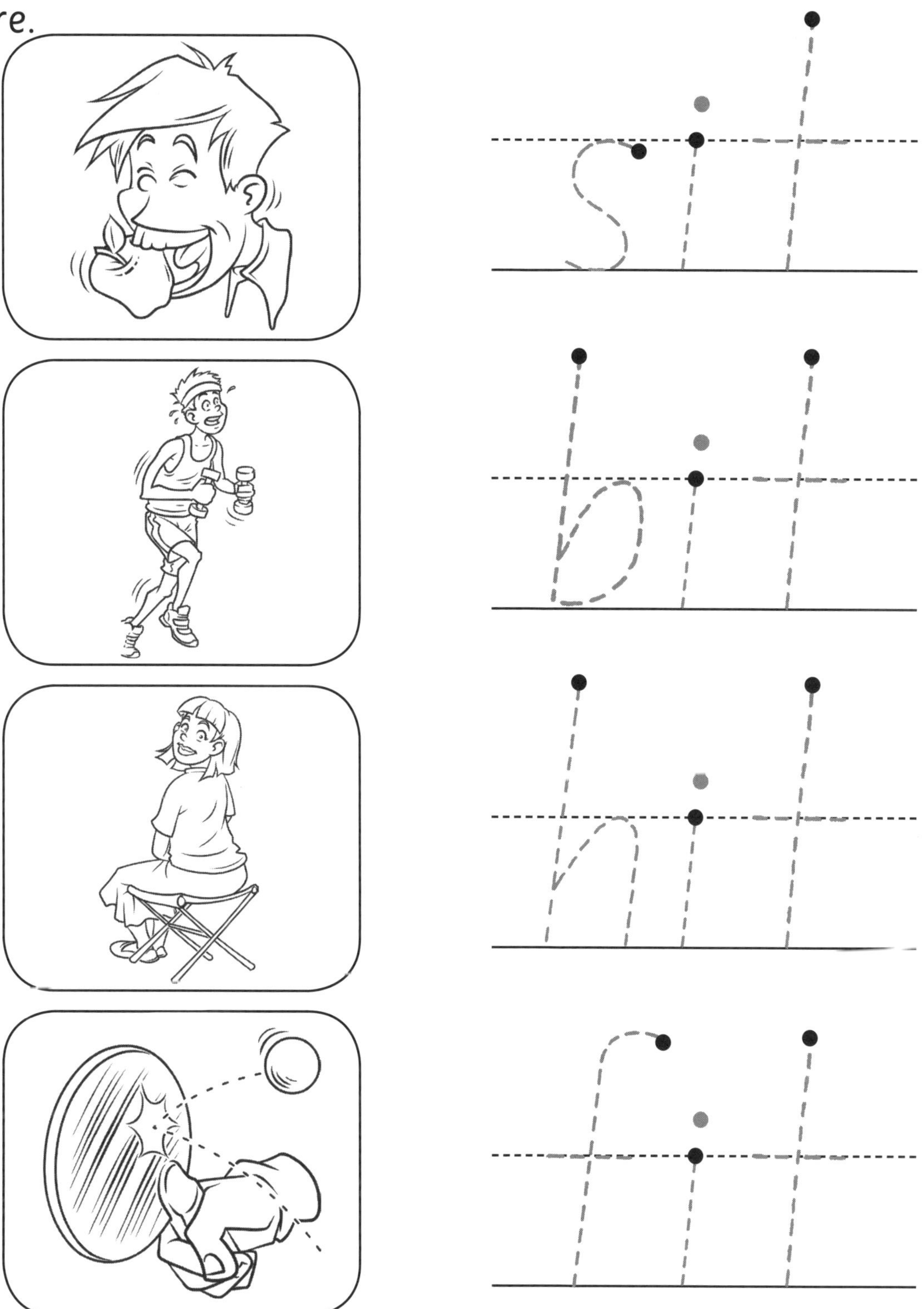

☑ Tick your best word.

it

Lesson 45 • Worksheet 3

Name

Sight words

1 Trace and write the words.

2 Find the matching words.

it	spin	swing
spin	swing	it
swing	it	spin

3 Guess the word by its shape.
Write each word in the boxes.

it spin swing

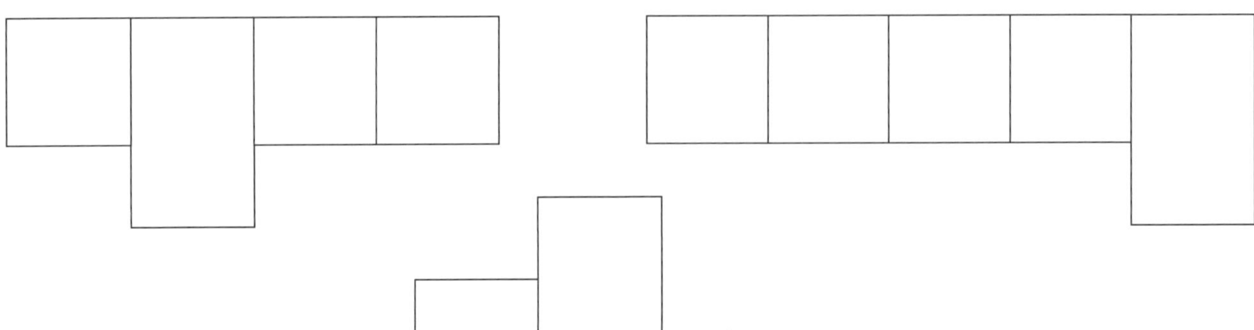

Name

Check

it

Lesson 45 • Worksheet 4

1 Use the wheel to make words.
Write the words.

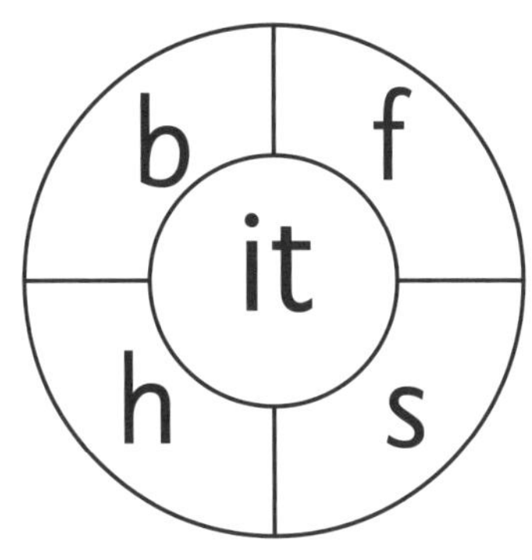

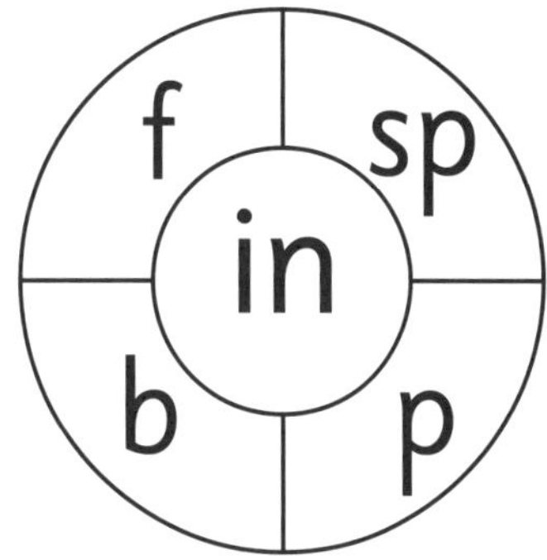

______________________ ______________________

______________________ ______________________

______________________ ______________________

______________________ ______________________

2 Colour the correct word. Cross out the wrong word.

Can you (sit / fin) on it?

Lesson 46 the sound **ig**

Learning objectives

Children will:

- identify the rime ig.
- read and write words using ig.
- read and write the words said and like.

Australian Curriculum Content Descriptions

Sound and letter knowledge

ACELA1439 listen to the sounds a student hears in the word, and write letters to represent those sounds; identify rhyme and syllables in spoken words; identify and manipulate sounds (phonemes) in spoken words; identify onset and rime in one-syllable spoken words

ACELA1440 identify familiar and recurring letters and the use of upper and lower case in written texts

Expressing and developing ideas

ACELA1435 learn that word order in sentences is important for meaning

ACELA1438 break words into onset and rime

ACELA1758 write consonant-vowel-consonant words by writing letters to represent the sounds in the spoken words; know that spoken words are written down by listening to the sounds heard in the word and then writing letters to represent those sounds

Sight words

I, like, it, said, my, the, has, a

Word families

fig, pig, rig, big, dig, jig, wig

Vocabulary words

castle, dress, ring, horse, throne, crown, queen

Extra assistance

When making word family lists, teach students to run through the alphabet and try each letter as a starting sound to go with the rime. They need to look for the "real" words. For example:

~~aig~~ big ~~cig~~ dig ~~eig~~ fig gig

Classroom activities

Find the Start

Give students a list of words with the first letter missing. Ask them to figure out which letter could be the starter for all the given words, for example:

_in _it _ig _id

Discuss the answers as a class. Was there more than one possible answer?

Mind the Gaps!

Write this sentence on the board:

"I like _____," said _____.

Ask students to read this sentence by themselves, write it down and fill in the gaps with words of their own. Discuss their individual sentences as a group.

Reading Eggs Lesson sequence	TEACH Content and skills	PRACTISE Children will:	APPLY
Hear: *Animated Lesson*	Introduce the rime ig using the song *Jig like a Pig*. Introduce the words said and like.	identify and read ig words. Identify said and like. Make sentences using said and like.	**Worksheet 1** Word families
Write: *Dot-to-Dot, Pick Up Bricks*	Reinforce correct letter formation. Recognise correct word order for a sentence.	write the word big. Choose the correct words to make a sentence.	**Worksheet 2** Read and write
Find: *Trains, Rhyming Squares*	Recognise letters in upper and lower case. Identify rhyming words.	match lower case and capital letters. Find images of rhyming words.	**Worksheet 3** Sight words
Vocabulary: *Word Windows, Jigsaw, The Theme Game, Wheel of Words, Break it Up*	Build vocabulary skills: Blend and recognise words. Recognise key vocabulary. Identify the number of phonemes in a word.	blend sounds to read words. Match pictures to words. Identify the number of sounds in a word.	**Worksheet 4** Check
Read: *Book*	Read aloud book.	listen, follow the reading and read along.	**Reading Eggs Story book** The Big Queen

Related Reading Eggs Activities, Interactives, Songs and Books

Music Café

Jig like a Pig

Reading Eggs Puzzle Park

Hidden Words
Song Lines
What is it?

Reading Eggs Posters

Reading Eggs Library Books

My Program Books

Interactives

Driving Tests

Spelling Bank

Critter Card

Big Pig

Teacher Toolkit

Spelling Activities

Grammar Lessons

Reading Eggs Apps

Eggy Sight words

ig

Lesson 46 · Worksheet 1

Name

Word families

1 Match each picture to a word.

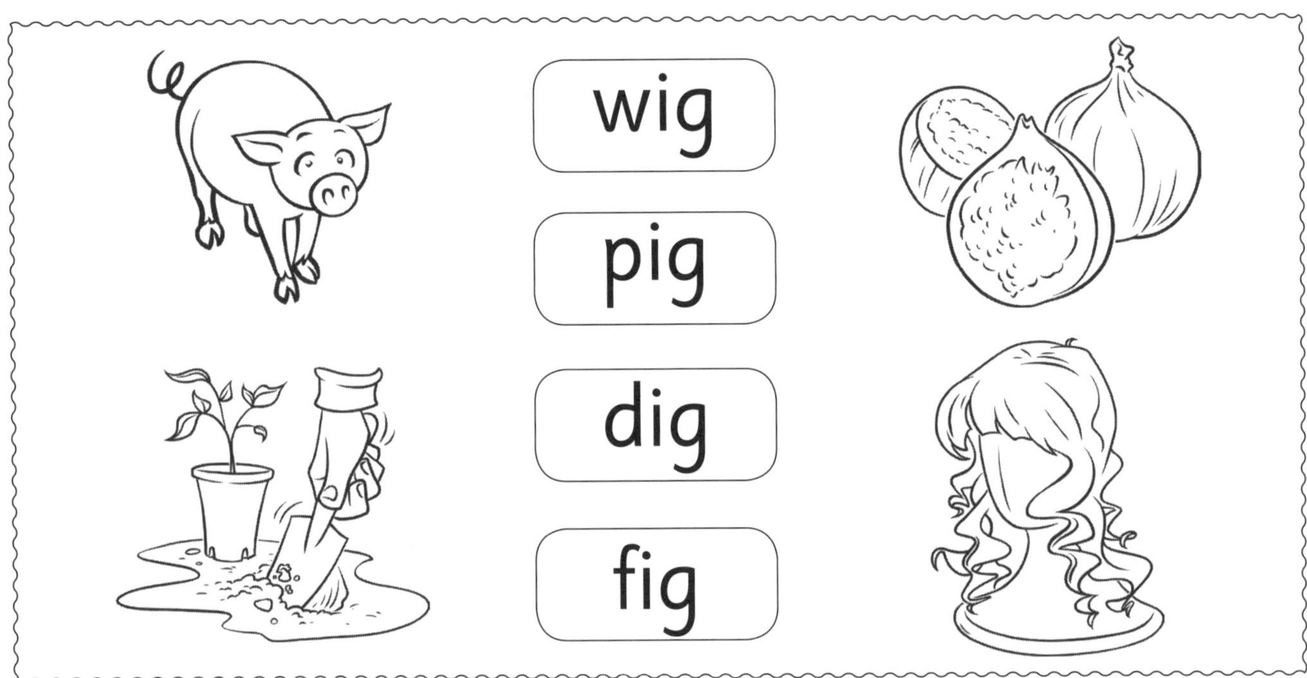

2 Say the word for each picture. Complete the word families.

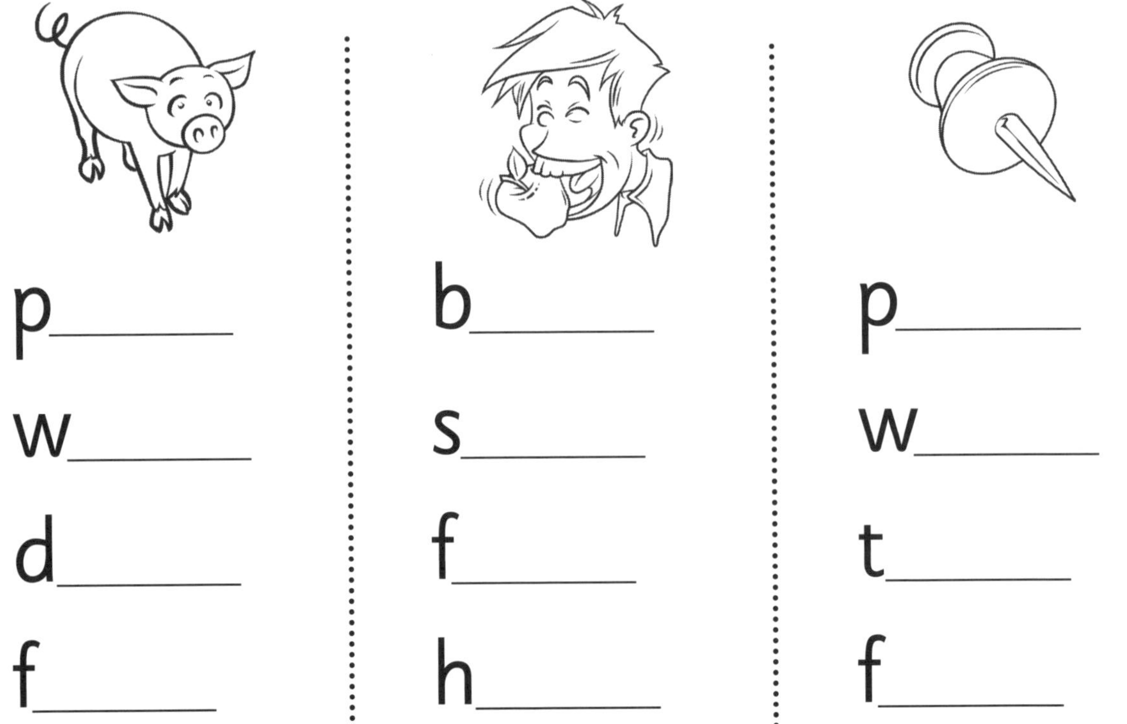

p______	b______	p______
w______	s______	w______
d______	f______	t______
f______	h______	f______

Name

1 Complete the sentence.

"This is Matt the ant,"

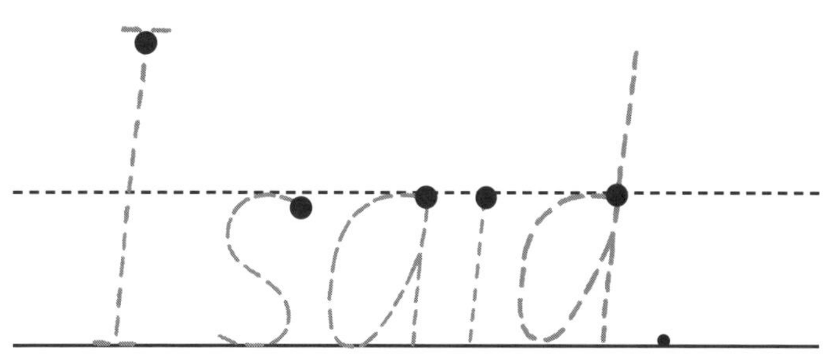

2 Complete the sentences.

big said like

I ________ my big horse.

I like my ________ bed.

"I like my big ring," she ________ .

Sight words

Lesson 46 • Worksheet 3

Name

1 Trace the words.

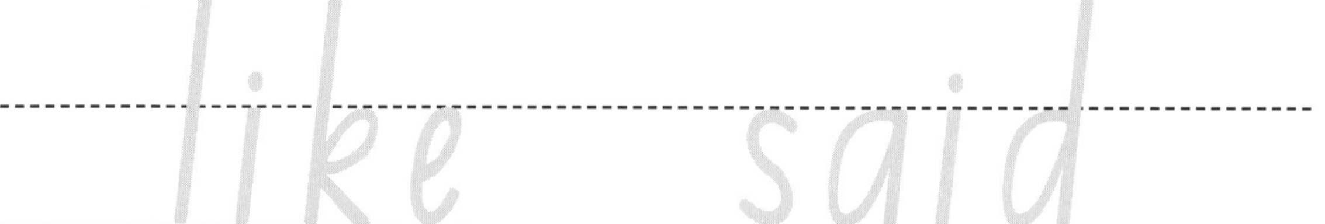

2 Join Big Pig to the word **like**.

3 Colour **like** = green, colour **said** = red.

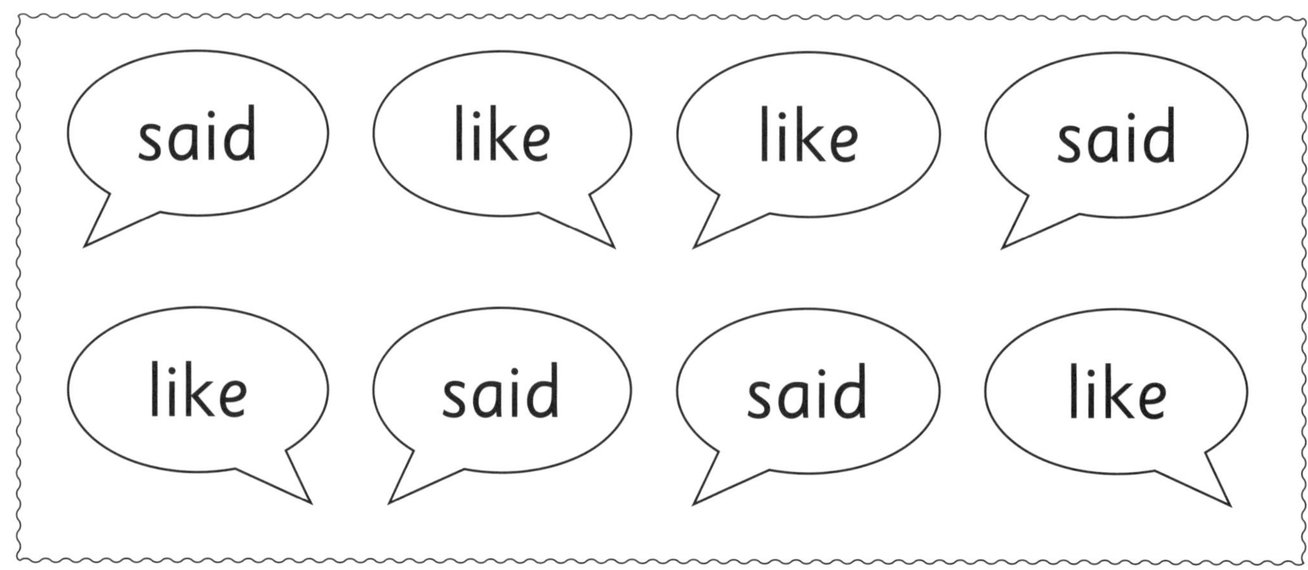

Name

it, ig, in

Word families

Lesson 46 · Worksheet 4

1 Complete the words. Match each word to its picture.

2 Guess the word by its shape. Write each word in the boxes.

like said big

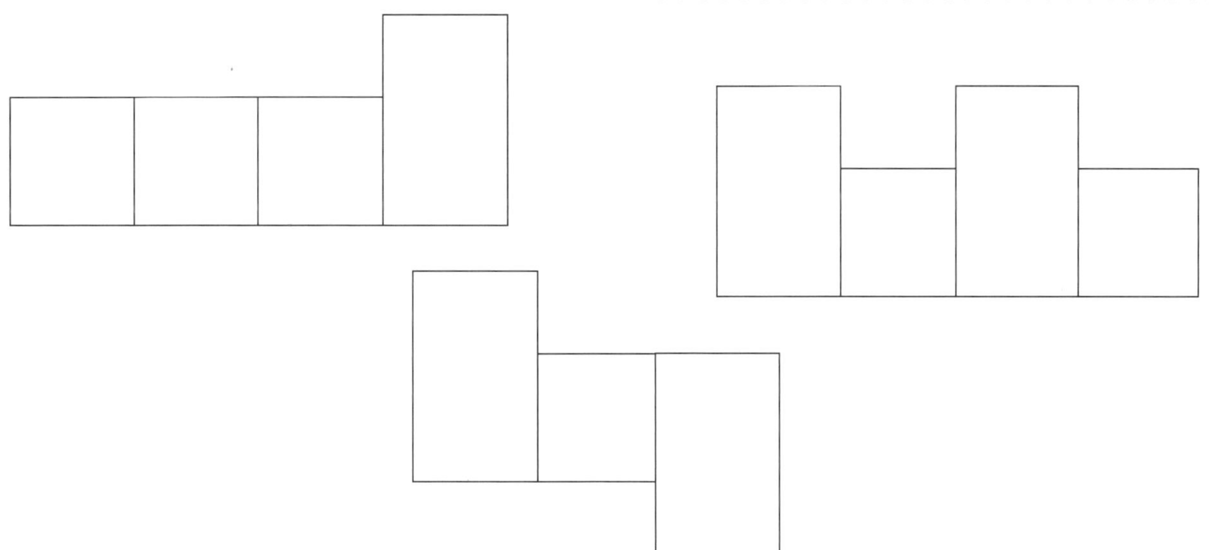

Lesson 47 the word **this**

Learning objectives

Children will:

- identify the word this.
- read and write sentences using this.

Australian Curriculum Content Descriptions

Sound and letter knowledge

ACELA1439 listen to the sounds a student hears in the word, and write letters to represent those sounds; identify and manipulate sounds (phonemes) in spoken words

ACELA1440 identify familiar and recurring letters and the use of upper and lower case in written texts

Expressing and developing ideas

ACELA1435 learn that word order in sentences is important for meaning

ACELA1438 build word families using onset and rime

ACELA1758 write consonant-vowel-consonant words by writing letters to represent the sounds in the spoken words; know that spoken words are written down by listening to the sounds heard in the word and then writing letters to represent those sounds

Sight words

this, is, yes, a, the, it, can, he

Word families

pig, big, wig, fig

Vocabulary words

bin, fish, kid, wag, too

Extra assistance

The sound th does not exist in some languages, so students from these backgrounds may struggle to pronounce it. Even native English-speaking children may struggle with this sound. It can be mispronounced as /d/, /t/, /s/ or /f/. To help students practise this sound, have them stick their tongue out between the top and bottom teeth and then pull it away, exaggerating the movement to reinforce it.

Classroom activities

Is This It?

Put a list of words on the board and ask students if you can put the word this in front of each word. Use singular and plural nouns, verbs and adjectives. See if the children can explain why some words work and some don't.

Mind the Gap!

Write these sentences on the board:

This is _____. This is a _____.

Ask students to read these sentences by themselves, write them down and fill in each gap with just one word. Discuss their individual sentences as a group.

Reading Eggs Lesson sequence	TEACH Content and skills	PRACTISE Children will:	APPLY
Hear: *Animated Lesson*	Introduce the word this.	identify the word this. Make sentences using the word this.	**Worksheet 1** Sight words
Write: *Make a Sentence*	Recognise correct word order for a sentence.	choose the correct words to make a sentence.	**Worksheet 2** Read and write
Find: *Fishing Boats, Know Your Alphabet, Alien Planets, Missing Sound*	Recognise a given word. Identify upper and lower case pairs of letters. Identify the correct onset letter to complete the word.	find the given word in a group. Match lower case letters to their capital. Choose the correct initial letter to make the word.	**Worksheet 3** Word families
Vocabulary: *Blend a Word, Book Ends, Sound Streamers, Picture Picker*	Build vocabulary skills: Blend and recognise words. Read basic vocabulary and identify key words. Identify sounds in words. Read and comprehend a sentence.	blend sounds to read words. Choose from a list of words to finish the sentence. Sound out and select letters to make words. Read a sentence and match to a picture.	**Worksheet 4** Check
Read: *Book*	Read aloud book.	listen, follow the reading and read along.	**Reading Eggs Story book** Wag it

Related Reading Eggs Activities, Interactives, Songs and Books

Music Café

In The Mix

In Time with Sam and Sid

Reading Eggs Puzzle Park

Hidden Words

Song Lines

What is it?

Reading Eggs Posters

Reading Eggs Library Books

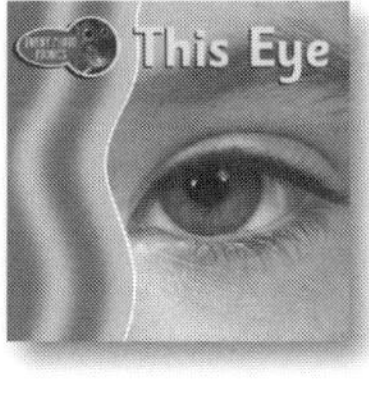

My Program Books

Interactives

Driving Tests

Spelling Bank

Critter Card

Scribble stick

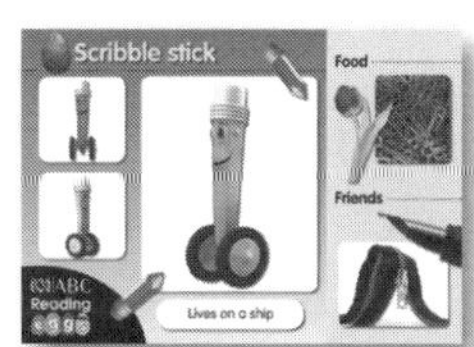

Teacher Toolkit

Spelling Activities

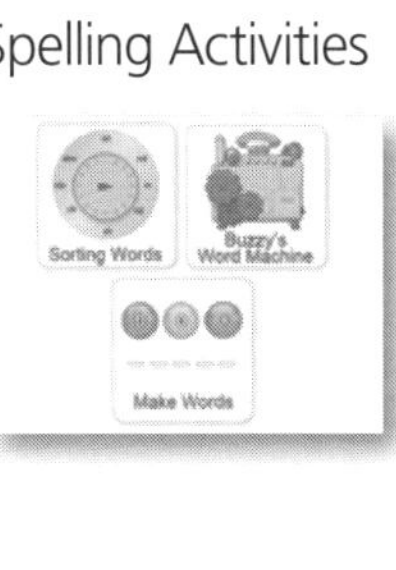

Reading Eggs Apps

Eggy Sight words

Name

Sight words

1 Trace.

2 Help Scribble stick find his way to his list.
Join up all the **this** words.

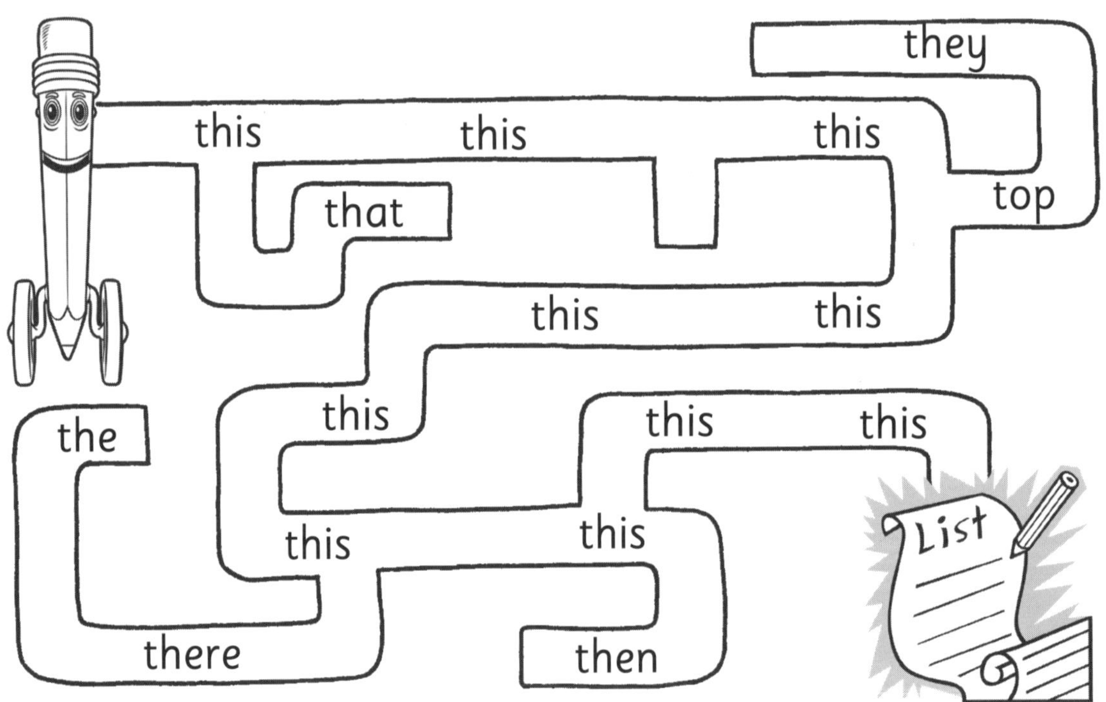

3 Circle the word **this**.

This is Sid the kid. This is the big pig. This is the big fish.

Colour a star each time you find **this**.

Name

Read and write

Lesson 47 • Worksheet 2

1 Complete each sentence. Draw a picture.

This is Sid the kid.

This is a big fish.

2 Colour the correct word. Cross out the wrong word.

This is the six / big pig.

Can / This 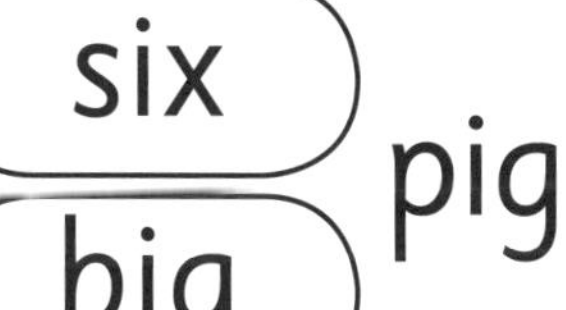 the big pig wag it?

Yes! The big pig the / can wag it.

Word families

Lesson 47 • Worksheet 3

Name

id, it, ix, ig

1 Draw lines to match the words that rhyme.

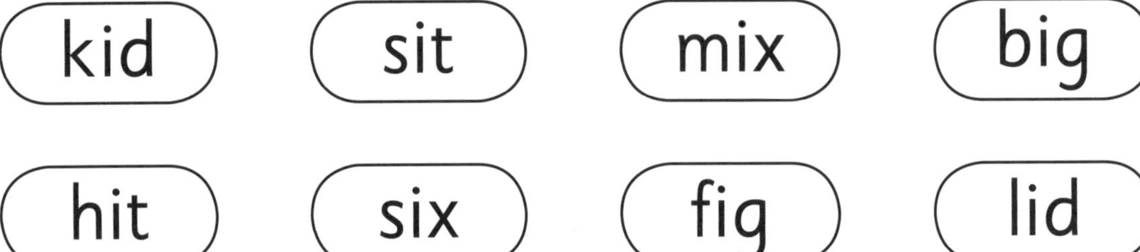

2 Say the word for each picture. Match it to its ending sound.

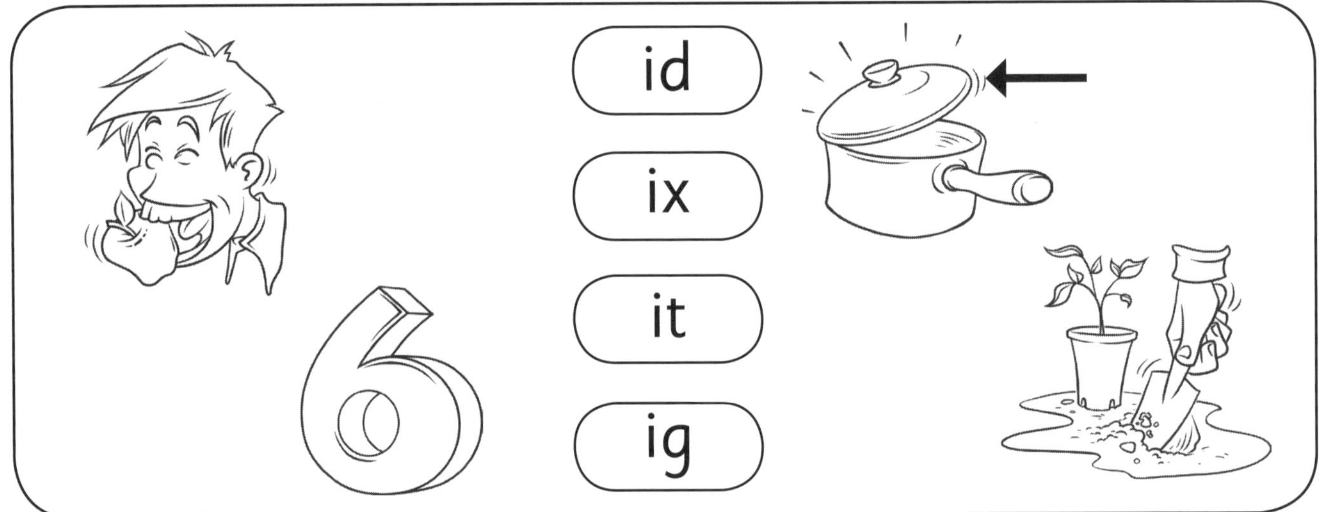

3 Draw:

a wig on Big pig.

six pink pigs.

Name

Check

1 Join the puzzle pieces. Write the words.

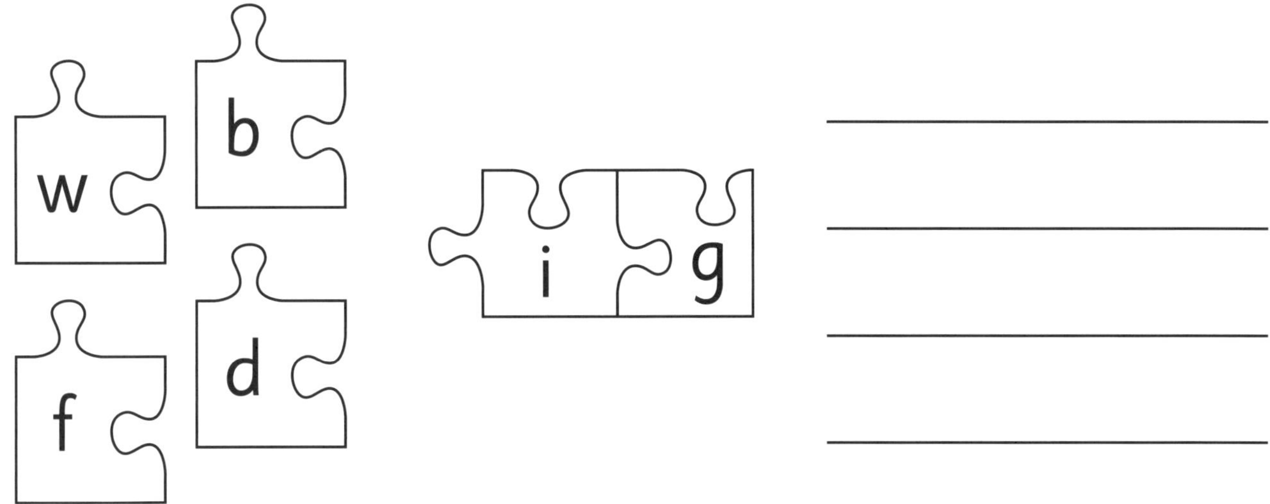

2 Colour the **id** words blue, the **it** words yellow and the **ix** words red.

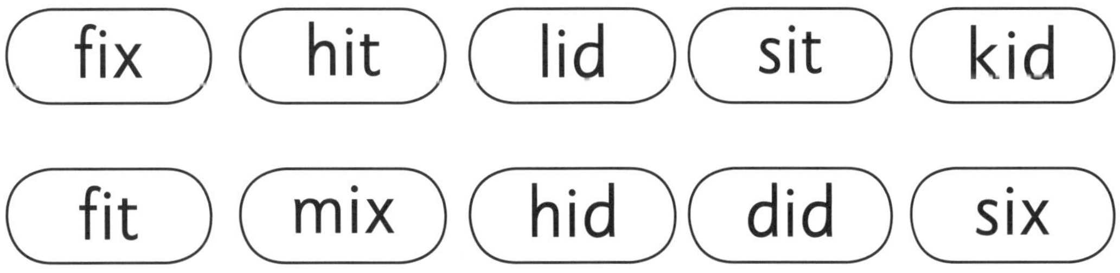

3 Complete the sentences.

This Can

________ Sam see the big pig?

________ is Sam the ant.

Lesson 48 the sound **ip**

Learning objectives

Children will:

- read and write words using ip.
- recognise the words big and little.
- identify some colour words.

Australian Curriculum Content Descriptions

Sound and letter knowledge

ACELA1439 listen to the sounds a student hears in the word, and write letters to represent those sounds; identify and manipulate sounds (phonemes) in spoken words; identify onset and rime in one-syllable spoken words

Expressing and developing ideas

ACELA1438 build word families using onset and rime

ACELA1758 recognise the most common sound made by each letter of the alphabet, including consonants and short vowel sounds; write consonant-vowel-consonant words by writing letters to represent the sounds in the spoken words; know that spoken words are written down by listening to the sounds heard in the word and then writing letters to represent those sounds

Word families

dip, lip, tip, sip, hip, nip, zip, pip, rip

Vocabulary words

pink, blue, black, little, big

Extra assistance

Some colour words can look very similar – blue and black for example. To practise identifying colours and their words, play a game of Bingo. Ask students to fill in a ten-square grid with colour words from a list you give them. After this, there is no talking until 'bingo'. Hold up an object which is all one colour. If students have that colour on their board they cross it off. Hold up more objects, until a student has crossed off all their words and calls out 'bingo'! Put the objects in a line and ask the students to name their colours out loud.

Classroom activities

Mix and Match

Put the consonant letters of the alphabet on the board in writing or magnetic letters. Write the sound ip on the board. Each student comes to the board and writes a word they can make using ip and another letter. Discuss their words with the class. Can anyone use two letters to make a new ip word?

Which Colour?

Put students in small groups of two or three. Give each group three sheets of paper with the word pink, blue or black written on each. Ask the students to think of as many things as they can that are pink, blue or black, and to draw them on the relevant sheet and label them. Bring the groups together to compare lists.

Reading Eggs Lesson sequence	TEACH Content and skills	PRACTISE Children will:	APPLY
Hear: *Animated Lesson*	Introduce the sound ip through words and the song *I'm an ip Frog*.	identify and read the ip sound in isolation and in words.	**Worksheet 1** Word families
Write: *Tiles*	Blend sounds to write words.	sound out and select letters to make words.	**Worksheet 2** Read and write
Find: *Climb the Ladder, Read and Colour, Golden Goose, Flock of Seagulls*	Recognise a given word. Identify colour words.	find the given word in a group. Match the colour words with their colours.	**Worksheet 3** Sight words
Vocabulary: *Word Windows, Groups, Make a Word*	Build vocabulary skills: Blend and recognise words. Recognise key vocabulary. Identify initial letters by sound and read words.	blend sounds to read and make words. Match pictures to words. Match pictures to their initial letter.	**Worksheet 4** Check
Read: *Book*	Read aloud book.	listen, follow the reading and read along.	**Reading Eggs Story book** Big and little

Related Reading Eggs Activities, Interactives, Songs and Books

Music Café

I'm an ip Frog

Reading Eggs Puzzle Park

Hidden Words
Song Lines
Animal Colours
Colour Code

Reading Eggs Posters

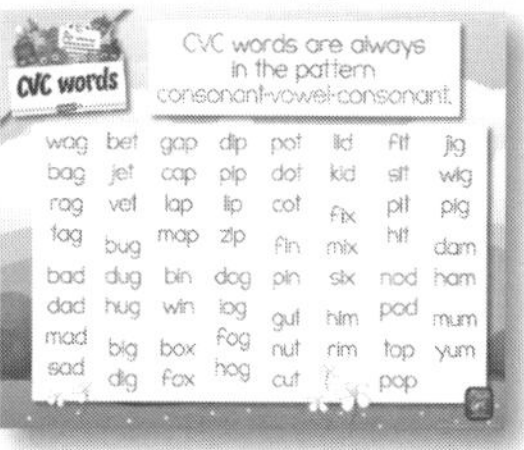

Reading Eggs Library Books

My Program Books

Interactives

Driving Tests

Spelling Bank

Critter Card

Thistle

Teacher Toolkit

Spelling Activities

Reading Eggs Apps

Eggy Sight words

Lesson 48 • Worksheet 1

Name

Word families

1 Trace.

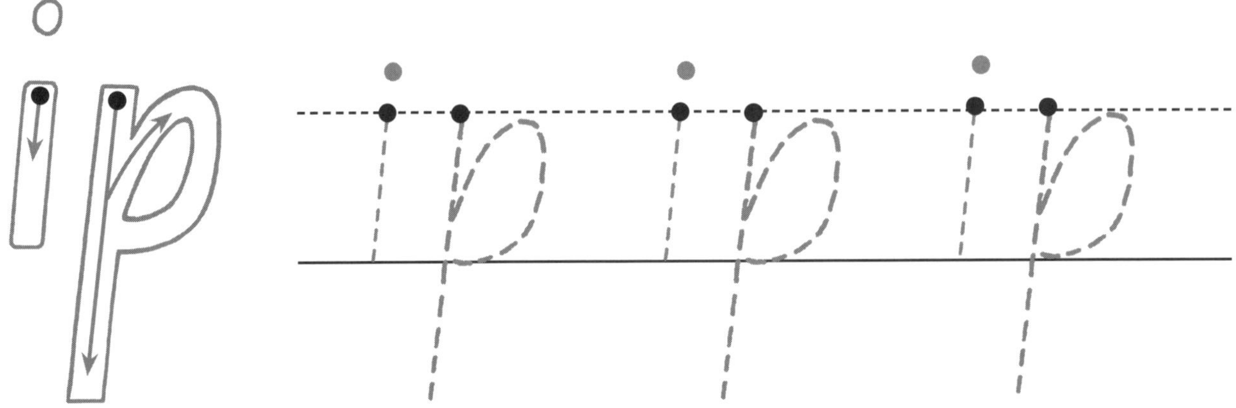

2 Colour the **ip** words.

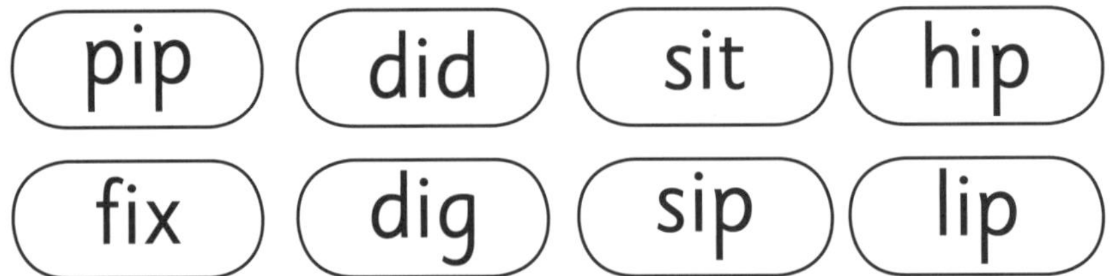

3 Match each picture to a word.

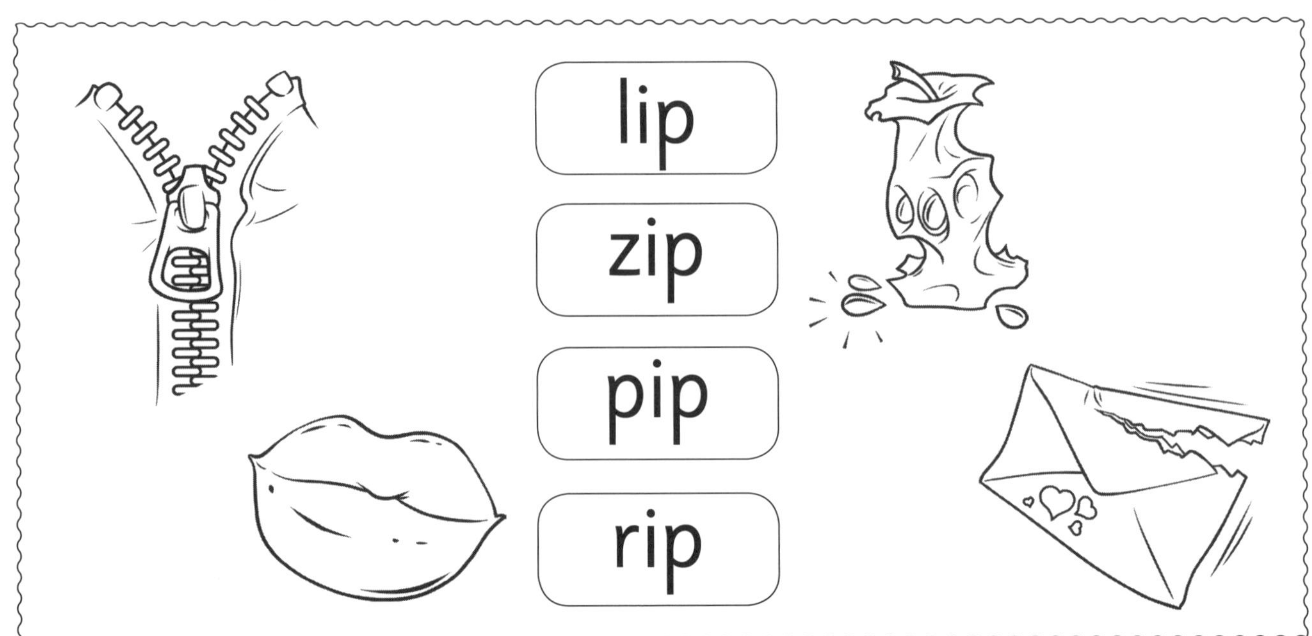

Name

Read and write

Lesson 48 · Worksheet 2

Name each picture. Complete the sentence.

pig zip pip bin six

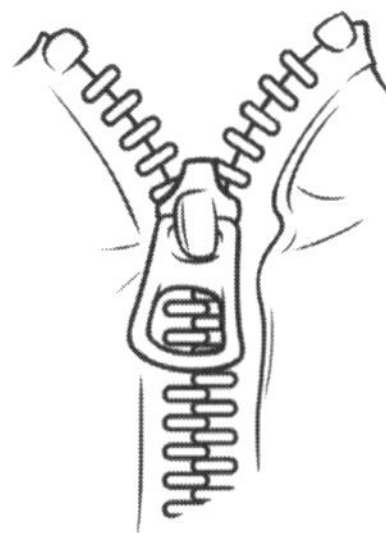

This is a __________.

This is a __________.

This is a __________.

This is a __________.

This is a __________.

Sight words

Lesson 48 · Worksheet 3

Name

1 Trace and write the words.

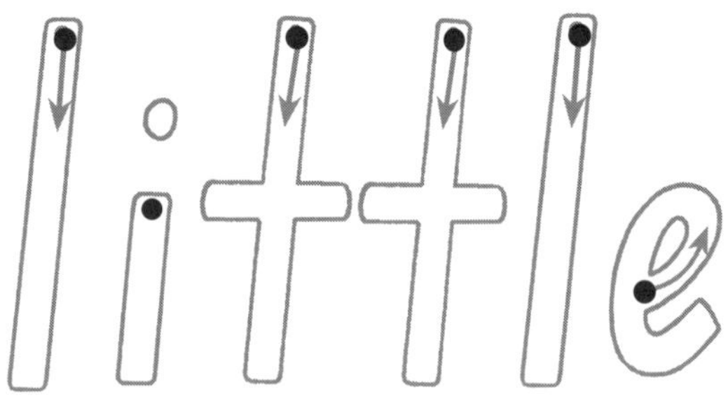

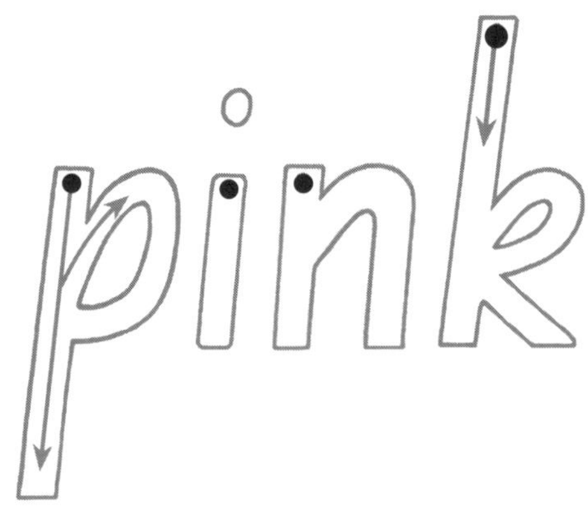

2 Help Thistle find his little cap. Colour the path of **little** words.

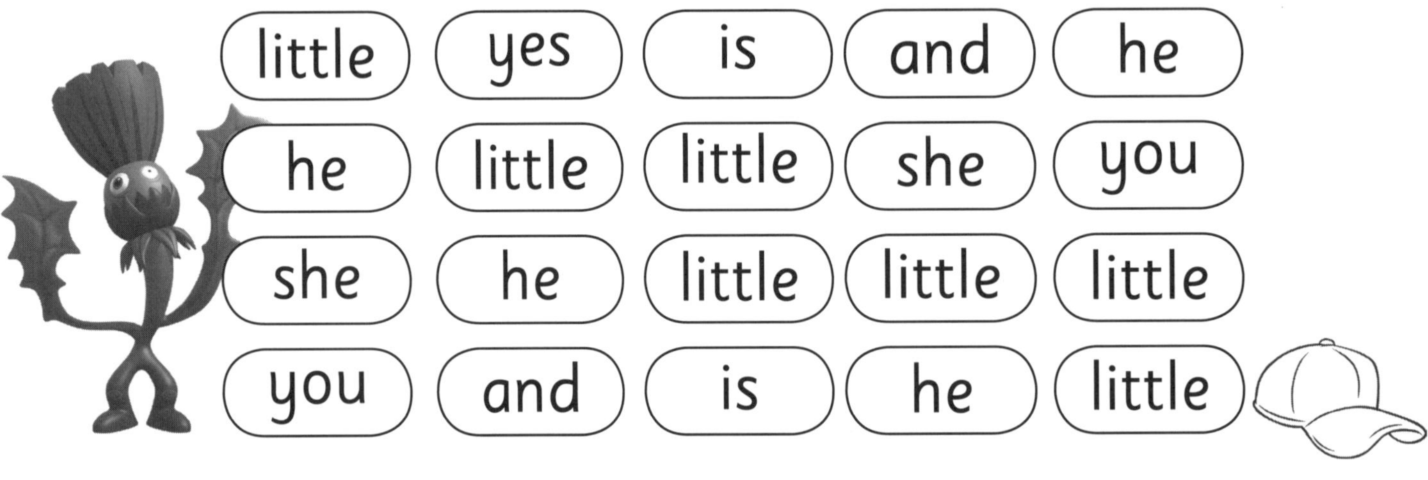

3 Guess the word by its shape.
Write each word in a box.

little pink pig

Name

Check

ip

Lesson 48 · Worksheet 4

1 Label each picture. Use the words.

bin
win
sip
rip
pin
tin

2 Find the words. Colour **little** = pink, **pip** = blue, **sip** = green.

l	i	t	t	l	e	p	i	p
s	i	p	l	i	t	t	l	e
p	i	p	s	i	p	p	i	p
l	i	t	t	l	e	s	i	p

3 Draw a picture for this sentence.

I can see six pips.

the sound **ill**

Learning objectives

Children will:

- identify the rime ill.
- read and write words using ill.

Australian Curriculum Content Descriptions

Sound and letter knowledge

ACELA1439 listen to the sounds a student hears in the word, and write letters to represent those sounds; identify and manipulate sounds (phonemes) in spoken words; identify onset and rime in one-syllable spoken words

Expressing and developing ideas

ACELA1438 break words into onset and rime; build word families using onset and rime

ACELA1758 write consonant-vowel-consonant words by writing letters to represent the sounds in the spoken words; know that spoken words are written down by listening to the sounds heard in the word and then writing letters to represent those sounds

Interpreting, analysing and evaluating

ACELY1649 navigate a text correctly, starting at the right place and reading in the right direction, returning to the next line as needed, matching one spoken word to one written word

Word families

pill, will, till, hill, gill, still, fill

Extra assistance

The sound at the end of ill is one sound made with two letters. To reinforce this idea, have students make crazy creatures by providing them with different animal heads with consonant sounds written on, bodies with vowels on them and a tail with **ll**. Students make words using three sounds creating crazy combination creatures and in the process reinforce the idea that **ll** is one sound.

Classroom activities

Say it Right!

Have a set of pictures of things ending with ill. Hold up a picture and say the word incorrectly, using the wrong vowel sound, eg hall for hill. Students need to call out the right word.

Bingo!

Give students a laminated board with 10 squares on it. Ask them to write a word in each square that ends with ill (use whiteboard markers). Say words that end with ill. Students put a cross on that word on their board. First one to 10 calls out 'bingo' and wins!

Reading Eggs Lesson sequence	**TEACH Content and skills**	**PRACTISE Children will:**	**APPLY**
Hear: *Animated Lesson*	Introduce the sound ill through words and the song *Jill Will.*	identify and read ill sound in isolation and in words.	**Worksheet 1** Ending sounds
Write: *Tiles, Word Ladder, Rumble Jumble*	Blend and write words. Unjumble letters for a given word.	blend sounds to make words. Write a word from jumbled letters.	**Worksheet 2** Read and write
Find: *Word family, 1, 2, 3, 4, Missing Sound*	Identify the correct onset letter to complete the word. Identify the order of a sequence of events.	choose the correct initial letter to make the word. Put pictures in order to show a sequence of events.	**Worksheet 3** Word families
Vocabulary: *Wheel of Words, Book Ends, Blend a Word*	Build vocabulary skills: Recognise key vocabulary. Read basic vocabulary and identify key words. Blend and recognise words.	match pictures to words. Choose from a list of words to finish the sentence. Blend sounds to read and make words.	**Worksheet 4** Check
Read: *Book*	Read aloud book.	listen, follow the reading and read along.	**Reading Eggs Story book** Word families for it, in, ig, id, ing

Related Reading Eggs Activities, Interactives, Songs and Books

Music Café

Jill Will

Reading Eggs Puzzle Park

Hidden Words

Song Lines

What is it?

Reading Eggs Posters

Reading Eggs Library Books

My Program Books

Interactives

Driving Tests

Spelling Bank

Critter Card

Sixty Six

Teacher Toolkit

Spelling Activities

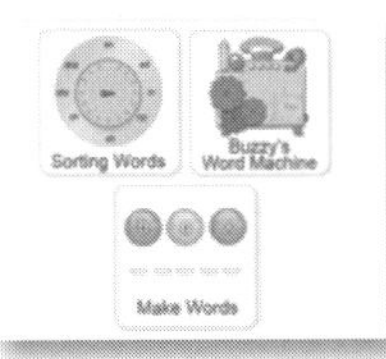

Reading Eggs Apps

Eggy Sight words

Lesson 49 • Worksheet 1

Name

Ending sounds

1 Trace.

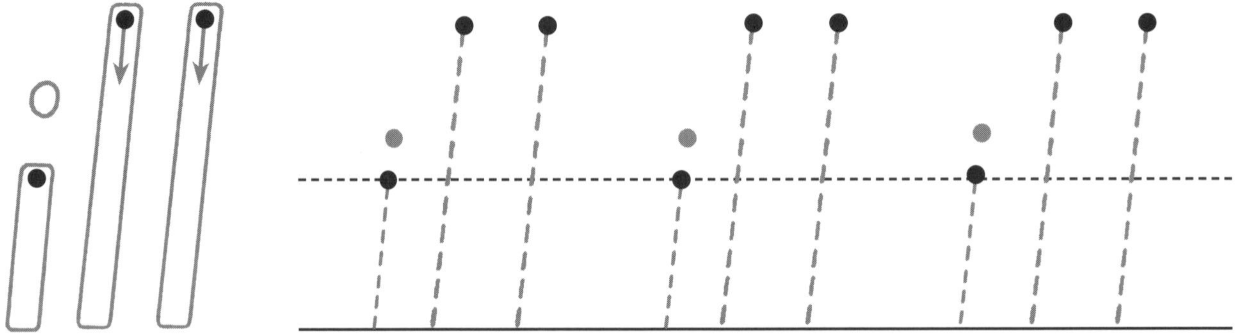

2 Join each sound to the word machine.
Write each word you make.

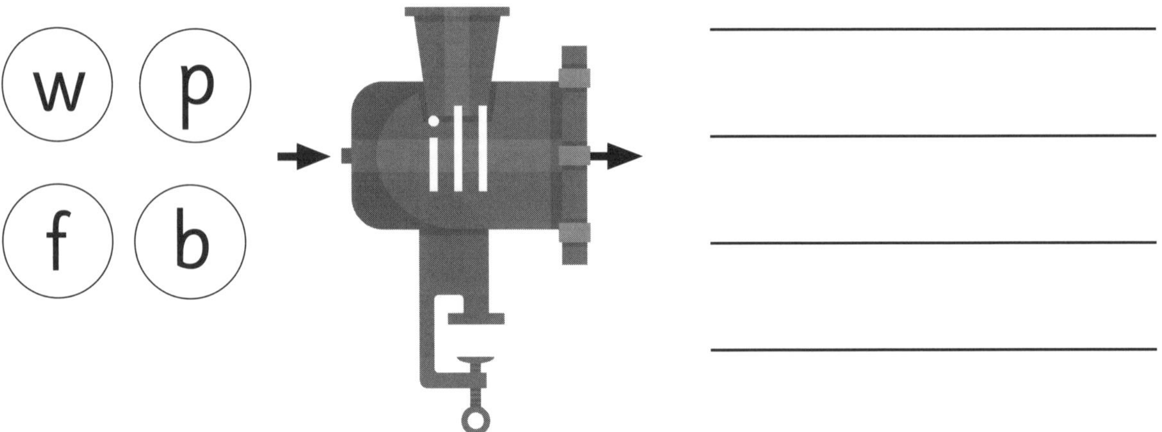

3 Write the words in alphabetical order.

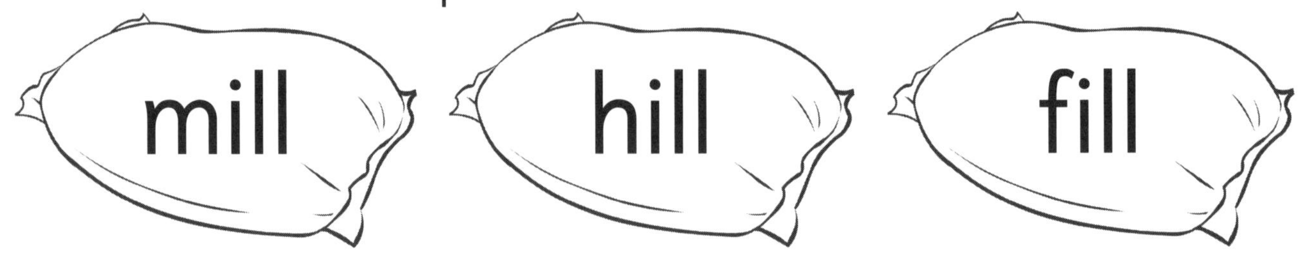

Name

Read and write

ill

Lesson 49 · Worksheet 2

1 Complete the sentence.

The castle is on a

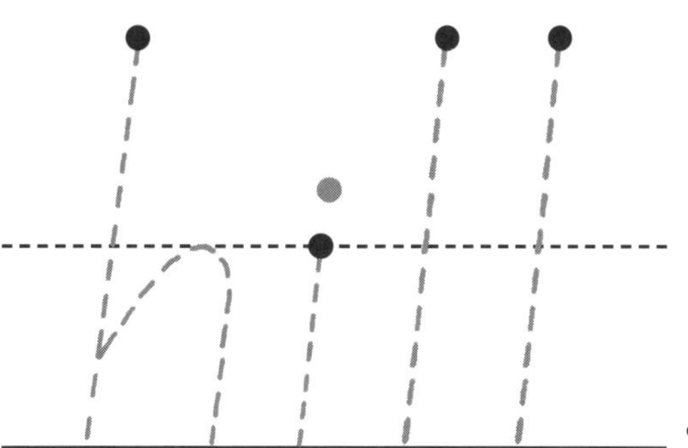

.

2 Colour the correct word. Cross out the wrong word.

"I am (il / ill)," said Sam the ant.

Sid (hid / hidd) six pins.

This fish has (bigg / big) fins.

3 Colour the **ill** words.

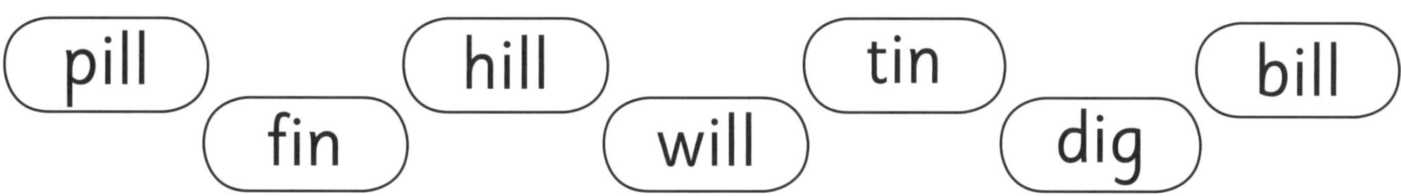

pill fin hill will tin dig bill

ill

Lesson 49 • Worksheet 3

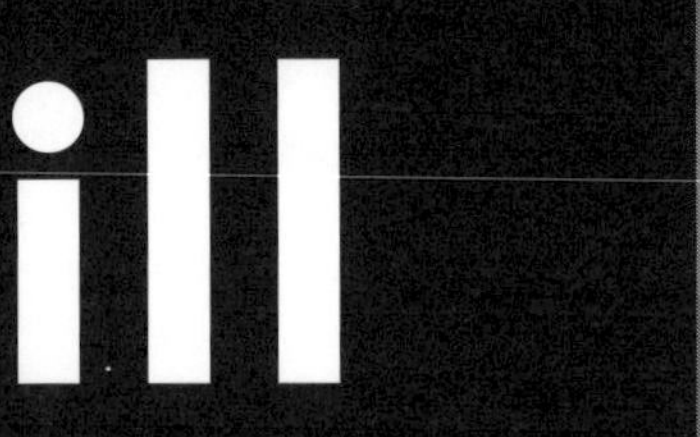

Name

Word families

1 Match each word to a picture.

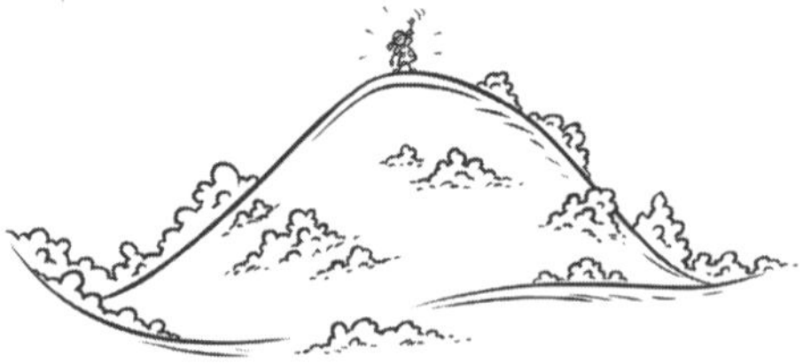

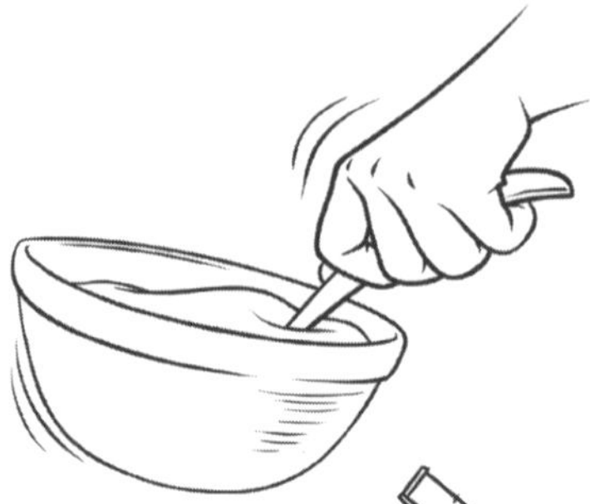

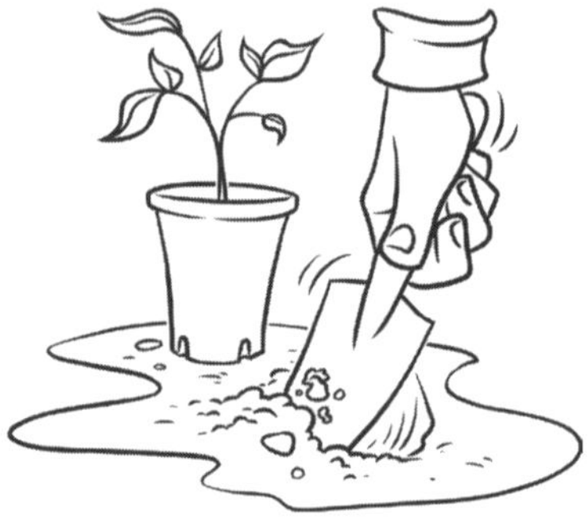

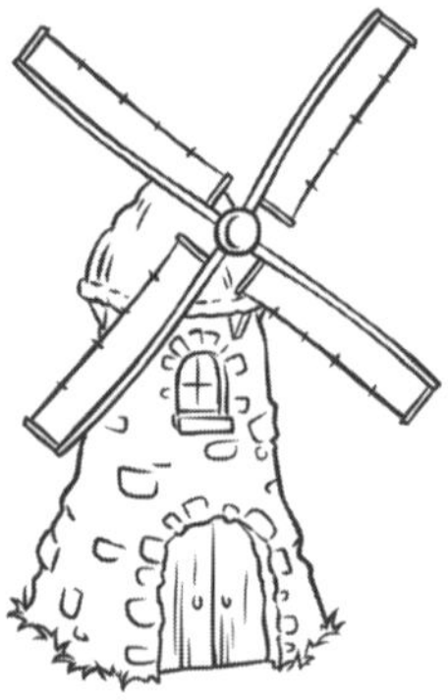

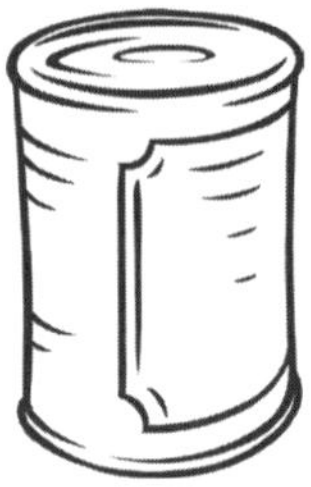

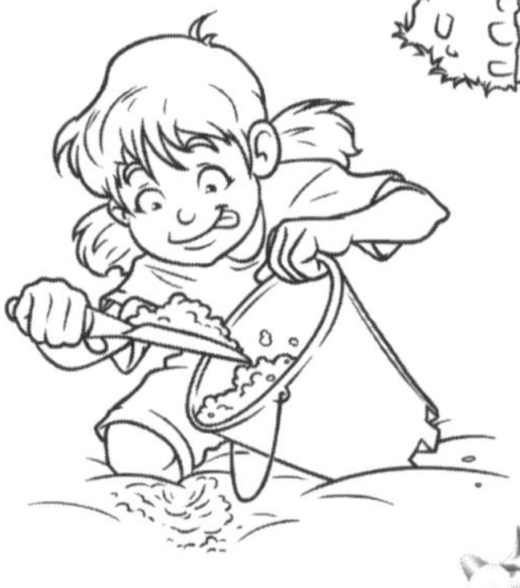

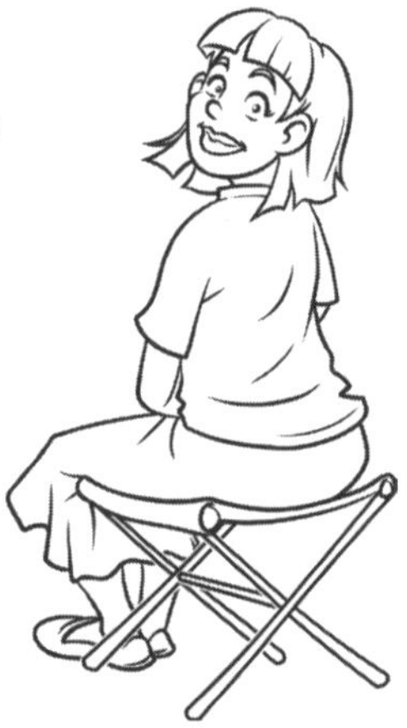

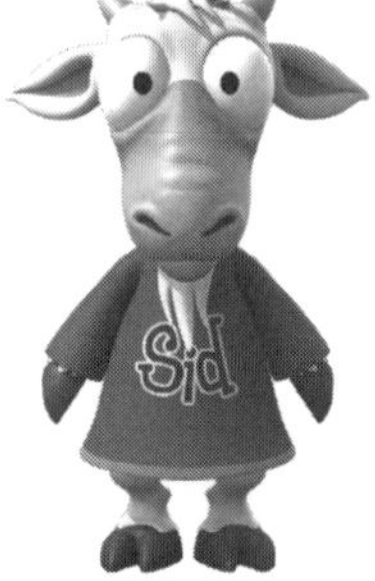

mix

hill

dig

Sid

mill

fill

sit

tin

2 Colour the odd one out.

hill fin will mill pill fill sill

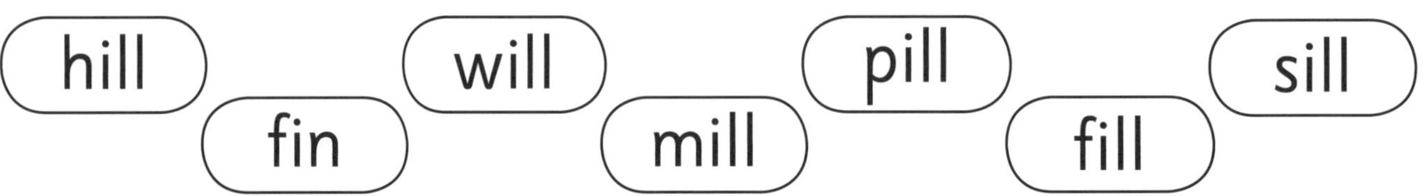

Name

Check

Lesson 49 • Worksheet 4

1 Complete the words. Match each word to its picture.

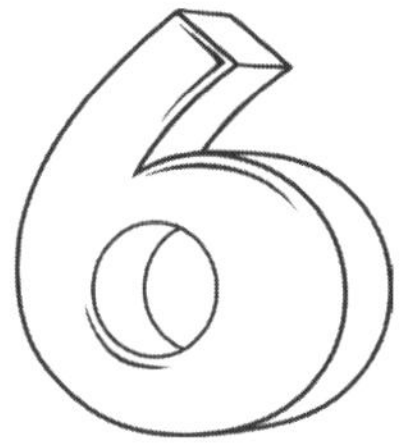

h______

s______

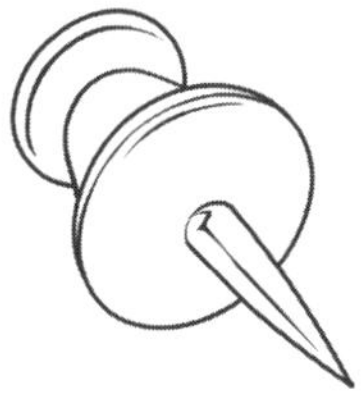

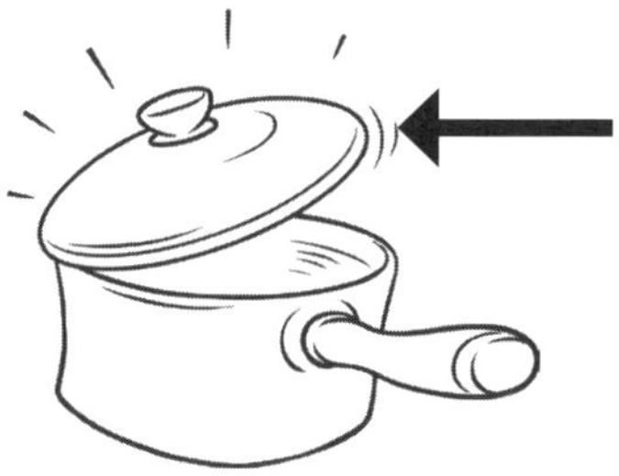

l______

p______

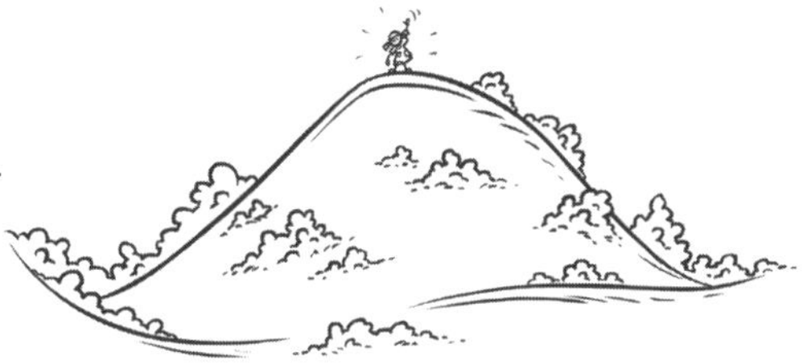

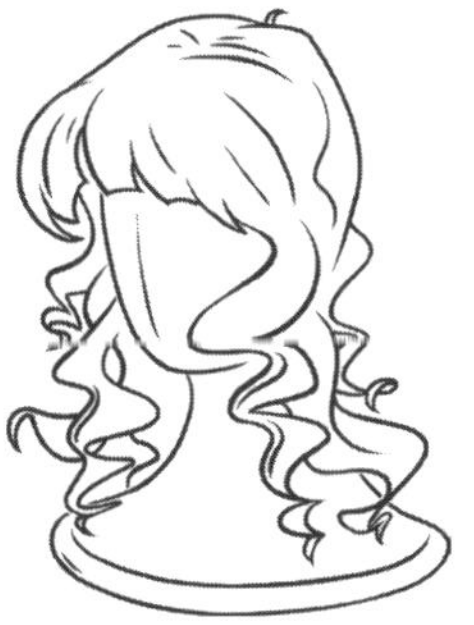

w______

h______

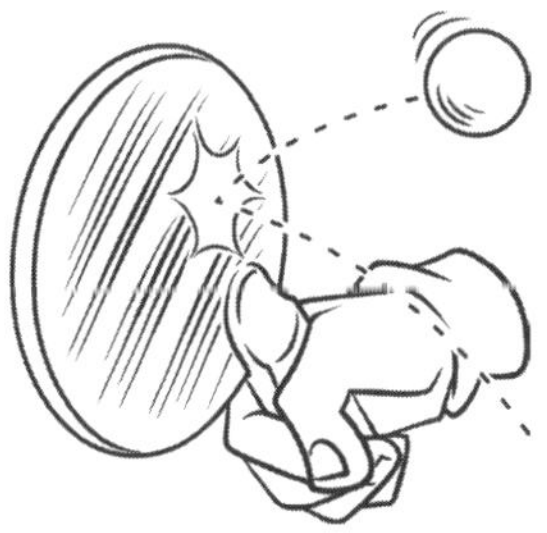

2 Guess the word by its shape. Write each word in the boxes.

pill mix dig

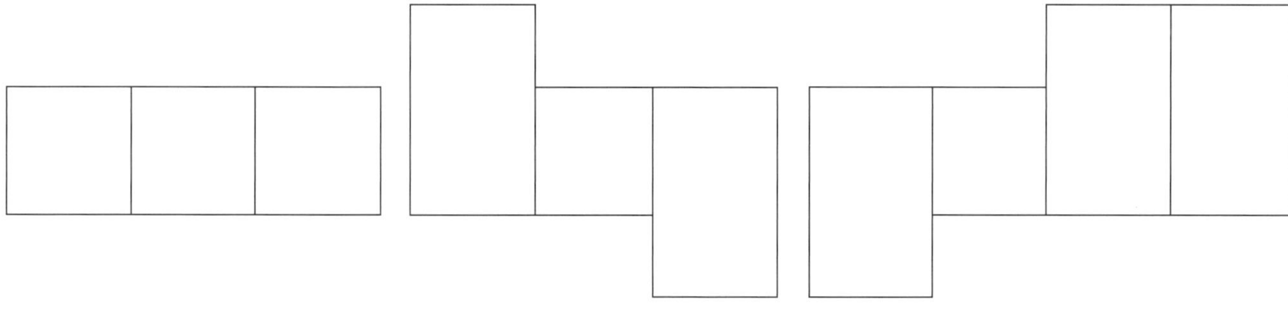

Lesson 50 the sound **ing**

Learning objectives

Children will:

- read and write words using ing.
- revise /i/ word families.
- recognise the sight words has, two and cannot.

Australian Curriculum Content Descriptions

Sound and letter knowledge

ACELA1439 listen to the sounds a student hears in the word, and write letters to represent those sounds;identify and manipulate sounds (phonemes) in spoken words; identify onset and rime in one-syllable spoken words

ACELA1440 identify familiar and recurring letters and the use of upper and lower case in written texts

Expressing and developing ideas

ACELA1435 learn that word order in sentences is important for meaning

ACELA1438 build word families using onset and rime

ACELA1758 know that spoken words are written down by listening to the sounds heard in the word and then writing letters to represent those sounds

Interpreting, analysing and evaluating

ACELY1649 navigate a text correctly, starting at the right place and reading in the right direction, returning to the next line as needed, matching one spoken word to one written word

Sight words

has, two, cannot, the, can, this, is, a, and

Word families

ip, id, ig, it, ill, in, ix, king, ring, wing, sing, swing

Vocabulary words

bird

Extra assistance

Students who speak another language may have trouble differentiating between /n/ and /ng/ endings. Give them opportunities to say and hear the difference. One way to do this is with a Spelling Bee. Give students a list of words ending with in and ing to learn for a week. Ask students one at a time to spell one of the words from the list. They have to listen for the ending when you say it and then they have to spell it correctly and say the word clearly.

Classroom activities

Flashcard Snap

Have at least two sets of flashcards of short i words. Shuffle and deal between two players. Keep cards face down. Players take turns to put a card from their pile onto a central pile, saying the word as they turn it over. If the two cards on top have the same ending, the players shout SNAP! The first to do so takes the central pile. Play continues until one player runs out of cards.

Reading Eggs Lesson sequence	**TEACH Content and skills**	**PRACTISE Children will:**	**APPLY**
Hear: *Animated Lesson*	Revise word families and blending onset and rime with the song *The Mousy House.*	choose the correct ending and initial letter to make the word.	**Worksheet 1** Word families
Write: *Make a Sentence*	Recognise correct word order for a sentence.	choose the correct words to make a sentence.	**Worksheet 2** Read and write
Find: *Today's Words, Frog Hops, Word family, Driving Trucks, Letter Lights, Fishing Boats, Time for 20*	Recognise a given word. Identify the correct onset letter to complete the word. Identify upper and lower case pairs of letters.	find the given word in a group. Choose the correct initial letter to make the word. Match lower case letters to their capital.	**Worksheet 3** Sight words
Vocabulary: *Word Windows, Break it Up*	Build vocabulary skills: Blend and recognise words. Identify the number of phonemes in a word.	blend sounds to read words. Identify the number of sounds in a word.	**Worksheet 4** Check
Read: *Book*	Read aloud book.	listen, follow the reading and read along.	**Reading Eggs Story book** The King can sing

Classroom activities

Find the Start

Give students a list of words with the first letter missing. Ask them to figure out which letter could be the starter for all the given words, for example:

_ing _ill _ip _it _ix

Discuss the answers as a class. Was there more than one possible answer?

Related Reading Eggs Activities, Interactives, Songs and Books

Music Café

The Mousy House

Reading Eggs Puzzle Park

More than One

Hidden Words

Song Lines

Reading Eggs Posters

Reading Eggs Library Books

My Program Books

Interactives

Driving Tests

Spelling Bank

Teacher Toolkit

Spelling Activities

Reading Eggs Apps

Eggy Sight words

Critter Card

Blue wing

ing

Lesson 50 • Worksheet 1

Name

Word families

1 Match each picture to a word.

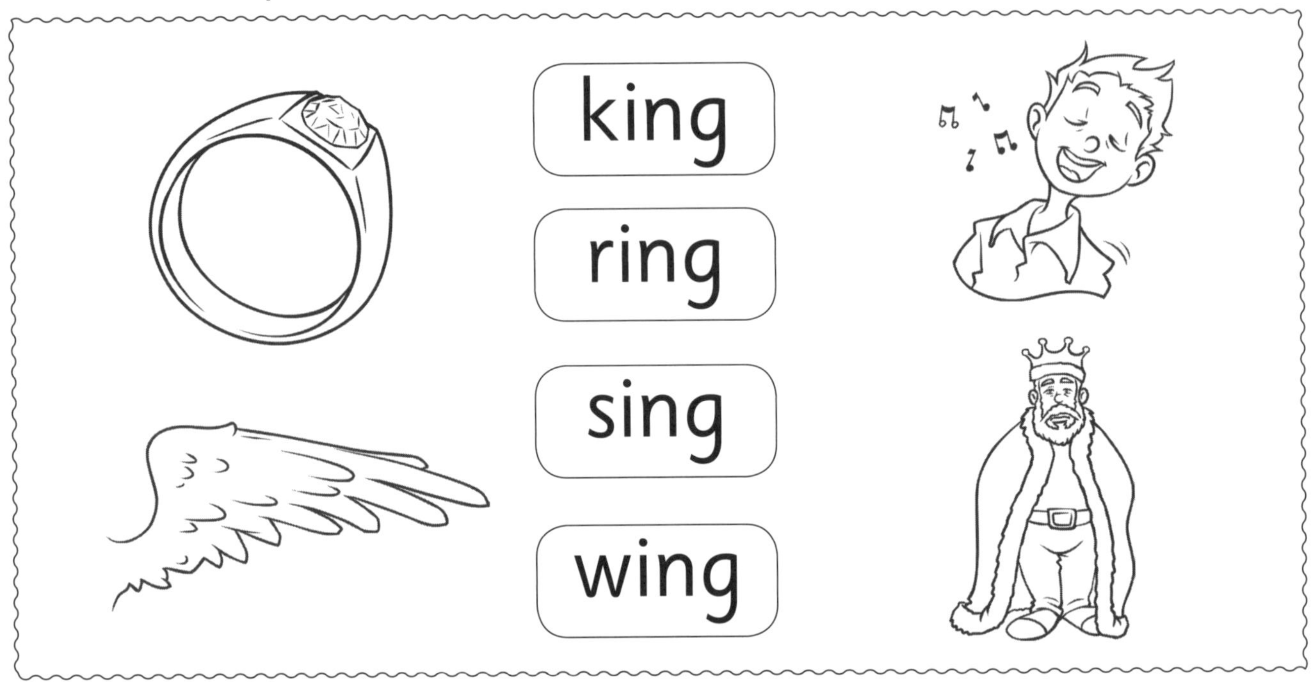

2 Colour the rings red if they end with the sound **ing**.

3 Colour the correct word. Cross out the wrong word.

The little bird can song / sing .

Name

Read and write

ing

Lesson 50 • Worksheet 2

1 Complete the sentence.

2 Complete the sentences.

wings ring sing

The king has a ________ .

The bird can ________ .

The bird has two ________ .

3 Circle the odd one out.

sing wing ring bird king

Sight words

Lesson 50 • Worksheet 3

Name

two, has, bird

1 Trace and write each word.

two has bird

2 Help Blue wing find her nest. Trace the path of **bird** words.

3 Colour **has** = blue, colour **two** = yellow.

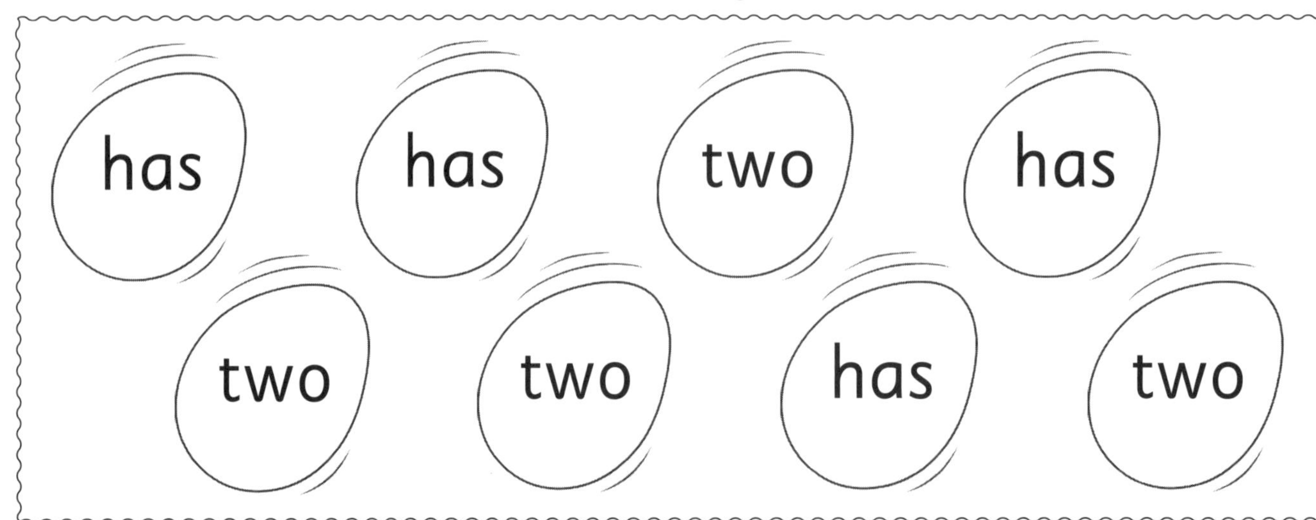

Name

Check

ing

Lesson 50 • Worksheet 4

Circle the picture that matches.

sing			
fin			
lip	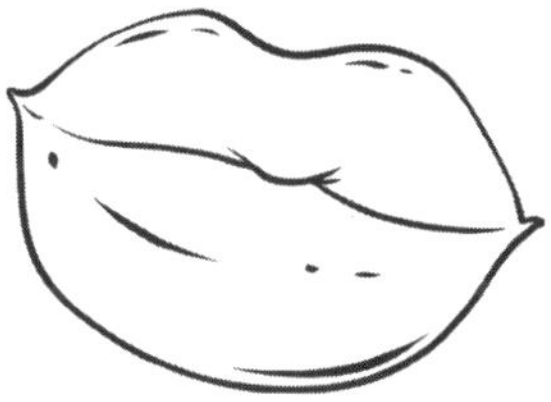		
pig			
mix			
hit			

Lesson 51 the word **go**

Learning objectives

Children will:

- identify the words go and by.
- read and write the words go and by.

Australian Curriculum Content Descriptions

Sound and letter knowledge

ACELA1439 listen to the sounds a student hears in the word, and write letters to represent those sounds; identify and manipulate sounds (phonemes) in spoken words

Creating texts

ACELY1653 follow clear demonstrations of how to construct each letter, learn to construct lower case letters

Expressing and developing ideas

ACELA1435 learn that word order in sentences is important for meaning

ACELA1758 recognise the most common sound made by each letter of the alphabet, including consonants and short vowel sounds; know that spoken words are written down by listening to the sounds heard in the word and then writing letters to represent those sounds

Sight words

go, by, you, can, see, the

Vocabulary words

pink, blue, black, six

Extra assistance

A fun game that can be adapted to reinforce sight word identification and practise pronunciation is Go Fish. Using a set of 15 or more pairs of sight word cards, deal five cards to each player; three players is best. The idea is to make matching pairs of sight words. Each player takes turns asking another player "Have you got a ___?" That player hands over the card for ___ if they have it or says "No, go fish!" if they don't. This means the player must pick up two more cards from the pile. Whenever they get a pair they lay it down in front of them. Play continues until someone runs out of cards.

Classroom activities

Make your own sentences

Write the sentence starter *I can go …* on the board. Ask students to write this sentence twice, once with a place at the end and the second time using an adverb like fast or slow. For a challenge, ask students if they can write it a third time using both, eg I can go home slowly.

Bingo!

Give students a laminated board with 10 squares on it. Ask them to write a word in each square from the list of known sight words (use whiteboard markers). Say words from the list. Students put a cross on that word on their board. First one to 10 calls out 'bingo' and wins!

Reading Eggs Lesson sequence	TEACH Content and skills	PRACTISE Children will:	APPLY
Hear: *Animated Lesson*	Introduce the words go and by through words and sentences.	identify the words go and by in isolation and use them in a sentence.	**Worksheet 1** Sight words
Write: *Dot-to-Dot, Pick Up Bricks*	Reinforce correct letter formation. Recognise correct word order for a sentence.	write the word by. Choose the correct words to make a sentence.	**Worksheet 2** Read and write
Find: *Read and Colour*	Identify colour words.	match the colour words with their colours.	**Worksheet 3** Vocabulary
Vocabulary: *Sound Streamers, Wheel of Words, Word Windows, Tiles, Picture Picker*	Build vocabulary skills: Identify sounds in words. Recognise key vocabulary. Blend and recognise words. Read and comprehend a sentence.	sound out and select letters to make words. Match pictures to words. Blend sounds to read and make words. Read a sentence and match to a picture.	**Worksheet 4** Check
Read: *Book*	Read aloud book.	listen, follow the reading and read along.	**Reading Eggs Story book** Can you see Sid?

Related Reading Eggs Activities, Interactives, Songs and Books

Reading Eggs Puzzle Park

More than One
Animal Colours
Colour Code
Squares
Fingers

Reading Eggs Posters

Reading Eggs Library Books

My Program Books

Interactives

Driving Tests

Spelling Bank

Teacher Toolkit

Spelling Activities

Reading Eggs Apps

Eggy Sight words

Critter Card

Go go gizmo

go

Lesson 51 • Worksheet 1

Name

Sight words

1 Trace and write the words.

go by

2 Join Go go gizmo to the **go** words.

3 Guess the word by its shape. Write each word in the boxes.

can go by you

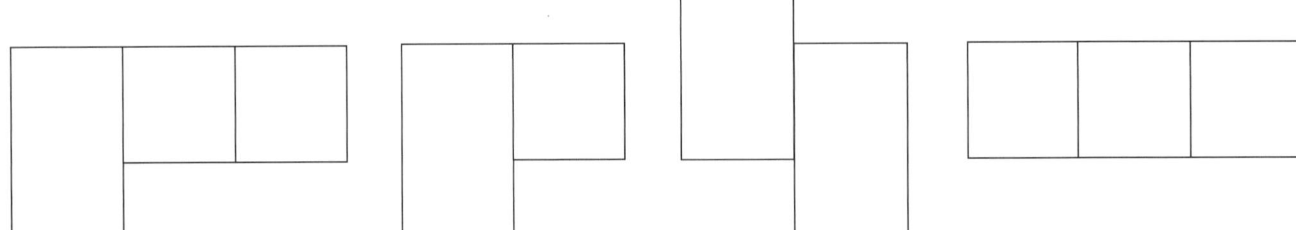

Name

Read and write

go

Lesson 51 • Worksheet 2

1 Complete each sentence.

Six big bees

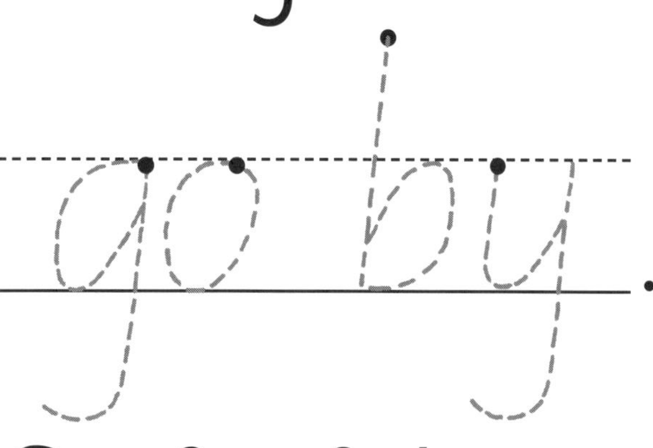

.

Six fat fish

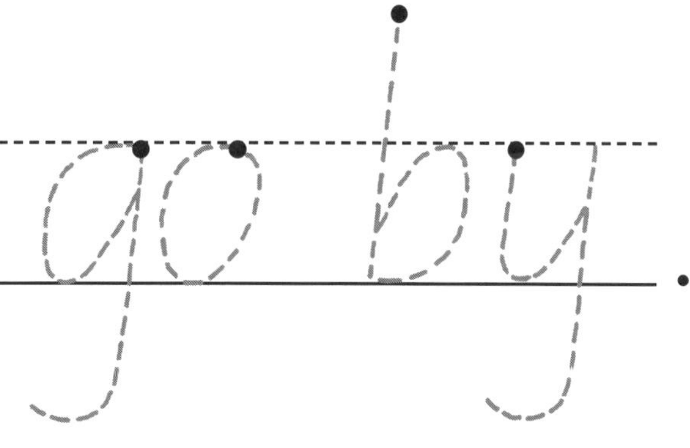

.

Six black bats

____________________.

2 Draw six more cans.

Vocabulary

Name

Lesson 51 • Worksheet 3

1 Read the words. Colour.

red blue green red
pink
yellow yellow
red
blue green
pink

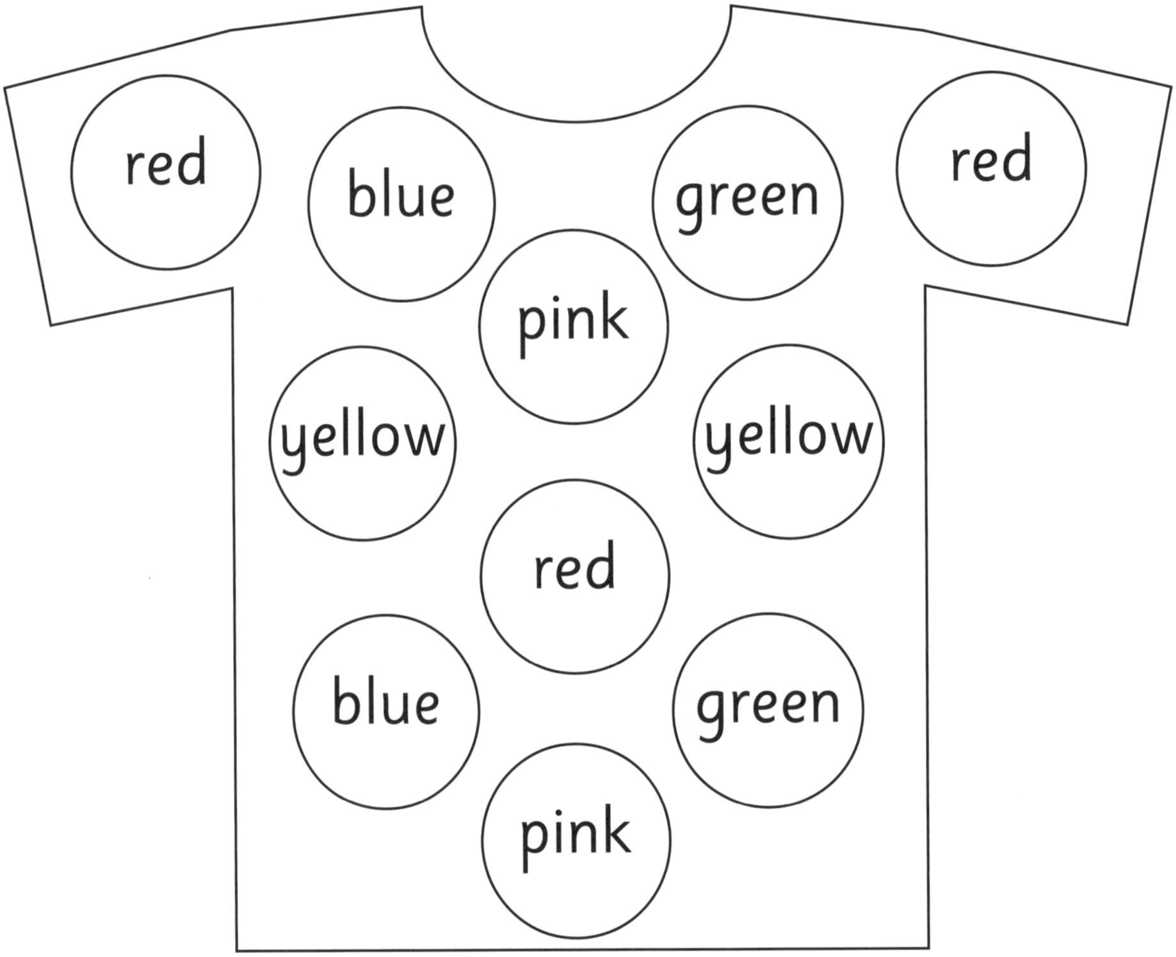

2 Match each word to a picture.

cats hats bees bats

Name

Check

go

Lesson 51 · Worksheet 4

1 Help Go go gizmo get to the rainbow. Draw a track of colour words.

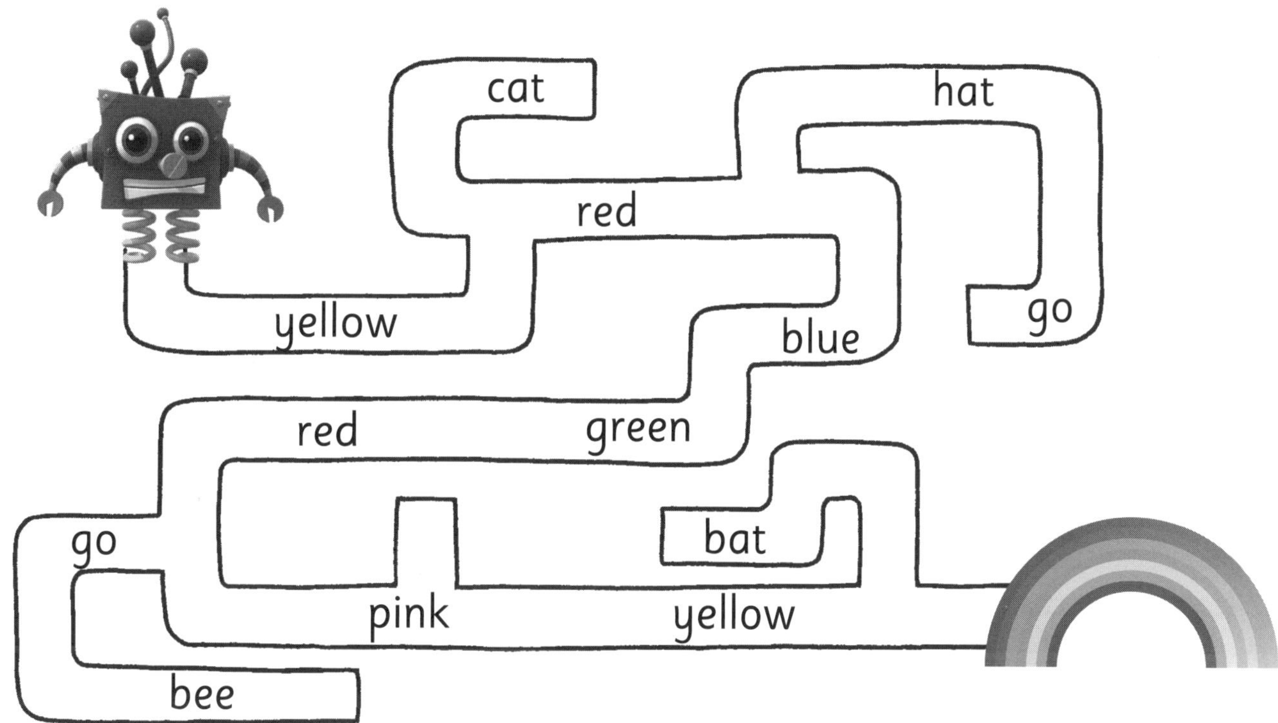

2 Complete the sentences.

go by Six

Six big bees go ________ .

________ fat Flobbies go by.

Six Sandy cans ________ by.

Lesson 52 the sound **ot**

Learning objectives

Children will:

- identify the rime ot.
- read and write the word look.

Australian Curriculum Content Descriptions

Sound and letter knowledge

ACELA1439 listen to the sounds a student hears in the word, and write letters to represent those sounds; identify rhyme and syllables in spoken words

Expressing and developing ideas

ACELA1435 learn that word order in sentences is important for meaning

ACELA1758 recognise the most common sound made by each letter of the alphabet, including consonants and short vowel sounds; know that spoken words are written down by listening to the sounds heard in the word and then writing letters to represent those sounds

Interpreting, analysing and evaluating

ACELY1649 navigate a text correctly, starting at the right place and reading in the right direction, returning to the next line as needed, matching one spoken word to one written word

Sight words

look, I, can, see, a, you, got

Word families

hot, dot, pot, cot

Vocabulary words

dolphin, turtle, ship, mermaid, seagull, whale, monster

Extra assistance

When teaching the sounds of the alphabet, we tend to use words that start with the given sound as examples. It is just as important to be able to recognise a sound at the end of a word. Finding rhyming words and making word families stresses the end sound. This can be reinforced using many letter-sound activities, but identifying the end sound rather than the initial sound.

Classroom activities

For Starters

Put the sound ot on the board in magnetic letters. Put all the letters of the alphabet around it. Students take turns to make ot words by simply changing the initial phoneme. Can anyone use more than one letter to start an ot word?

Which Hat?

Place three hats on the floor with the labels at, it and ot. Discuss the sounds. Have a pile of objects or pictures of objects that end with at, it and ot. Each student chooses one and works out which hat it must go in. Discuss their choice with the class.

Reading Eggs Lesson sequence	TEACH Content and skills	PRACTISE Children will:	APPLY
Hear: *Animated Lesson*	Introduce the sound ot through the song *Sid the Kid thinks ot*. Introduce the word look.	identify the ot sound. Identify the word look in a group and use it in a sentence.	**Worksheet 1** Sight words
Write: *Pick Up Bricks*	Recognise correct word order for a sentence.	choose the correct words to make a sentence.	**Worksheet 2** Vocabulary
Find: *Missing Sound*	Identify the correct onset letter to complete the word.	choose the correct initial letter to make the word.	**Worksheet 3** Word families
Vocabulary: *Blend a Word, Jigsaw, Rhyming Squares, Today's Words, The Theme Game, Tiles*	Build vocabulary skills: Blend and recognise words. Recognise key vocabulary. Identify rhyming words.	blend sounds to read and make words. Match pictures to words. Find images of rhyming words. Tap on the word being said.	**Worksheet 4** Check
Read: *Book*	Read aloud book.	listen, follow the reading and read along.	**Reading Eggs Story book** Look! Can you see?

Related Reading Eggs Activities, Interactives, Songs and Books

Music Café

Sid the Kid thinks ot

Reading Eggs Puzzle Park

Hidden Words
Song Lines
What is it?

Reading Eggs Posters

Reading Eggs Library Books

My Program Books

Interactives

Driving Tests

Spelling Bank

Teacher Toolkit

Spelling Activities

Reading Eggs Apps

Eggy Sight words

Critter Card

Dotty sun spot

Sight words

Lesson 52 • Worksheet 1

Name

look, got

1 Trace and write each word.

2 Help Dotty sun spot find her pot. Follow the path of **got** words.

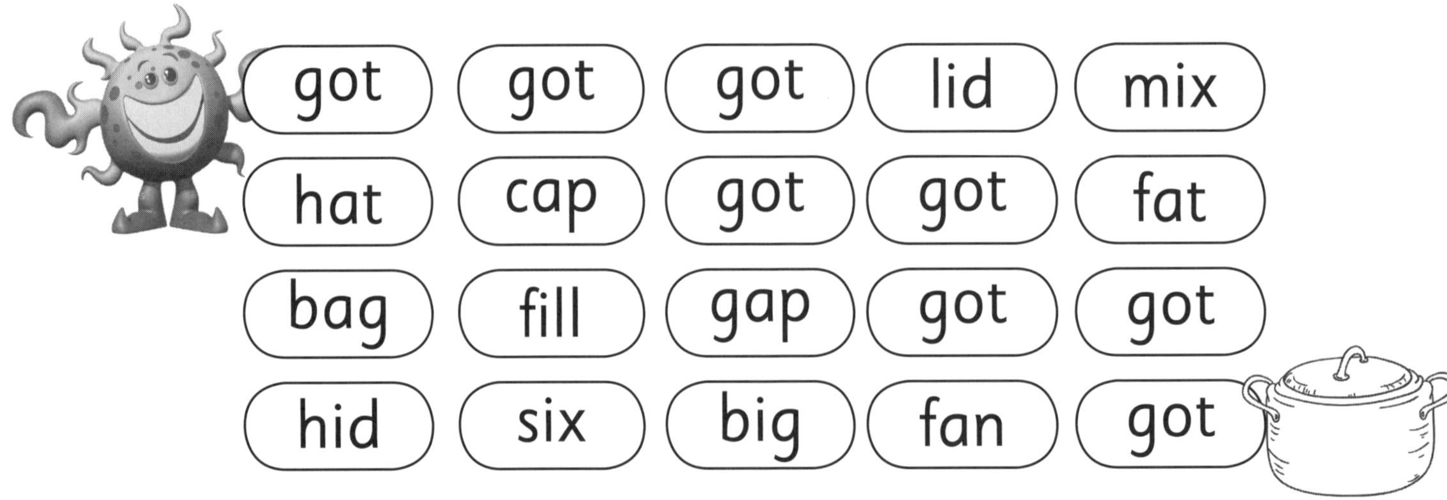

3 Circle the matching words in each row.

look	can	has	look
got	it	got	in

Name

Vocabulary

Lesson 52 · Worksheet 2

1 Match each word to a picture.

mermaid

seagull

turtle

ship

dolphin

whale

2 Colour the correct word. Cross out the wrong word.

This is a whale mermaid.

I can see a seagull ship.

Can you see the dolphin turtle?

ot

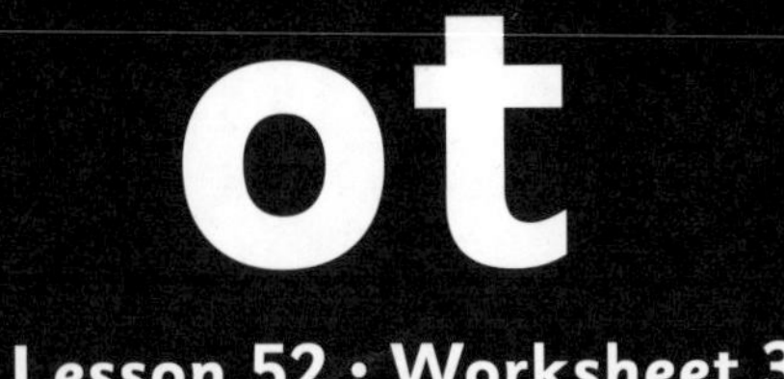

Lesson 52 · Worksheet 3

Name

Word families

1 Match each word to a picture.

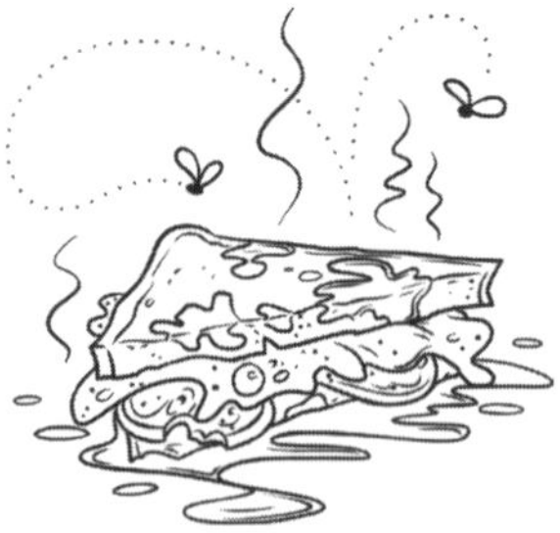

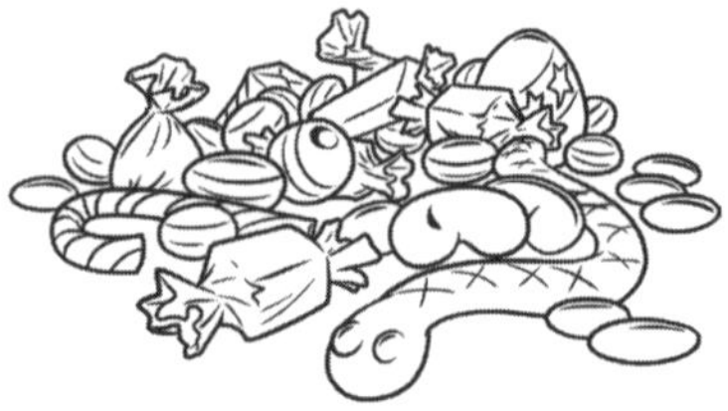

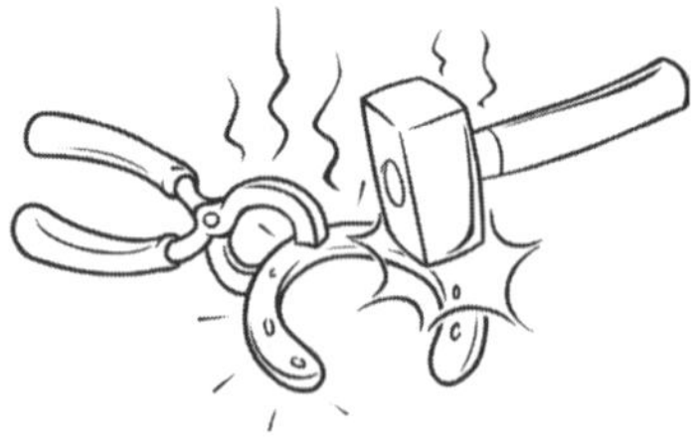

hot

dot

pot

cot

rot

lots

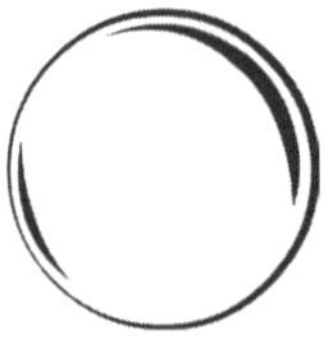

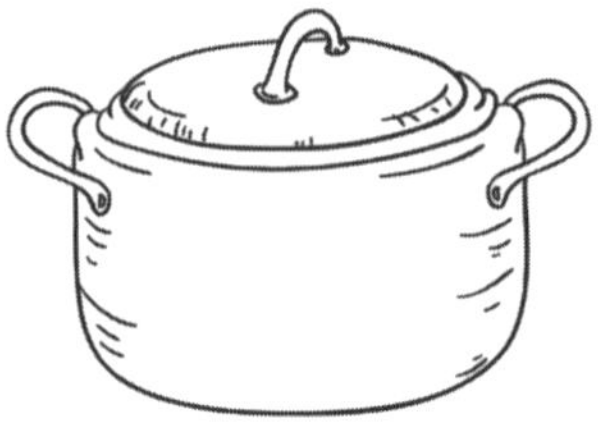

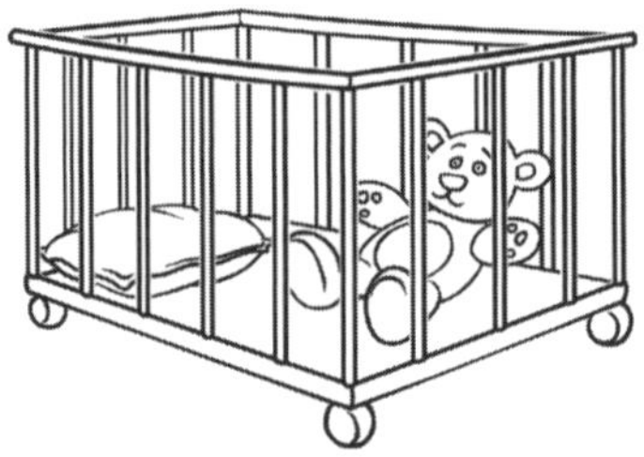

2 Draw:

dots on the dog.	a hot pot.

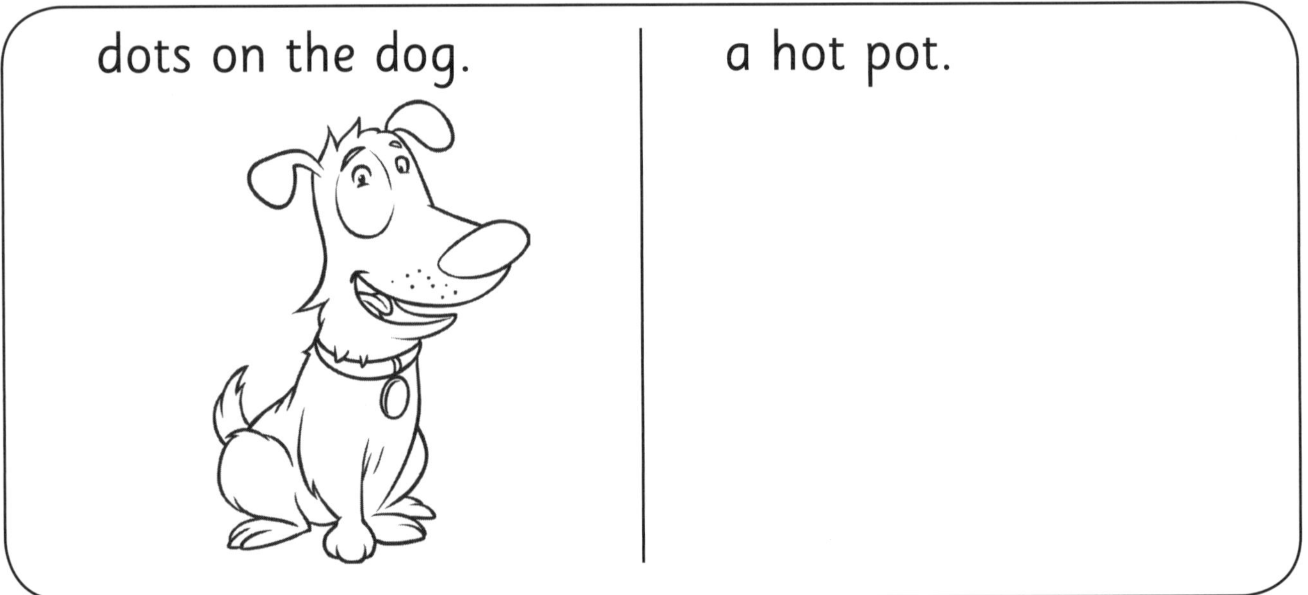

Name

Check

ot

Lesson 52 • Worksheet 4

1 Label each picture. Use the words.

pot cot ship hot mermaid whale

2 Trace and copy each word.

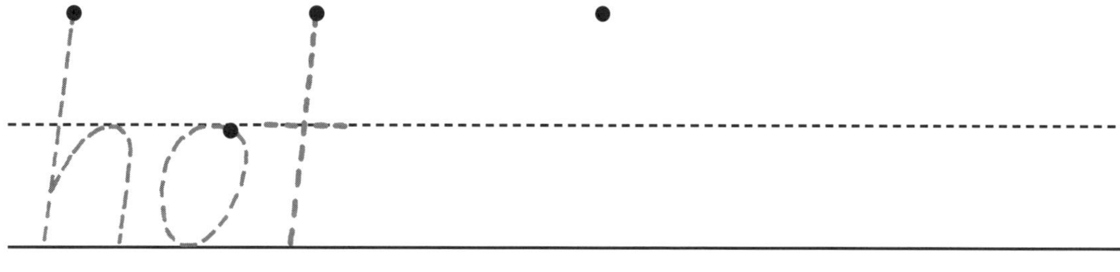

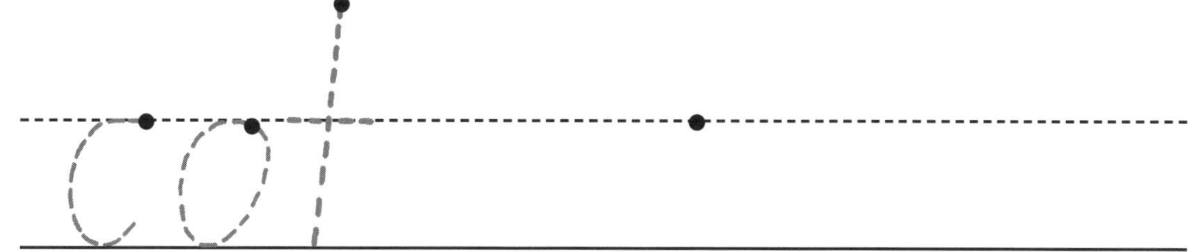

Lesson 53 the sound **og**

Learning objectives

Children will:

- identify the rime og.
- read and write words using og.

Australian Curriculum Content Descriptions

Sound and letter knowledge

ACELA1439 listen to the sounds a student hears in the word, and write letters to represent those sounds; identify and manipulate sounds (phonemes) in spoken words; identify onset and rime in one-syllable spoken words

Creating texts

ACELY1653 follow clear demonstrations of how to construct each letter, learn to construct lower case letters

Expressing and developing ideas

ACELA1435 learn that word order in sentences is important for meaning

ACELA1438 build word families using onset and rime

ACELA1758 write consonant-vowel-consonant words by writing letters to represent the sounds in the spoken words; know that spoken words are written down by listening to the sounds heard in the word and then writing letters to represent those sounds

Sight words

of, this, got, a, lots, the, had, to, go, at, and

Word families

dog, log, fog, cog, frog, sock, rock, shop, mop

Vocabulary words

pet, sack, seed

Extra assistance

Students who speak Spanish and some Asian languages at home may not distinguish between the short vowel sounds /o/, /u/ and /a/. Use consonant-vowel-consonant words to reinforce vowel sounds. Give students a list of words with the consonants there and the vowels missing. Say the words out loud and the students have to fill in the middle sound. This is a good way to assess who is having trouble distinguishing them.

Classroom activities

Brainstorm

Brainstorm a list of words that end with the og sound. Start with single letter onsets. Then ask if anyone knows of any other beginnings such as fr and cl.

Say it Right!

Have a set of pictures of things ending with og. Hold up a picture and say the word incorrectly, using the wrong vowel sound, eg hag for hog, or the wrong initial sound, eg dog for frog. Students need to call out the right word.

Reading Eggs Lesson sequence	**TEACH Content and skills**	**PRACTISE Children will:**	**APPLY**
Hear: *Animated Lesson*	Introduce the sound og through the song *Tom the Dog thinks og*.	identify the sound og in isolation and the word dog.	**Worksheet 1** Vocabulary
Write: *Dot-to-dot, Make a Sentence*	Reinforce correct letter formation of lower case letters. Recognise correct word order for a sentence.	write the word dog. Choose the correct words to make a sentence.	**Worksheet 2** Read and write
Find: *Word family, Missing Sound, Golden Goose*	Identify the correct onset letter to complete the word. Recognise a given word.	choose the correct initial letter to make the word. Find the given word in a group.	**Worksheet 3** Word families
Vocabulary: *Word Windows, Jigsaw, Wheel of Words, Tiles*	Build vocabulary skills: Blend and recognise words. Recognise key vocabulary.	blend sounds to read and make words. Match pictures to words.	**Worksheet 4** Check
Read: *How does it end?, Book*	Read and comprehend a sentence. Read aloud book.	read a beginning and match it to the correct ending. Listen, follow the reading and read along.	**Reading Eggs Story book** Tom the dog

Related Reading Eggs Activities, Interactives, Songs and Books

Music Café

Tom the Dog thinks og

Reading Eggs Puzzle Park

More than one
Hidden Words
Song Lines
What is it?

Reading Eggs Posters

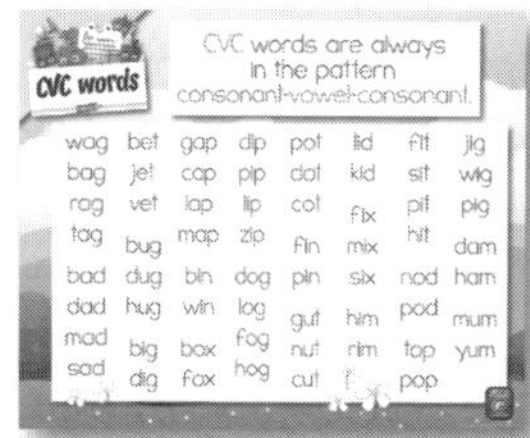

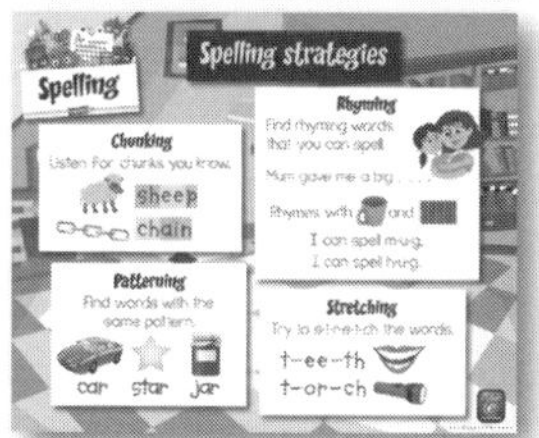

Reading Eggs Library Books

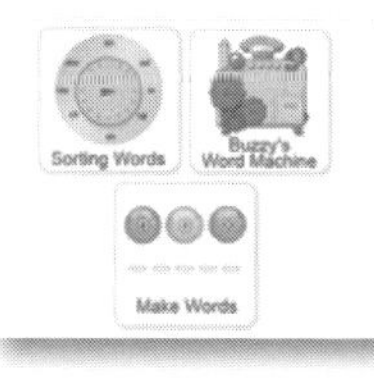

My Program Books

Interactives

Driving Tests

Spelling Bank

Teacher Toolkit

Spelling Activities

Reading Eggs Apps

Eggy Sight words

Critter Card

Hedgehog dog

og

Name

Vocabulary

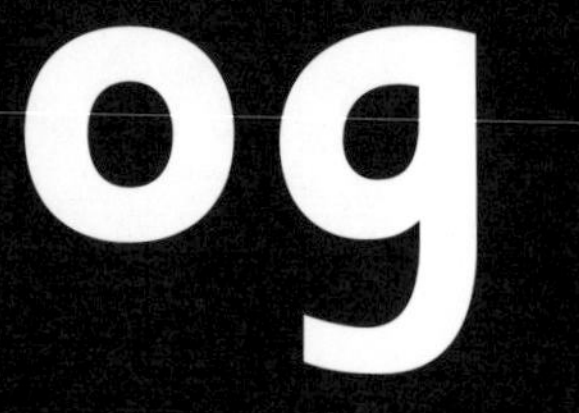

Lesson 53 • Worksheet 1

1 Match each word to a picture.

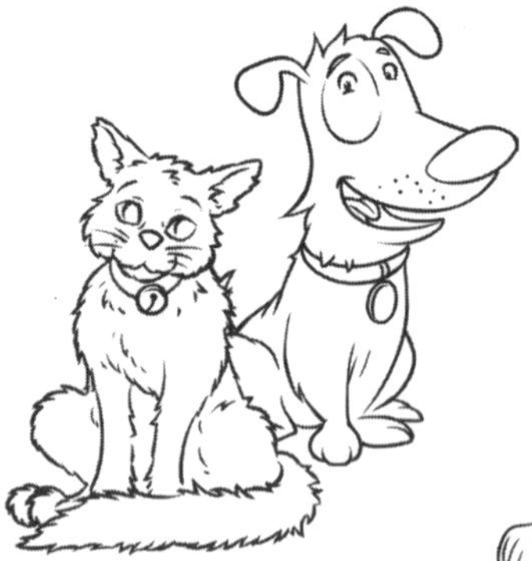

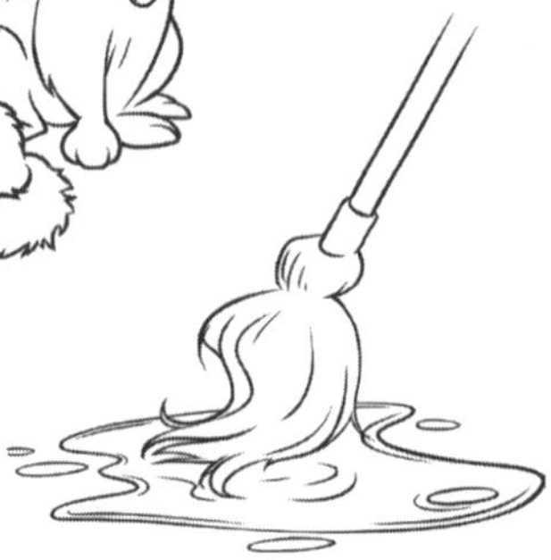

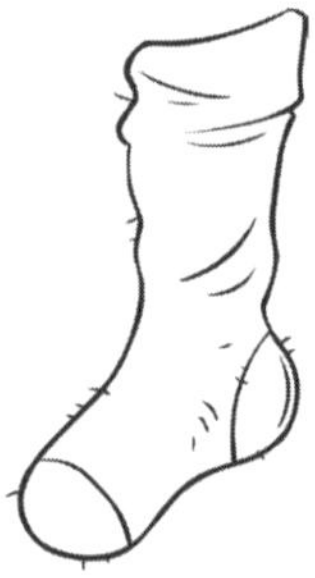

frog

pets

shop

sock

rock

mop

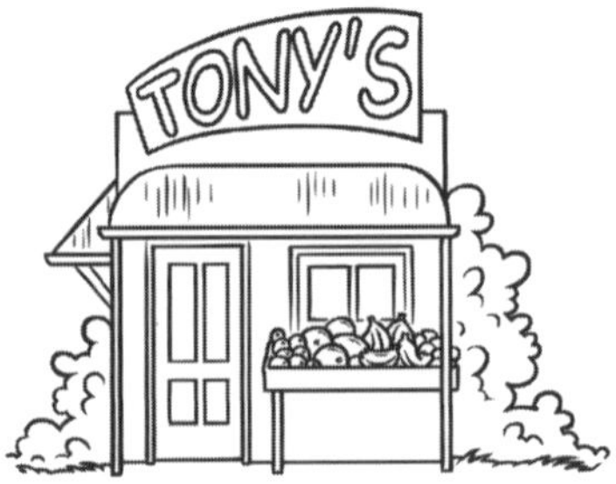

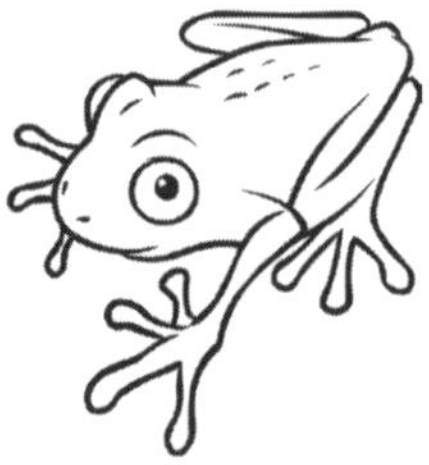

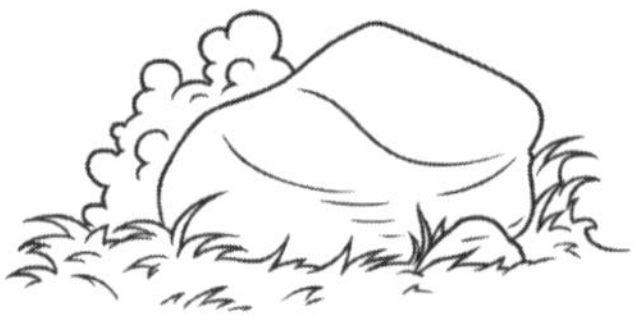

2 Draw a frog on a log.

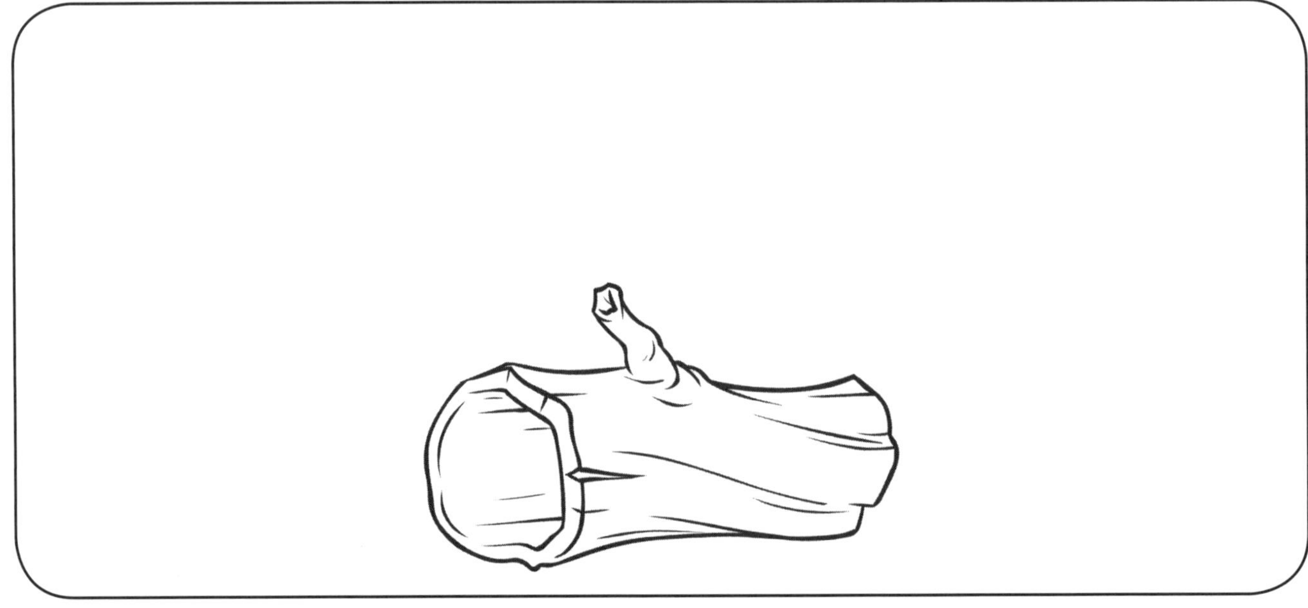

Name

og

Lesson 53 • Worksheet 2

Read and write

1 Complete each sentence.

This pet got a

____________________.

This pet got lots of

____________________.

This pet got a

____________________.

2 Colour **ot** words red. Colour **og** words green. Write them.

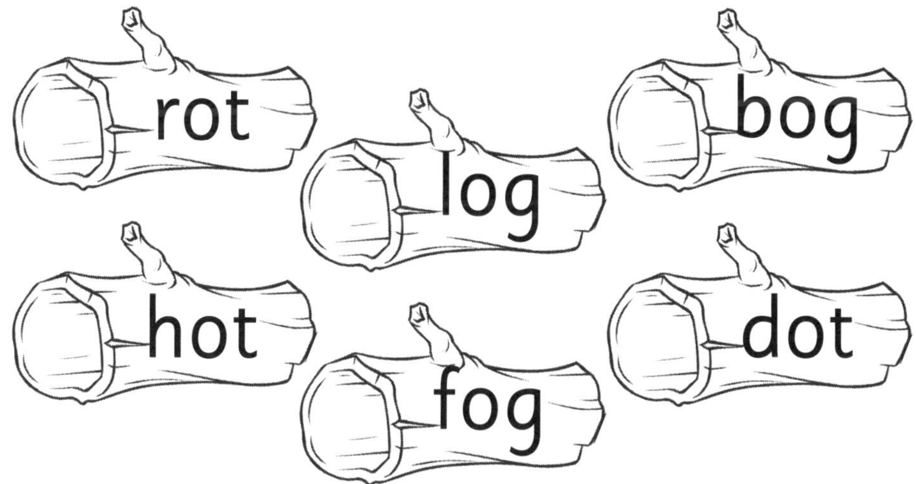

og

Lesson 53 • Worksheet 3

Name

Word families

1 Trace.

og og og og

2 Complete the words.
Use Hedgehog dog's letters.

____og

____og

____og

____og

____og

3 Colour the right word. Cross out the wrong word.

frog

log

log

dog

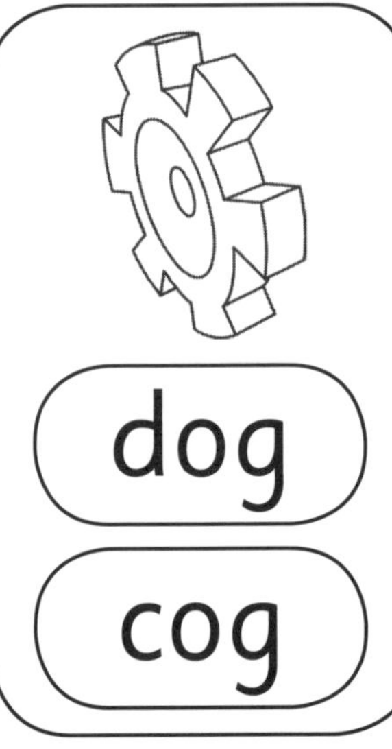

dog

cog

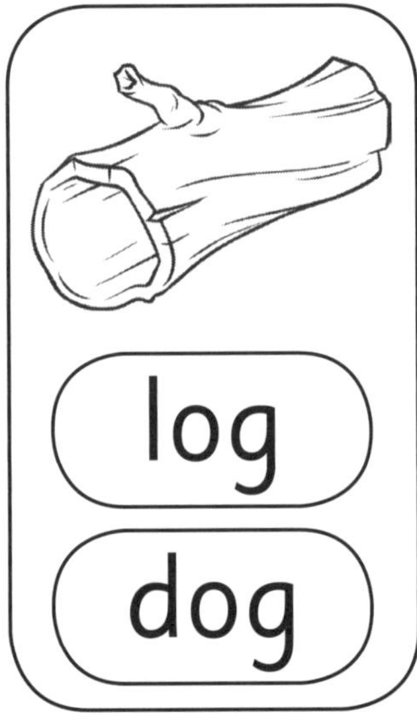

log

dog

Name

Check

og

Lesson 53 • Worksheet 4

1 Find the words. Colour **rock** = red, **sock** = green, **shop** = blue.

s	o	c	k	s	h	o	p
s	h	o	p	r	o	c	k
s	o	c	k	s	h	o	p
r	o	c	k	s	o	c	k

2 Make a word with each letter on the fridge.

_____og

_____og

_____og

_____og

_____og

3 Draw a picture for this sentence.

Tom the dog has lots of socks.

Lesson 54 the sound **op**

Learning objectives

Children will:

- identify the rime op.
- read and write words using op.

Australian Curriculum Content Descriptions

Sound and letter knowledge

ACELA1439 listen to the sounds a student hears in the word, and write letters to represent those sounds; identify and manipulate sounds (phonemes) in spoken words

Creating texts

ACELY1653 follow clear demonstrations of how to construct each letter, learn to construct lower case letters

Expressing and developing ideas

ACELA1435 learn that word order in sentences is important for meaning

ACELA1438 build word families using onset and rime

ACELA1758 write consonant-vowel-consonant words by writing letters to represent the sounds in the spoken words; know that spoken words are written down by listening to the sounds heard in the word and then writing letters to represent those sounds

Sight words

got, play, can, the, we, all, in

Word families

pop, top, mop, hop

Vocabulary words

playground

Extra assistance

As students move beyond basic sight words and the easy consonant-vowel-consonant words, it is important to reinforce the strategy of sounding out new words, for both reading and spelling. Many words are spelt phonetically, especially words used for beginner reading books, so sounding out each letter can help decode a new word. When spelling a new word, encourage students to sound it out and spell it phonetically. Praise the parts they get right while correcting any mistakes.

Classroom activities

Make It!

Give each student some playdough or plasticine or clay to make the rime op. Then ask them to shape an onset letter to make a word. How many op words can they make out of their materials? They could also collect natural items such as leaves and twigs to combine with their modelling material to make op words.

Reading Eggs Lesson sequence	**TEACH Content and skills**	**PRACTISE Children will:**	**APPLY**
Hear: *Animated Lesson*	Introduce the sound op through the song *Tom the Dog thinks op*.	identify the sound op in isolation and the word pop.	**Worksheet 1** Word families
Write: *Dot-to-Dot, Make a Sentence*	Reinforce correct letter formation of lower case letters. Recognise correct word order for a sentence.	write the word got. Choose the correct words to make a sentence.	**Worksheet 2** Read and write
Find: *Word family, Letter Lights, Leaping Penguins, Time for 20, Send a Letter*	Identify the correct onset letter to complete the word. Recognise upper and lower case letters. Recognise a given word.	choose the correct initial letter to make the word. Match the capital and lower case letters. Find the given word in a group.	**Worksheet 3** Sight words
Vocabulary: *Word Windows, Break it Up*	Build vocabulary skills: Blend and recognise words. Identify the number of phonemes in a word.	blend sounds to read and make words. Identify the number of sounds in a word.	**Worksheet 4** Check
Read: *Book Ends, Book*	Read sentences and identify key vocabulary. Read aloud book.	choose from a list of words to finish the sentence. Listen, follow the reading and read along.	**Reading Eggs Story book** The playground

Classroom activities

Which Hat?

Place three hats on the floor with the labels op, og and ot. Discuss the sounds. Have a pile of objects or pictures of objects that end with op, og and ot. Each student chooses one and works out which hat it must go in. Discuss their choice with the class.

Related Reading Eggs Activities, Interactives, Songs and Books

Music Café

Tom the Dog thinks op

Reading Eggs Puzzle Park

Hidden Words

Song Lines

What is it?

Animal Fun

Reading Eggs Posters

Reading Eggs Library Books

My Program Books

Interactives

Driving Tests

Spelling Bank

Teacher Toolkit

Spelling Activities

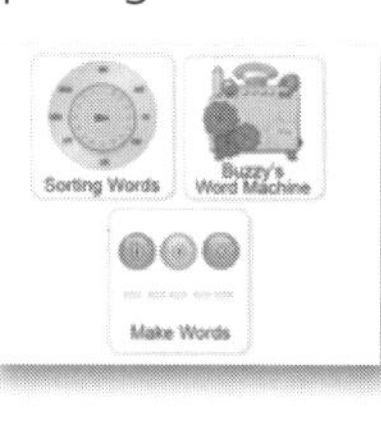

Reading Eggs Apps

Eggy Sight words

Critter Card

Buzzle top

op

Lesson 54 • Worksheet 1

Name

Word families

1 Colour the op words. Write them.

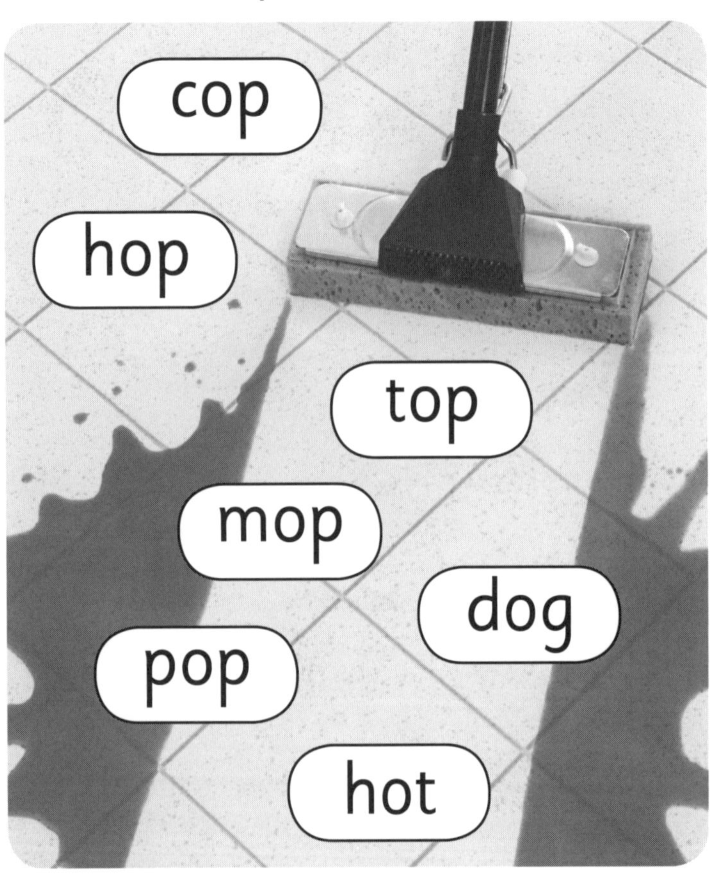

cop

2 Write the words on the correct log.

hop bog dot mop cot fog

op

og

ot

Name

Read and write

op

Lesson 54 • Worksheet 2

1 Match each word to a picture.

2 Complete the sentences.

stop hop mop

Lollipop Mop likes to ________ .

Sixty Six has to ________ .

Kangako likes to ________ .

Play

Lesson 54 • Worksheet 3

Name

Sight words

1 Trace and write the word.

play

2 Join Buzzle top to the **play** words.

3 Circle the matching words in each row.

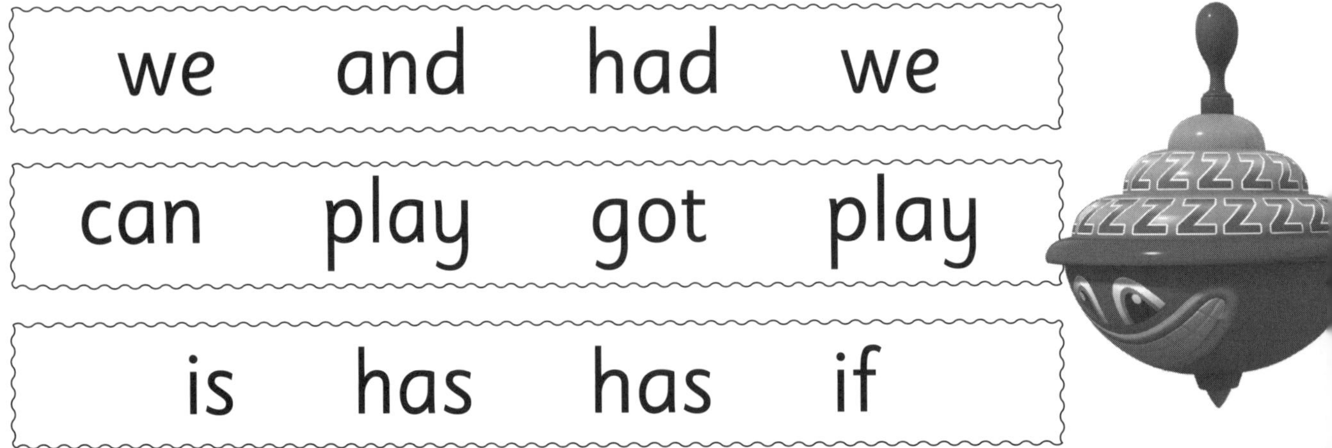

Name

Check

1 Complete each sentence with **play**.

Zee the bee can

---.

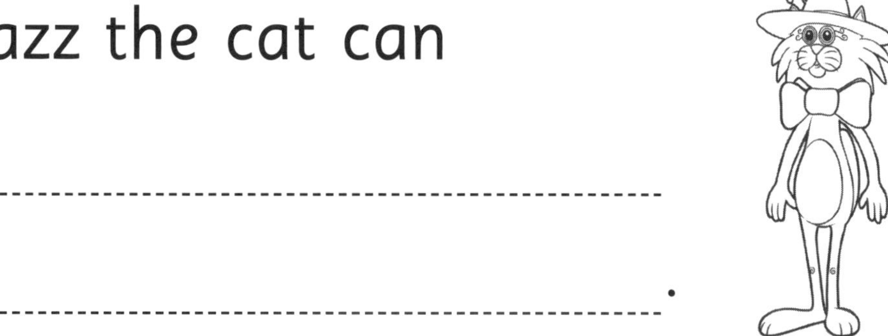

Jazz the cat can

---.

2 Use the word wheels to make words. Write the new words.

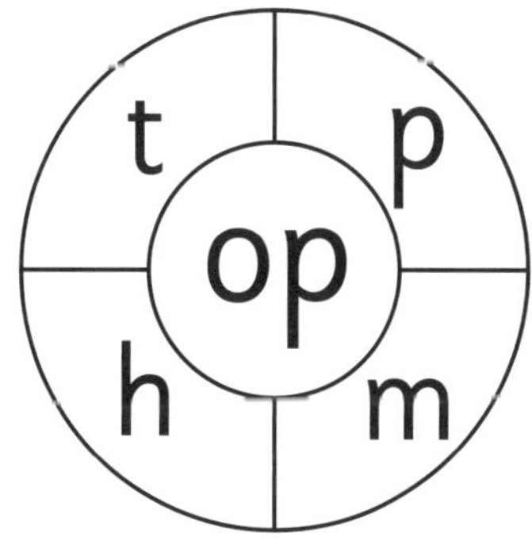

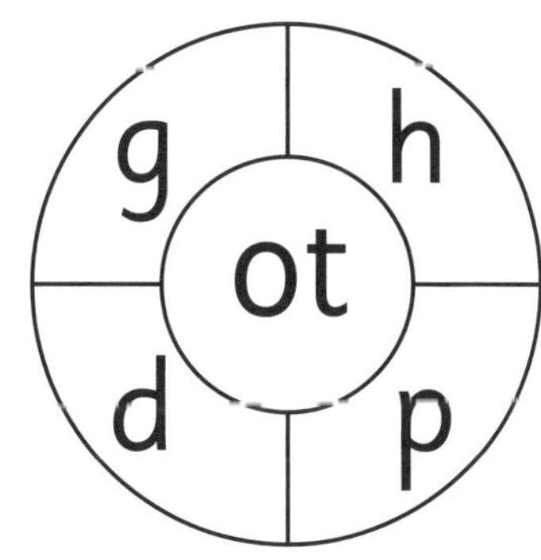

h d
og
l b

________________ ________________ ________________

________________ ________________ ________________

________________ ________________ ________________

________________ ________________ ________________

Lesson 55 the sound o

Learning objectives

Children will:

- identify the short o rimes.
- read and write words using the short o sound.

Australian Curriculum Content Descriptions

Sound and letter knowledge

ACELA1439 listen to the sounds a student hears in the word, and write letters to represent those sounds; identify and manipulate sounds (phonemes) in spoken words

ACELA1440 identify familiar and recurring letters and the use of upper and lower case in written texts

Expressing and developing ideas

ACELA1435 learn that word order in sentences is important for meaning

ACELA1438 build word families using onset and rime

ACELA1758 recognise the most common sound made by each letter of the alphabet, including consonants and short vowel sounds; write consonant-vowel-consonant words by writing letters to represent the sounds in the spoken words; know that spoken words are written down by listening to the sounds heard in the word and then writing letters to represent those sounds

Sight words

got, a, he, lots, of, the, on,

Word families

dog, hog, log, fog, jog, cog, bog, pop, mop, hop, top, stop, shop, rock, cot, pot, dot, hot, not, nod

Vocabulary words

popcorn

Extra assistance

When students are learning to sound out and spell words for their own writing, a good strategy is to think of rhyming words. If they know how to spell top, it is easier to spell shop. They know how to spell the ending, now they just have to work out the beginning. Word families can be useful for helping students identify rhyming words and to see that many have the same ending.

Classroom activities

Find the Sound

Give each student three cards with the sounds ot, og and op. Say a word and ask students to listen to the end sound. They should hold up the card which makes that final sound. Use clear, recognisable words such as hot, pop, bog.

Reading Eggs Lesson sequence	TEACH Content and skills	PRACTISE Children will:	APPLY
Hear: *Animated Lesson*	Review the sounds og and op through the songs *Tom the Dog thinks op and og.*	sort and match words by their sounds.	**Worksheet 1** Word families
Write: *Word Ladder, Make a Sentence, Pick Up Bricks*	Identify sounds in a word and write the word. Recognise correct word order for a sentence.	sound out a word and select letters to spell it correctly. Choose the correct words to make a sentence.	**Worksheet 2** Read and write
Find: *Power Words, Climb the Ladder, Trains*	Recognise key vocabulary. Identify upper and lower case letters.	match words to pictures. Find the given word in a group. Match lower case and capital letters.	**Worksheet 3** Sight words
Vocabulary: *Blend a Word, Sound Streamers, Tiles*	Build vocabulary skills: Blend and recognise words. Identify sounds in words.	blend sounds to read and make words. Sound out and select letters to make words. Match pictures to initial letters and words.	**Worksheet 4** Check
Read: *Book*	Read aloud book.	listen, follow the reading and read along.	**Reading Eggs Story book** Top Dog

Classroom activities

Bingo!

Give students a laminated board with ten squares on it. Ask them to write a word in each square from a list of short o sound words (use whiteboard markers). Say words from the list. Students put a cross on that word on their board. First one to 10 calls out 'bingo' and wins!

Related Reading Eggs Activities, Interactives, Songs and Books

Music Café

Tom the Dog thinks op

Tom the Dog thinks og

Reading Eggs Puzzle Park

More than one

Hidden Words

Song Lines

What is it?

Reading Eggs Posters

Reading Eggs Library Books

My Program Books

Interactives

Driving Tests

Spelling Bank

Teacher Toolkit

Spelling Activities

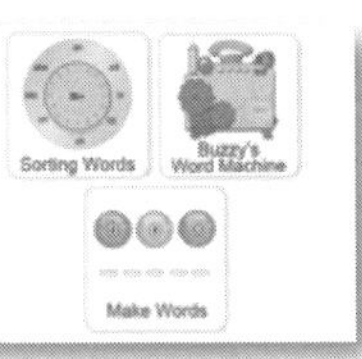

Reading Eggs Apps

Eggy Sight words

Critter Card

Lollipop mop

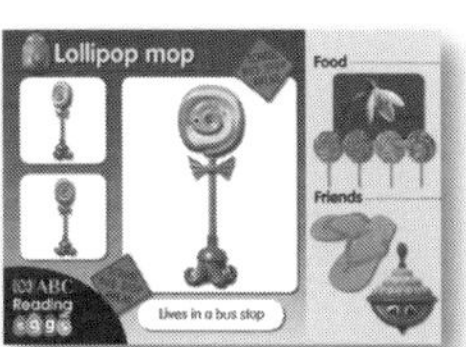

Name

Word families

1 Colour the right word. Cross out the wrong word.

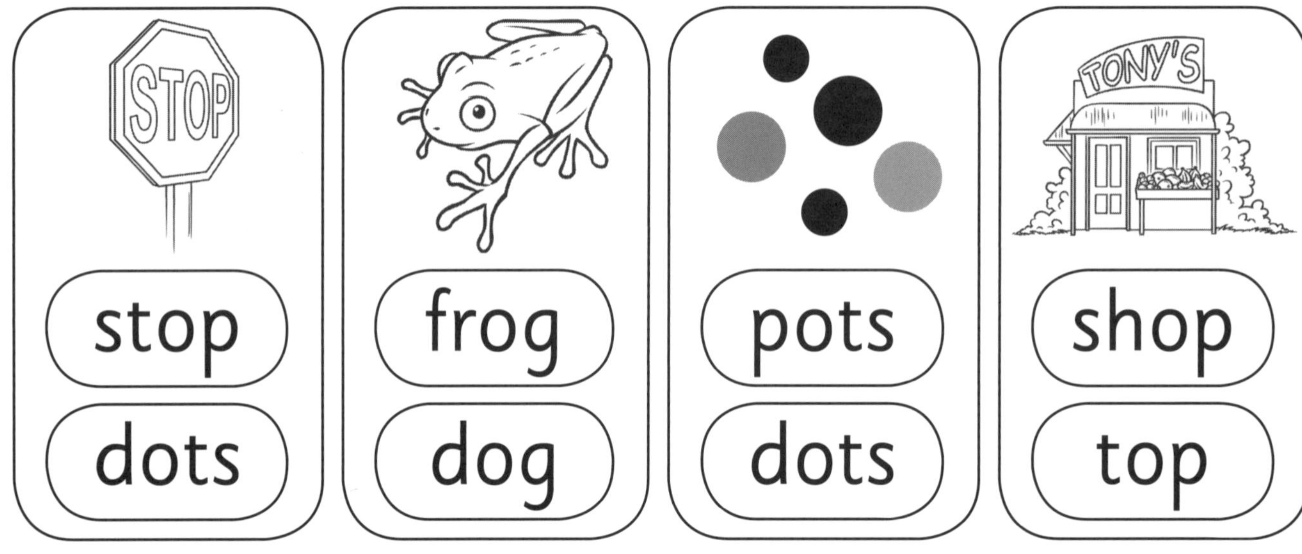

2 Complete the words.
Use Lollipop mop's letters.

Name

O

Lesson 55 • Worksheet 2

Read and write

1 Complete each sentence.

pops hot dog pot log

Top Dog got a

--- .

The popcorn

--- .

He hops onto a

--- .

Top Dog got a

--- .

Name

Sight words

1 Trace and write the word.

lots

2 Colour **lots** = red, **got** = green, **top** = yellow.

got

top

got

lots

lots

top

top

lots

3 Draw lots of popcorn in the pan.

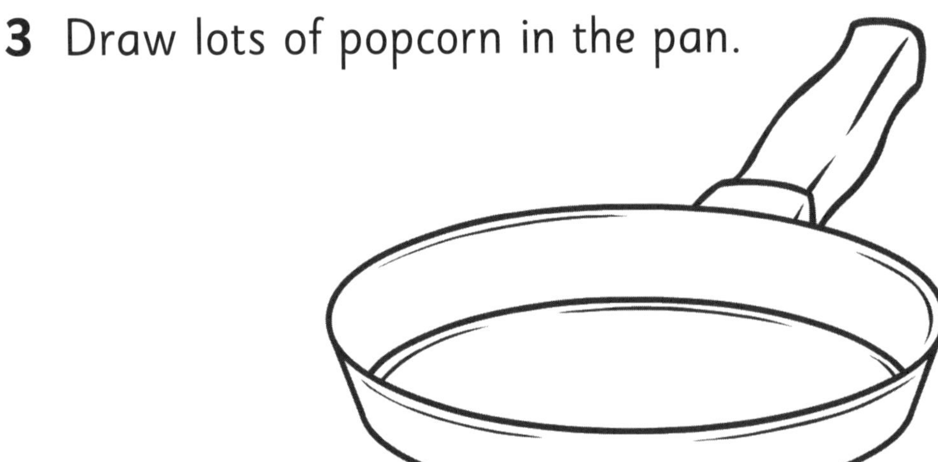

Name

Check

o

Lesson 55 · Worksheet 4

1 Say the name of each picture. Circle the end sound.

ot op og

ot op og

ot op og

ot op og

ot op og

ot op og

2 Colour the word **lots**.

hot pots lots tops mops

3 Write a sentence using Lollipop mop's word.

lots

Lesson 56 the word **are**

Learning objectives

Children will:

- identify the words are, not and said.
- read the words are, not and said.
- recognise words for red, yellow and green.

Australian Curriculum Content Descriptions

Sound and letter knowledge

ACELA1439 identify and manipulate sounds (phonemes) in spoken words

ACELA1440 identify familiar and recurring letters and the use of upper and lower case in written texts

Expressing and developing ideas

ACELA1758 recognise the most common sound made by each letter of the alphabet, including consonants and short vowel sounds; know that spoken words are written down by listening to the sounds heard in the word and then writing letters to represent those sounds

Interpreting, analysing and evaluating

ACELY1649 navigate a text correctly, starting at the right place and reading in the right direction, returning to the next line as needed, matching one spoken word to one written word

Sight words

are, said, not, this, is, you, yes, I, am, the, no, like, to

Vocabulary words

happy, red, yellow, green

Extra assistance

A reading strategy that can help beginners with independent reading is to look at the pictures for clues to work out unknown words. Sometimes knowing what sound it starts with and seeing the item or action in a picture is enough to help a child decipher the rest of the word. Most early reading books have a lot of quite literal pictures to help their readers.

Classroom activities

Which Colour?

Put students in small groups of two or three. Give each group three sheets of paper with the word red, green or yellow written on each. Ask the students to think of as many things as they can that are red, green or yellow, and to draw them on the relevant sheet and label them. Bring the groups together to compare lists.

Sentence Shuffle

Write an enlarged version of the sentence *I am not happy!* and read it with the children. Students then create other endings for the *I am not …* sentence starter, for example:

I am not five. I am not a boy. I am not tall.

Reading Eggs Lesson sequence	**TEACH Content and skills**	**PRACTISE Children will:**	**APPLY**
Hear: *Animated Lesson*	Introduce the word are through sentences.	identify and read the word are in isolation and in a sentence.	**Worksheet 1** Sight words
Match: *Know Your Alphabet*	Identify upper and lower case letters.	match lower case and capital letters.	**Worksheet 2** Read and write
Find: *Flock of Seagulls, Frog Logs, Today's Words, Wheel of Words, Golden Goose*	Recognise key vocabulary.	find the given word in a group.	**Worksheet 3** Vocabulary
Vocabulary: *Blend a Word, Read and Colour, Break It Up*	Build vocabulary skills: Blend and recognise words. Identify colour words. Identify the number of phonemes in a word.	blend sounds to read words. Match the colour words with their colours. Identify the number of sounds in a word.	**Worksheet 4** Check
Read: *Book*	Read aloud book.	listen, follow the reading and read along.	**Reading Eggs Story book** Are you happy?

Related Reading Eggs Activities, Interactives, Songs and Books

Reading Eggs Puzzle Park

Hidden Words
Song Lines
Animal Colours
Colour Code

Reading Eggs Posters

Reading Eggs Library Books

My Program Books

Interactives

Driving Tests

Spelling Bank

Teacher Toolkit

Spelling Activities

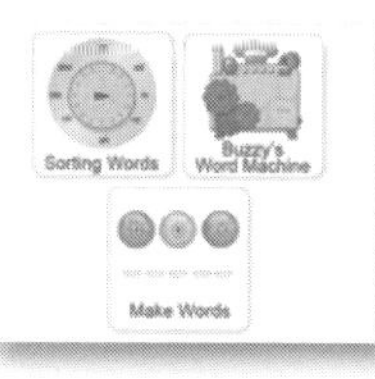

Reading Eggs Apps

Eggy Sight words

Critter Card

Wobble blob

are

Lesson 56 • Worksheet 1

Name

Sight words

1 Trace and write the words.

are not said

2 Join Grumble goz to the **happy** words.

happy   not   happy

are   happy   are

said   happy

3 Guess the word by its shape.
Write each word in the boxes.

are not happy

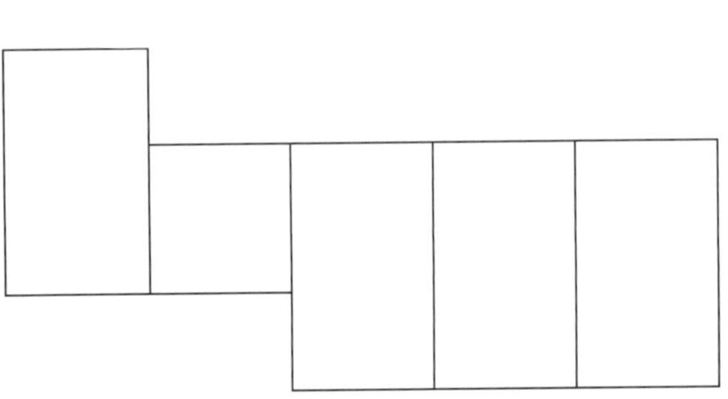

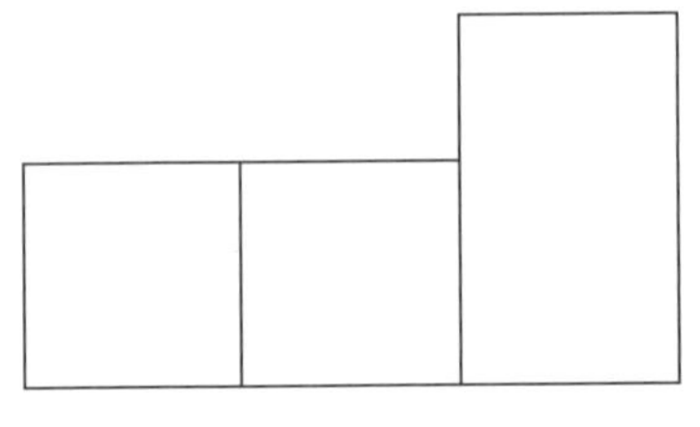

Name

Read and write

are

Lesson 56 · Worksheet 2

1 Match each sentence to a picture.

Are you happy, Frogfish?

Are you happy, Sam the ant?

Are you happy, Grumble goz?

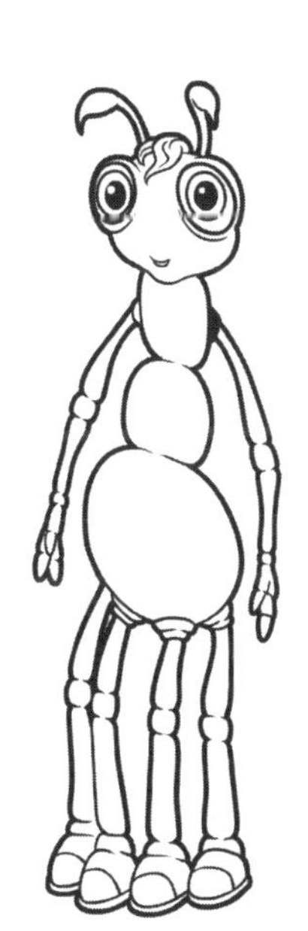

Are you happy, Zee the bee?

Vocabulary

Name

Lesson 56 • Worksheet 3

1 Match each word to a picture.

2 Colour the flag.

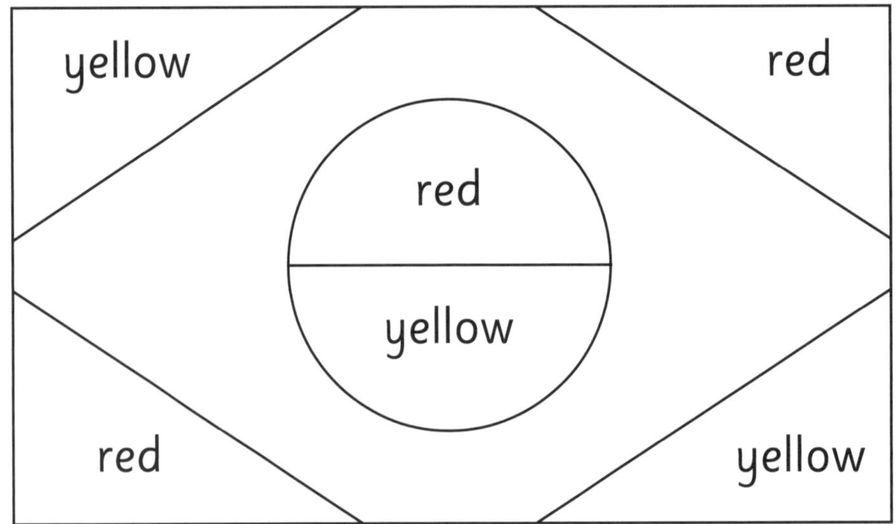

3 Join each critter to their name.

Name

Check

are

Lesson 56 • Worksheet 4

1 Read and trace.

Are you happy?

Yes I am.

Draw yourself.

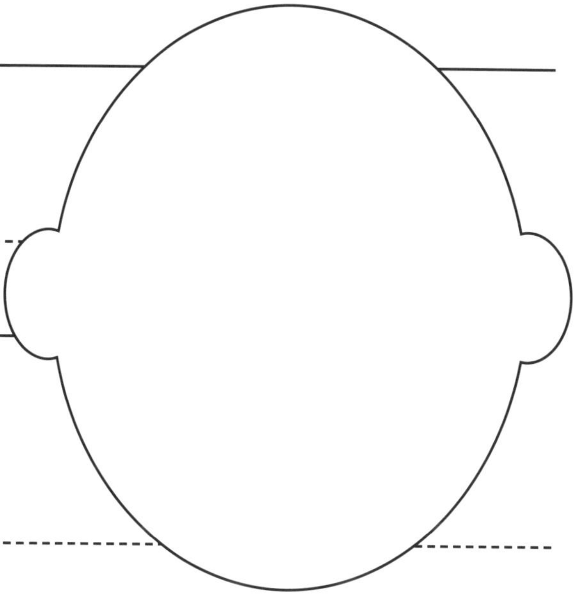

2 Circle the correct word. Cross out the wrong word.

This The is a Frogfish.

Is Are you happy, Frogfish?

"Yes, I am happy," he say said .

Lesson 57 the words **his** and **her**

Learning objectives

Children will:

- identify the words his, her and we.
- use the words his, her and we in sentences.
- read and write words within a theme.

Australian Curriculum Content Descriptions

Sound and letter knowledge

ACELA1439 identify rhyme and syllables in spoken words; identify and manipulate sounds (phonemes) in spoken words

Creating texts

ACELY1653 follow clear demonstrations of how to construct each letter, learn to construct lower case letters

Expressing and developing ideas

ACELA1435 learn that word order in sentences is important for meaning

ACELA1438 build word families using onset and rime

ACELA1758 recognise the most common sound made by each letter of the alphabet, including consonants and short vowel sounds; know that spoken words are written down by listening to the sounds heard in the word and then writing letters to represent those sounds

Interpreting, analysing and evaluating

ACELY1649 navigate a text correctly, starting at the right place and reading in the right direction, returning to the next line as needed, matching one spoken word to one written word

Sight words

his, her, we, said, like, it, she, this, is, a, the, he, all

Vocabulary words

lady, princess, prince, queen, king, dog, crown, game, bone, horse, castle, party

Extra assistance

Some children may use gender specific pronouns interchangeably or may use only one. Some students may not know when to use the possessive his and hers over he and she. Quite often you will find that they are using he's and she's instead of his and hers in spoken language – he's bag, she's brush. Give them opportunities to practise choosing the right one, both verbally and in written language.

Classroom activities

Bingo!

Give students a laminated board with 10 squares on it. Ask them to write a word in each square from the list: his, her, we, are, not, look, go, by, has, this, said, like, it (use whiteboard markers). Say words from the list. Students put a cross on that word on their board. First one to 10 calls out 'bingo' and wins!

Reading Eggs Lesson sequence	TEACH Content and skills	PRACTISE Children will:	APPLY
Hear: *Animated Lesson*	Introduce the words his and her through the song *His and Hers*. Introduce the word we.	identify and read the words his and her and match to pictures. Identify the word we and use in sentences.	**Worksheet 1** Sight words
Write: *Dot-to-Dot, Pick Up Bricks*	Reinforce correct letter formation of lower case letters. Recognise correct word order for a sentence.	write the word her. Choose the correct words to make a sentence.	**Worksheet 2** Read and write
Find: *Rhyming Squares, Missing Sound*	Identify rhyming words. Identify the correct onset letter to complete the word.	find images of rhyming words. Choose the correct initial letter to make the word.	**Worksheet 3** Vocabulary
Vocabulary: *The Theme Game, Word Windows, Wheel of Words*	Build vocabulary skills: Recognise key vocabulary. Blend and recognise words.	match pictures to words. Blend sounds to read words.	**Worksheet 4** Check
Read: *Picture Picker, Book*	Read and comprehend a sentence. Read aloud book.	read a sentence and match to a picture. Listen, follow the reading and read along.	**Reading Eggs Story book** We like

Classroom activities

Flashcard Snap

Have a set of flashcards with lower case and capital letters. Shuffle and deal between two players. Keep cards face down. Players take turns to put a card from their pile onto a central pile, sounding out the letter they turn over. If the two cards on top match, the players shout SNAP! The first to do so takes the central pile. Play continues until one player runs out of cards.

Related Reading Eggs Activities, Interactives, Songs and Books

Music Café

His and Hers

Reading Eggs Puzzle Park

Hidden Words

Song Lines

What is it?

Reading Eggs Posters

Reading Eggs Library Books

My Program Books

Interactives

Driving Tests

Spelling Bank

Teacher Toolkit

Spelling Activities

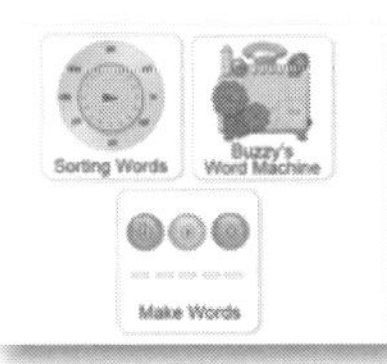

Reading Eggs Apps

Eggy Sight words

Critter Card

Rockee robot

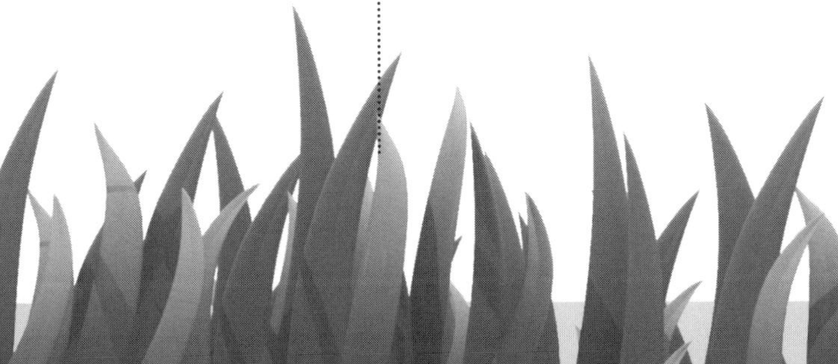

his her

Name

Sight words

Lesson 57 · Worksheet 1

1 Trace and write each word.

his her

2 Complete the labels.

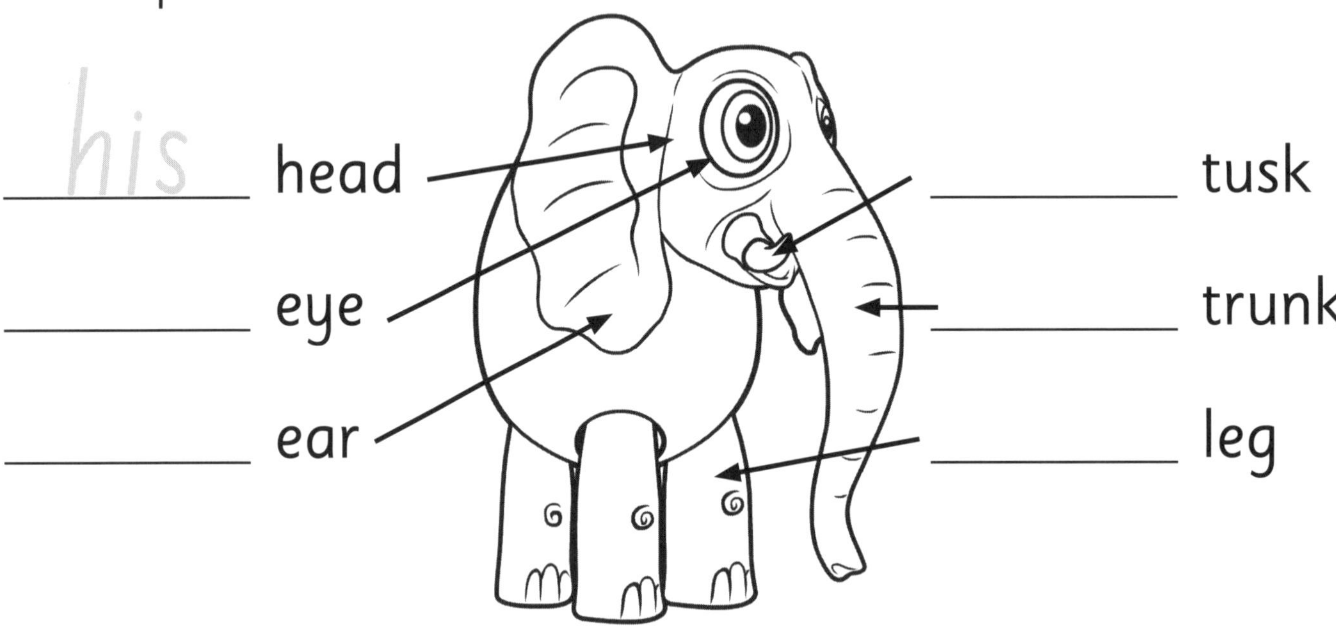

3 Help Airy Fairy find her wand. Colour the path of **her** words.

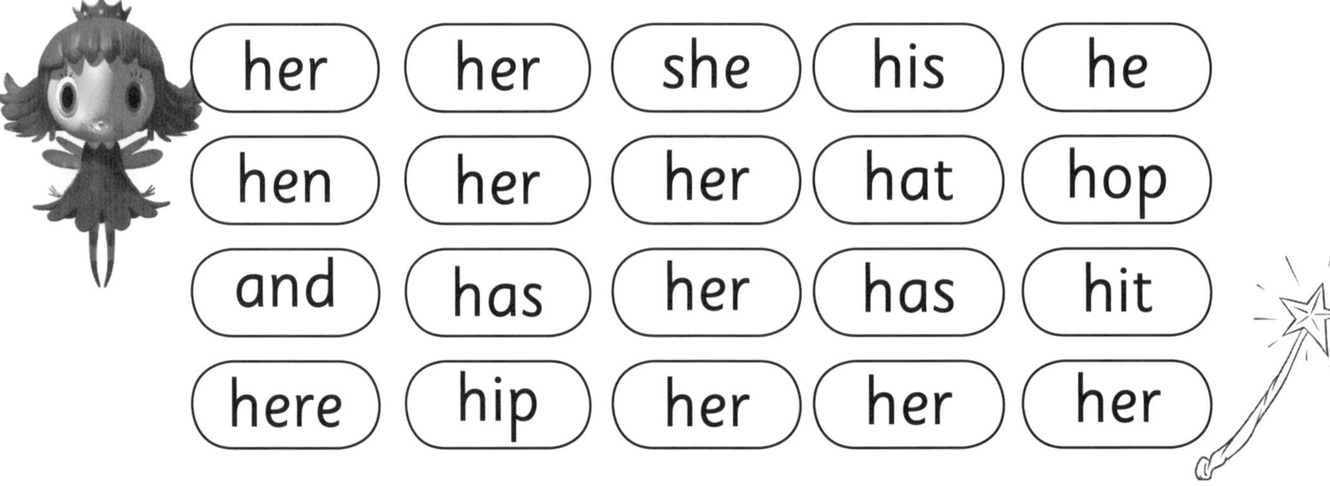

Name

Read and write

his her

Lesson 57 • Worksheet 2

1 What does each person like? Read and draw.

This is the Princess. She likes her horse.	This is the King. He likes his castle.
This is the Queen. She likes her crown.	This is the Prince. He likes his game.

2 Trace and finish the sentence.

Vocabulary

Name

Lesson 57 • Worksheet 3

1 Match each word to a picture.

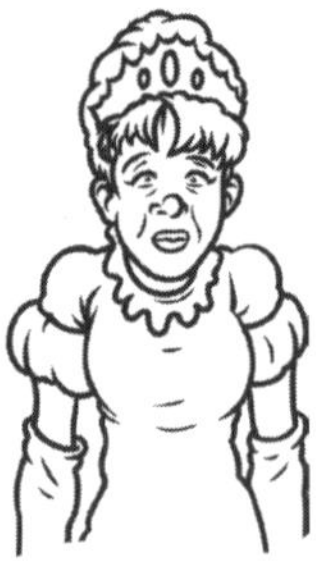
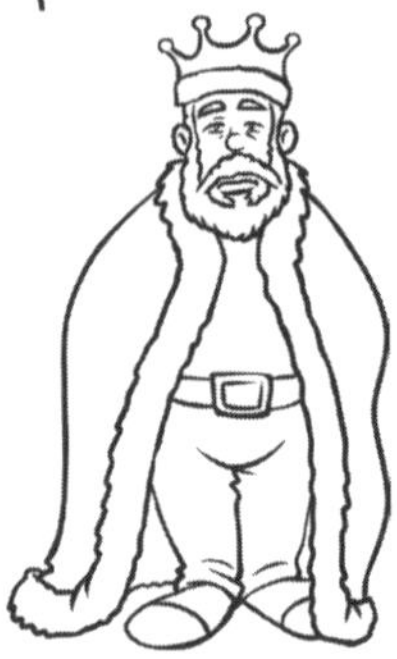
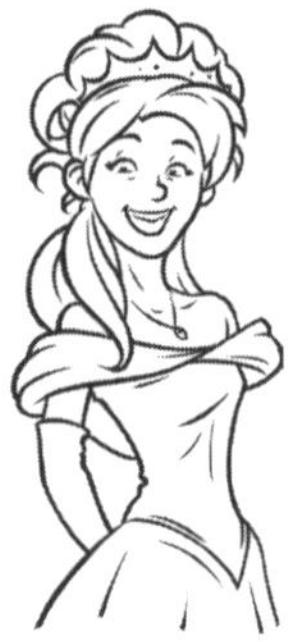

queen

prince

king

princess

knight

horse

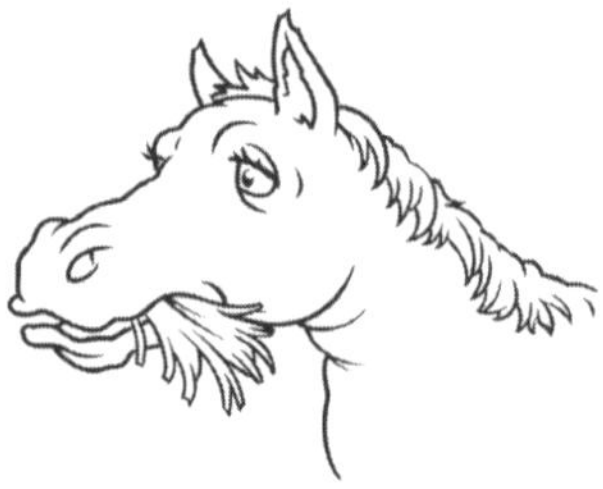
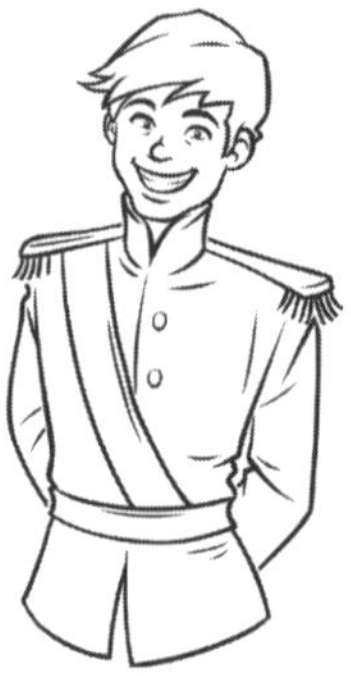
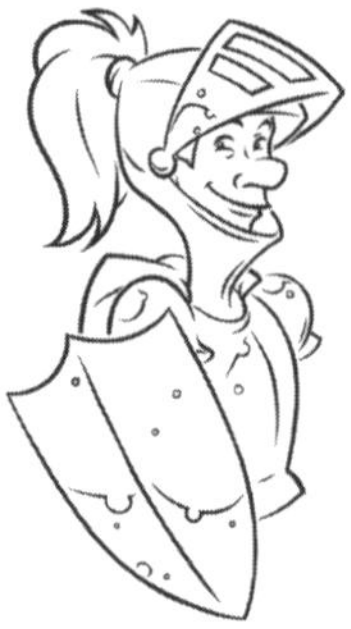

2 Colour the **royal** words. = red. Colour the **sea** words. = blue.

queen

mermaid

turtle

ship

princess

knight

prince

whale

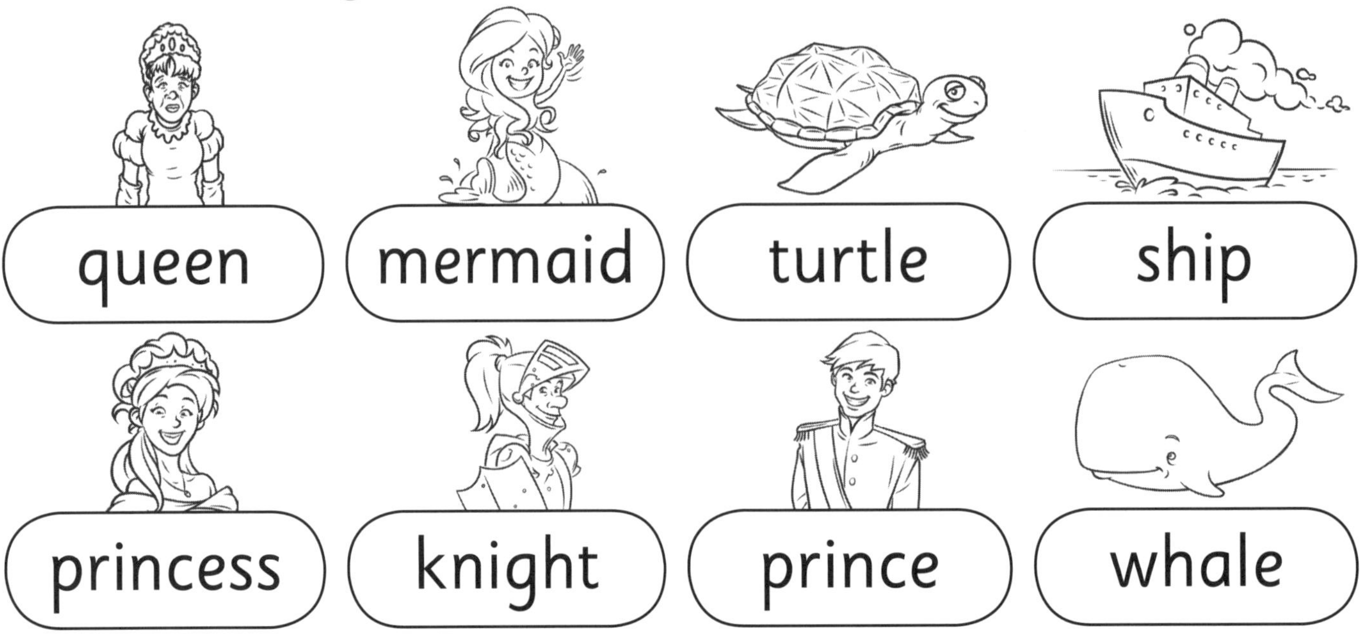

Name

Check

his her

Lesson 57 • Worksheet 4

1 Guess the word by its shape.
Write each word in the boxes.

his her like

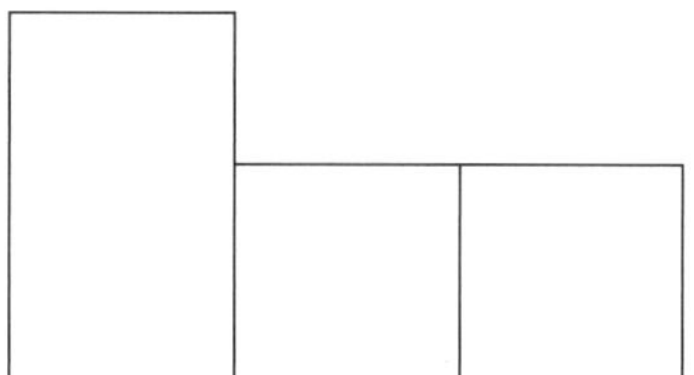

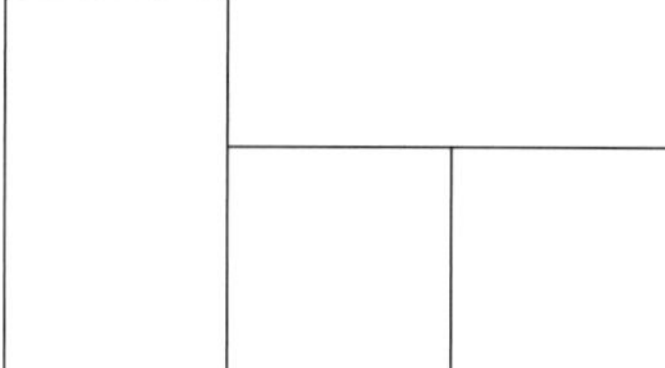

2 Crack the code!

e = ▲
h = ■
i = ●
r = ★
s = ◗
t = ✿

■ ▲ ★ ____________

✿ ■ ▲ ____________

● ◗ ____________

■ ● ◗ ____________

✿ ■ ● ◗ ____________

3 Complete the sentences.

her This his

__________ is the King.

He likes __________ castle.

The Queen likes __________ crown.

Lesson 58 the sound **ock**

Learning objectives

Children will:

- identify the rimes od, ock and ox.
- read and write words using od, ock and ox.

Australian Curriculum Content Descriptions

Sound and letter knowledge

ACELA1439 listen to the sounds a student hears in the word, and write letters to represent those sounds; identify and manipulate sounds (phonemes) in spoken words; identify onset and rime in one-syllable spoken words

ACELA1440 identify familiar and recurring letters and the use of upper and lower case in written texts

Expressing and developing ideas

ACELA1438 build word families using onset and rime

ACELA1758 recognise the most common sound made by each letter of the alphabet, including consonants and short vowel sounds; write consonant-vowel-consonant words by writing letters to represent the sounds in the spoken words, know that spoken words are written down by listening to the sounds heard in the word and then writing letters to represent those sounds

Word families

sock, lock, rock, dock, fox, box, rod, top

Extra assistance

The sounds ocks and ox give students an opportunity to explore rhyming sounds that are spelt differently. Divide a large piece of paper or the board in half. Write ocks at the top of one side and ox at the top of the other side. Now go through the alphabet one consonant at a time. Does each sound make a word when put with the phonemes /o/k/s/? Which spelling does it go with?

Classroom activities

Find the Start

Give students a list of words with the first letter missing. Ask them to figure out which letter could be the starter for all the given words, for example:

_ot _ock _og _op

Could there be more than one starter letter that works for them all?

Mix and Match

Put the consonant letters of the alphabet on the board in writing or magnetic letters. Write the sounds ox, ock and od on the board. Each student comes to the board and writes a word they can make using a rime and an onset letter. Discuss their words with the class.

Reading Eggs Lesson sequence	TEACH Content and skills	PRACTISE Children will:	APPLY
Hear: *Animated Lesson*	Introduce the sound od through the song *Tom the Dog thinks od.*	recognise the sound od.	**Worksheet 1** Word families
Write: *Rumble Jumble, Word Ladder*	Unjumble letters for a given word. Identify sounds in a word and write the word.	write a word from jumbled letters. Sound out a word and select letters to spell it correctly.	**Worksheet 2** Read and write
Find: *Frog Logs, Word family, Letter Lights, Catching Frogs*	Recognise a given word. Identify the correct onset letter to complete the word. Recognise upper and lower case letters.	find the given word in a group. Choose the correct initial letter to make the word. Match the capital and lower case letters.	**Worksheet 3** Vocabulary
Vocabulary: *Blend a Word, Jigsaw, Sound Streamers, Tiles*	Build vocabulary skills: Blend and recognise words. Recognise key vocabulary. Identify sounds in words.	blend sounds to read and make words. Match pictures to words. Sound out and select letters to make words.	**Worksheet 4** Check
Read: *Book*	Read aloud book.	listen, follow the reading and read along.	**Reading Eggs Story book** Fox, rocks, socks and tops

Related Reading Eggs Activities, Interactives, Songs and Books

Music Café

Tom the Dog thinks od

Reading Eggs Puzzle Park

More than One
Hidden Words
Song Lines
What is it?

Reading Eggs Posters

Reading Eggs Library Books

My Program Books

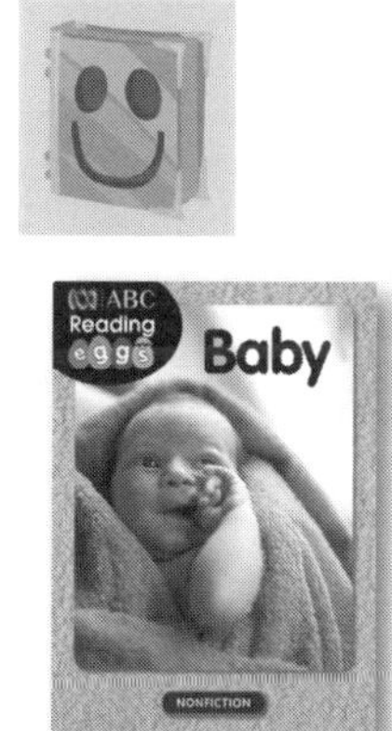

Interactives

Driving Tests

Spelling Bank

Teacher Toolkit

Spelling Activities

Reading Eggs Apps

Eggy Sight words

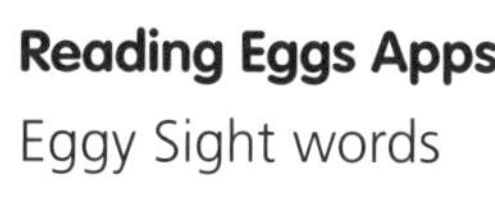

Critter Card

Tick tock clock

Name

Word families

Lesson 58 · Worksheet 1

1 Trace.

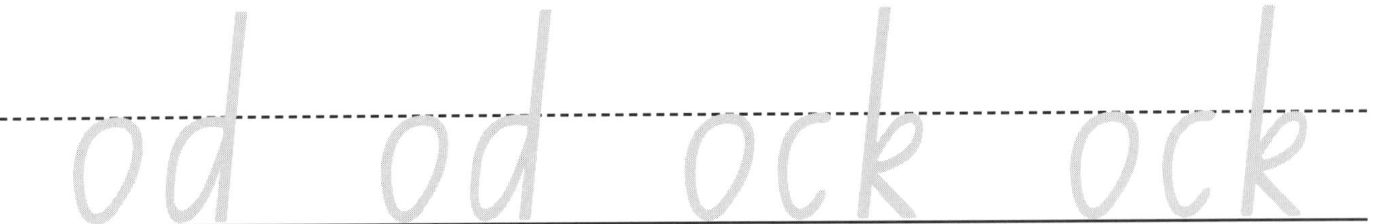

2 Complete the words. Use Tick tock clock's letters.

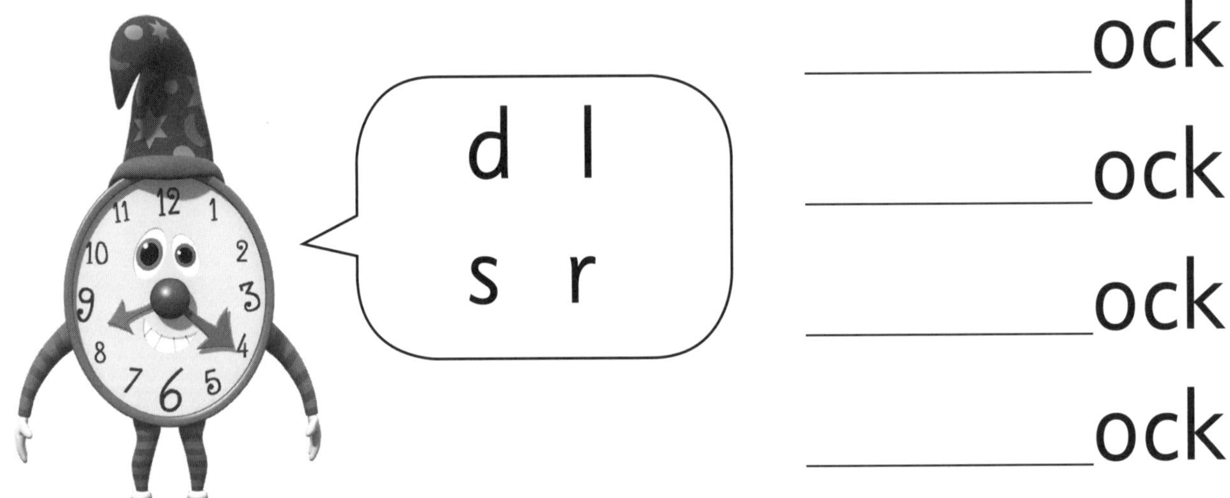

3 Colour the right word. Cross out the wrong word.

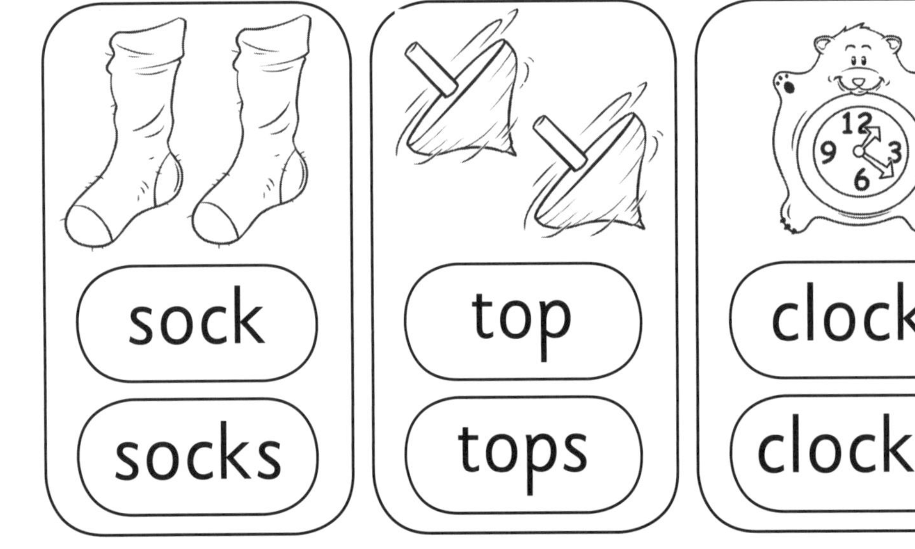

Name

Read and write

ock

Lesson 58 · Worksheet 2

1 Complete each sentence.

The fox got lots of

________________________________ .

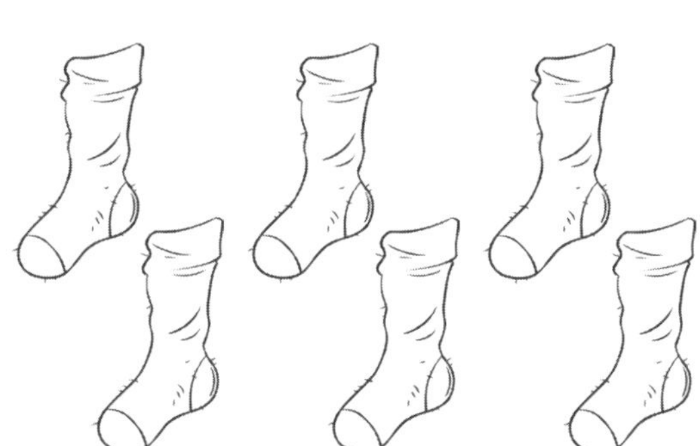

The fox got lots of

________________________________ .

2 Colour the **ock** words = red, colour the **od** words = green.

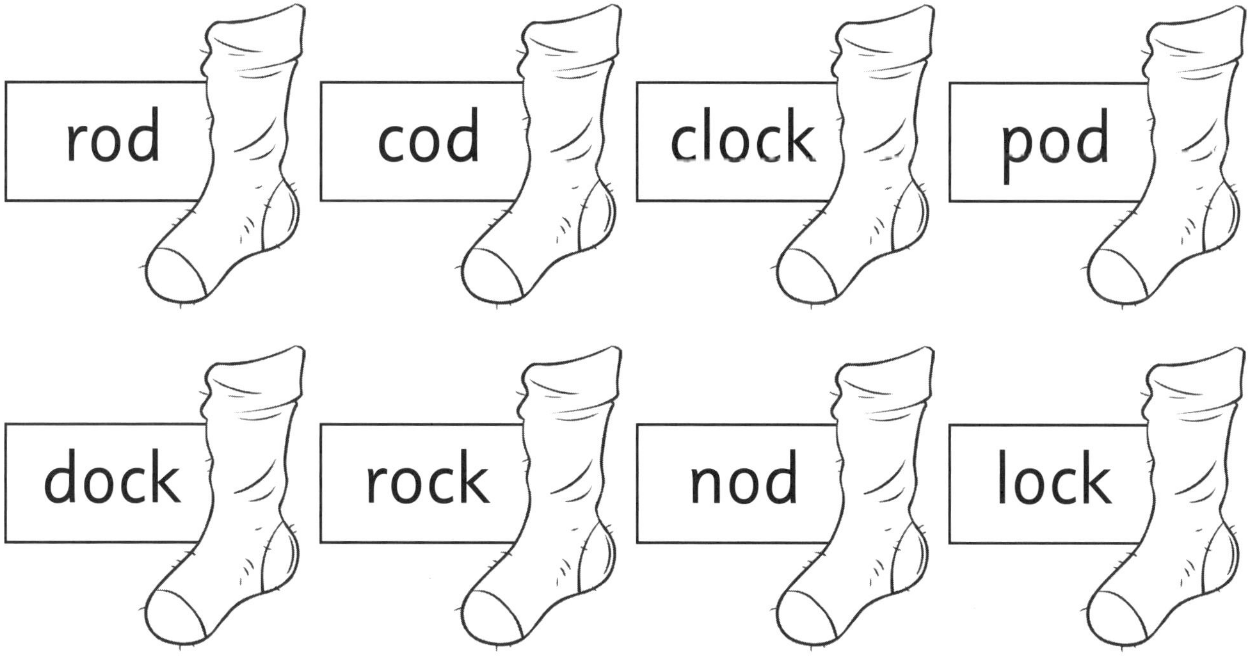

Lesson 58 • Worksheet 3

Name

Vocabulary

1 Join each sound to the word machine.
Write each word you make.

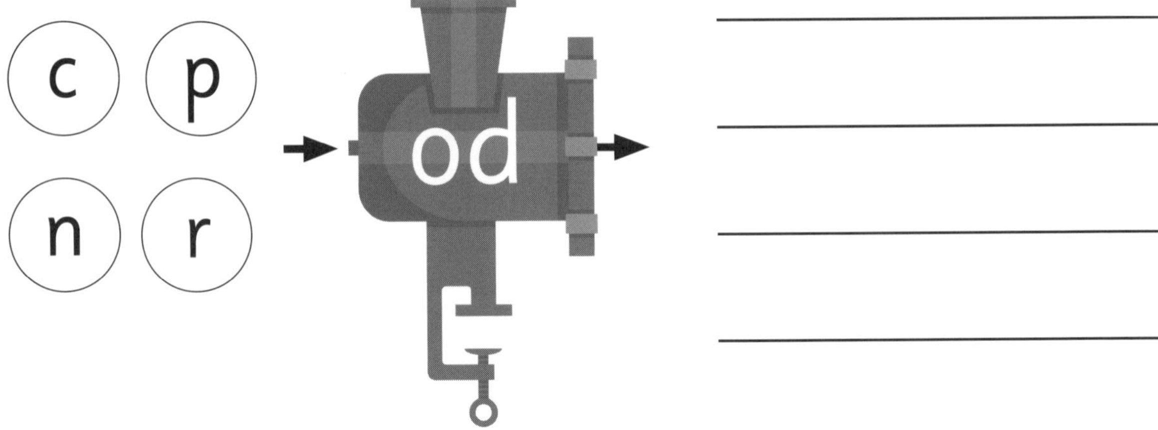

2 Match each word to a picture.

Name

Check

ock

Lesson 58 · Worksheet 4

1 Find the words. Colour **sock** = red, **nod** = green, **pod** = pink.

n	o	d	s	o	c	k
s	o	c	k	p	o	d
p	o	d	s	o	c	k
s	o	c	k	n	o	d

2 Make a word with the letters on the fridge.

_____od _____ock

_____od _____ock

3 Draw a picture for this sentence.

There are lots of rocks in this box.

Lesson 59 the sound **od**

Learning objectives

Children will:

- identify the rimes od and ot.
- recognise the sight word very.
- read and write words with y at the end.

Australian Curriculum Content Descriptions

Sound and letter knowledge

ACELA1439 listen to the sounds a student hears in the word, and write letters to represent those sounds; identify and manipulate sounds (phonemes) in spoken words; identify onset and rime in one-syllable spoken words

Expressing and developing ideas

ACELA1435 learn that word order in sentences is important for meaning

ACELA1758 recognise the most common sound made by each letter of the alphabet, including consonants and short vowel sounds; know that spoken words are written down by listening to the sounds heard in the word and then writing letters to represent those sounds

Interpreting, analysing and evaluating

ACELY1649 navigate a text correctly, starting at the right place and reading in the right direction, returning to the next line as needed, matching one spoken word to one written word

Sight words

very

Word families

pot, cot, hot, dot, rot, got, pod, rod, cod, fox, box, rocks, socks

Vocabulary words

puppy, lucky, bossy, happy, muddy, cherry, silly, fish, horse, seagull, mouse, bear, duck

Extra assistance

An effective strategy for reading new words is chunking. This is where the student divides the word into recognisable sections, not just individual letters. For example, cherry is ch-e-rr-y. When reading the word, the student needs to recognise the /ch/ sound is not /c/ /h/ and they don't make the /r/ sound twice.

Classroom activities

Is it very?

Put a list of words on the board and ask students if you can put the word very in front of each word. Use singular and plural nouns, verbs, adverbs and adjectives. See if the children can find a rule to explain when words can be 'very'.

Reading Eggs Lesson sequence	**TEACH Content and skills**	**PRACTISE Children will:**	**APPLY**
Hear: *Animated Lesson*	Revise the rimes od and ot with the songs *Tom the Dog thinks od* and *Sid thinks ot.*	identify the sound in each picture to make word families.	**Worksheet 1** Word families
Write: *Make a Sentence, Pick Up Bricks*	Recognise correct word order for a sentence.	choose the correct words to make a sentence.	**Worksheet 2** Vocabulary
Find: *Car and Puddles*	Recognise a given word.	find the given word in a group.	**Worksheet 3** Sight words
Vocabulary: *Blend a Word, Jigsaw, The Theme Game, Word Windows, Break it Up, Tiles*	Build vocabulary skills: Blend and recognise words. Recognise key vocabulary. Identify the number of phonemes in a word.	blend sounds to read and make words. Match pictures to words. Identify the number of sounds in a word.	**Worksheet 4** Check
Read: *Book Ends , Book*	Read basic vocabulary and identify key words. Read aloud book.	choose from a list of words to finish the sentence. Listen, follow the reading and read along.	**Reading Eggs Story book** Barry is bossy

Classroom activities

Mind the Gap!

Write this sentence on the board: Barry is a very bossy bear.

Give students an animal each and ask them to write a sentence like the one above using their animal. Have them illustrate their sentence to show the description they gave their animal.

Related Reading Eggs Activities, Interactives, Songs and Books

Music Café

Tom the Dog thinks od

Sid thinks ot

Reading Eggs Puzzle Park

Hidden Words

Song Lines

Animal Fun

Describe it

Reading Eggs Posters

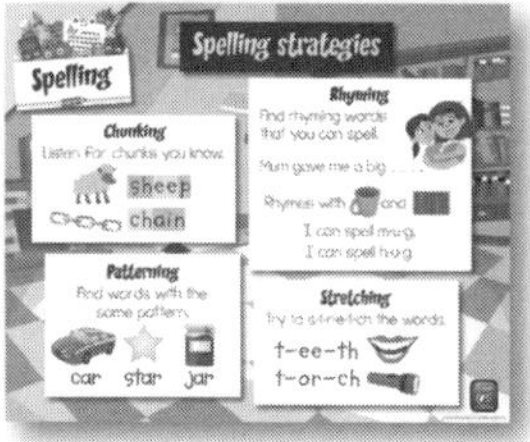

Reading Eggs Library Books

My Program Books

Interactives

Driving Tests

Spelling Bank

Teacher Toolkit

Spelling Activities

Reading Eggs Apps

Eggy Sight words

Critter Card

Socky fox

od

Name

Word families

Lesson 59 • Worksheet 1

1 Label each picture.

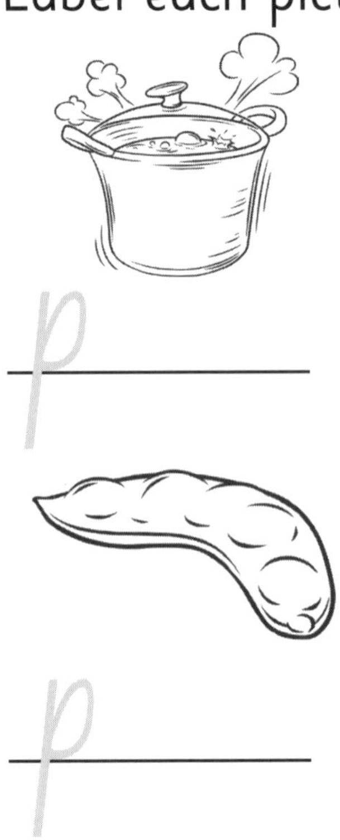

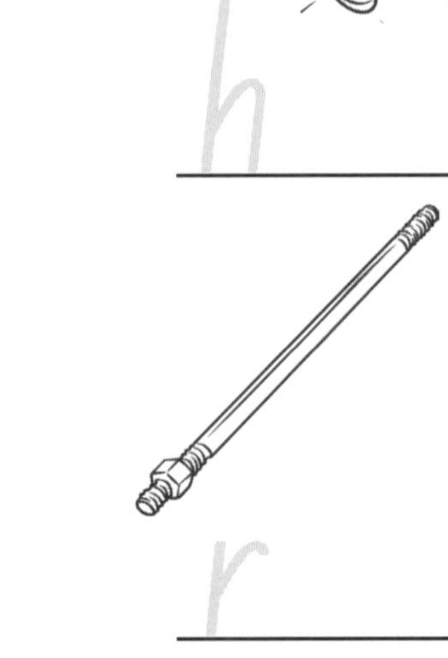

p______ c______ h______

p______ c______ r______

2 Colour **od** words = blue, **ot** words = red.

nod | not | pot | pod | spot

3 Draw:

a rod for this cod.

spots on this pot.

Name

Vocabulary

Lesson 59 • Worksheet 2

Match each word to a picture.

Sight words

Lesson 59 • Worksheet 3

Name

very

1 Trace and write the word.

very

2 Help Socky fox find his sock. Follow the path of **very** words.

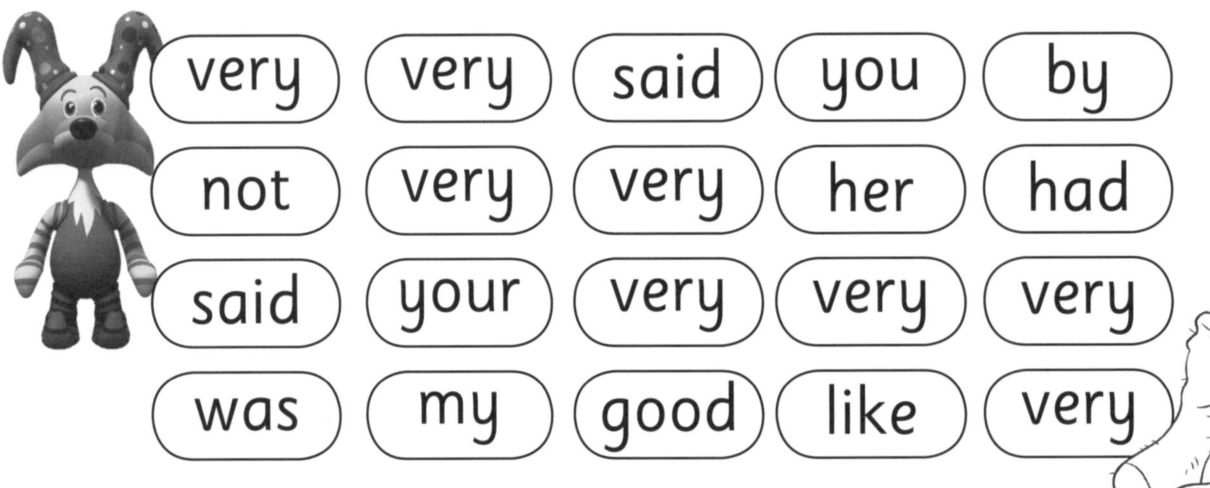

3 Circle the matching words in each row.

her	her	like	his
very	my	your	very
was	this	said	said

Name

Check

Lesson 59 · Worksheet 4

1 Complete the sentences.

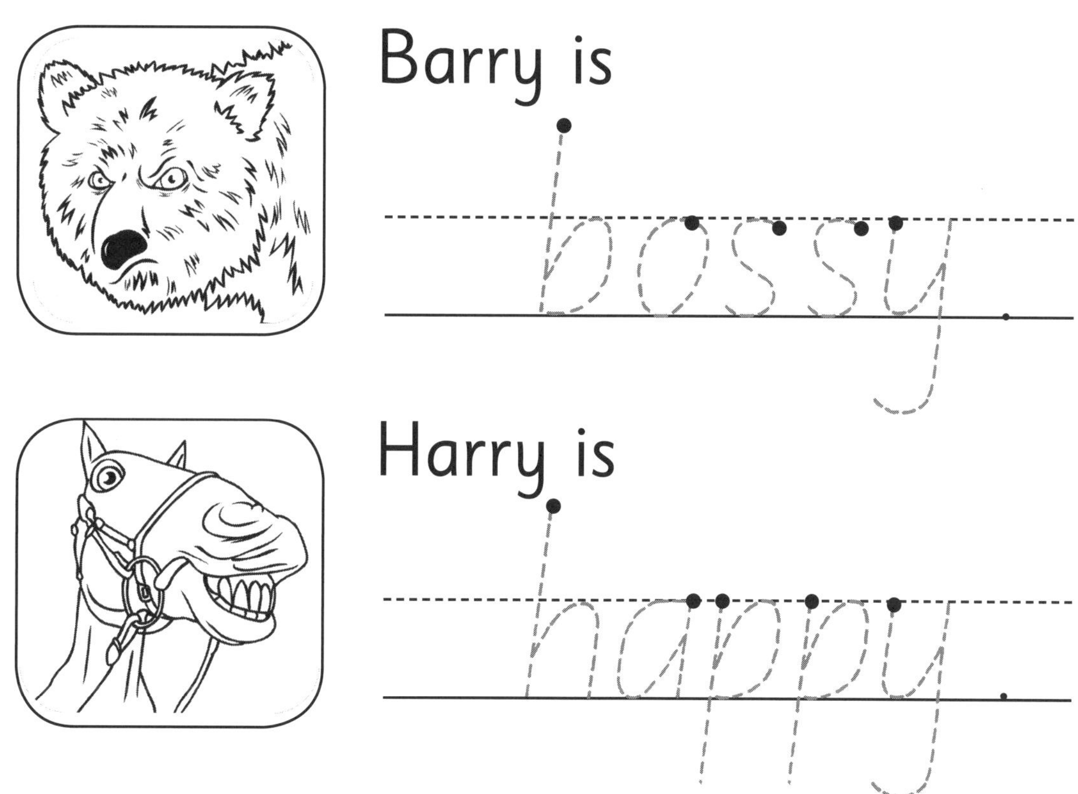

2 Colour the correct word. Cross out the wrong word.

Barry is (happy) (very) bossy.

This (pot) (put) is very hot.

There is a cod on this (red) (rod) .

Lesson 60 Review

Learning objectives

Children will:

- review the short o rimes – ot, og, od, op, ock, ox.
- read and write words using short o rimes.

Australian Curriculum Content Descriptions

Sound and letter knowledge

ACELA1439 listen to the sounds a student hears in the word, and write letters to represent those sounds; identify and manipulate sounds (phonemes) in spoken words; identify onset and rime in one-syllable spoken words

ACELA1440 identify familiar and recurring letters and the use of upper and lower case in written texts

Expressing and developing ideas

ACELA1438 build word families using onset and rime

ACELA1758 recognise the most common sound made by each letter of the alphabet, including consonants and short vowel sounds; write consonant-vowel-consonant words by writing letters to represent the sounds in the spoken words; know that spoken words are written down by listening to the sounds heard in the word and then writing letters to represent those sounds

Sight words

am

Word families

pod, rod, cod, dog, cog, jog, hog, log, frog, fog, clock, dock, sock, lock, rock, dot, cot, hot, pot, rot, lot, spot, top, mop, hop, pop, stop, drop, shop, fox, box

Extra assistance

Learning word families can provide students with an opportunity to start writing some rhymes of their own. Encourage them to write short sentences that end with rhyming words. Emphasise that the sentences should be related, for example:

The dog went for jog.

Then he sat on a log.

Classroom activities

Word Wheel

Give each student two circles of cardboard, one larger than the other, joined through the centre with a split pin. On the visible edge of the larger circle write the consonant letters b, d, f, h, n, p, r. On the smaller circle write the rimes ot, og, op, od, ock, ox, so they will match up with the outer letters and make words. Have students turn the circles and write out the words they make.

Reading Eggs Lesson sequence	**TEACH Content and skills**	**PRACTISE Children will:**	**APPLY**
Hear: *Animated Lesson*	Revise word families and blending onset and rime with the song *The Mousy House*.	choose the correct ending and initial letter to make the word.	**Worksheet 1** Word families 1
Write: *Missing Sound*	Identify the correct onset letter to complete the word.	choose the correct initial letter to make the word.	**Worksheet 2** Read and write
Find: *Fishing Boats, Kick A Goal, Know Your Alphabet, 1, 2, 3, 4, Time for 20*	Recognise a given word. Identify upper and lower case pairs of letters. Identify the order of a sequence of events.	match words to pictures. Find the given word in a group. Match lower case letters to their capital. Put pictures in order.	**Worksheet 3** Word families 2
Vocabulary: *Find Your Treasure, Sound Streamers, Tiles*	Build vocabulary skills: Recognise key vocabulary. Identify sounds in words. Blend and recognise words.	match pictures to words. Sound out and select letters to make words. Blend sounds to make words.	**Worksheet 4** Check
Read: *Book Ends , Book*	Read basic vocabulary and identify key words. Read aloud book.	choose from a list of words to finish the sentence. Listen, follow the reading and read along.	**Reading Eggs Story book** Word families for ot, og, op, ock

Classroom activities

Flashcard Snap

Have at least two sets of flashcards for the sight words learnt so far. Shuffle and deal between two players. Keep cards face down. Players take turns to put a card from their pile onto a central pile, saying the word as they turn it over. If the two cards on top are the same, the players shout SNAP! The first to do so takes the central pile. Play continues until one player runs out of cards.

Related Reading Eggs Activities, Interactives, Songs and Books

Music Café

The Mousy House

Reading Eggs Puzzle Park

More than one
Hidden Words
Song Lines
What is it?

Reading Eggs Posters

Reading Eggs Library Books

My Program Books

Interactives

Driving Tests

Spelling Bank

Teacher Toolkit

Spelling Activities

Reading Eggs Apps

Eggy Sight words

Critter Card

Tom the dog

Review

Lesson 60 • Worksheet 1

Name

Word families 1

Make word families. Complete each word.

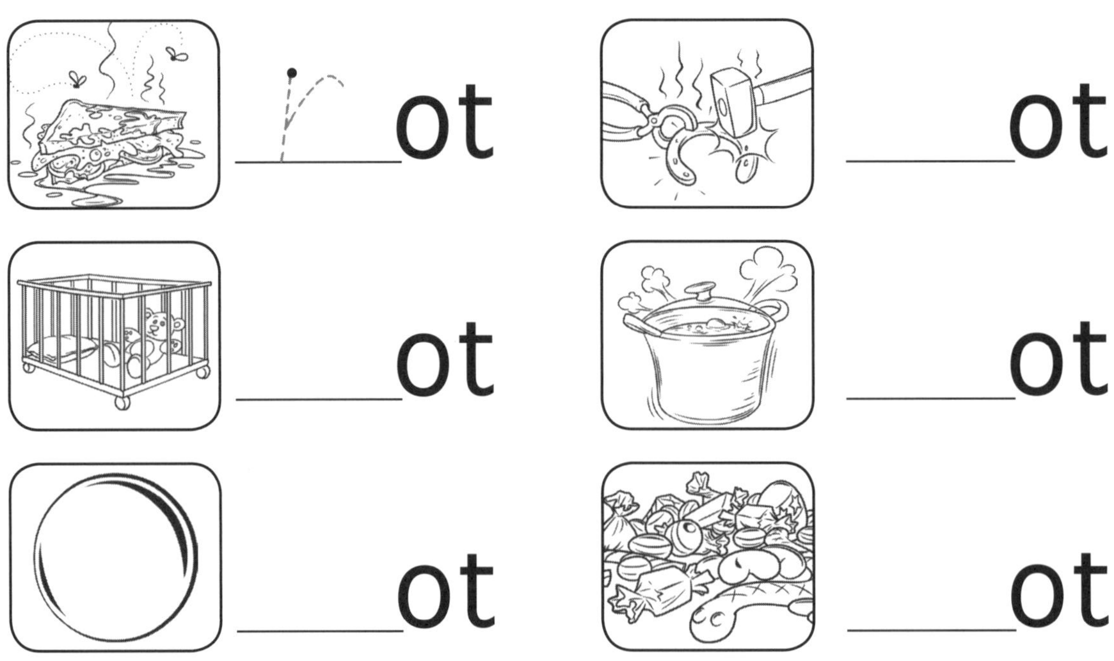

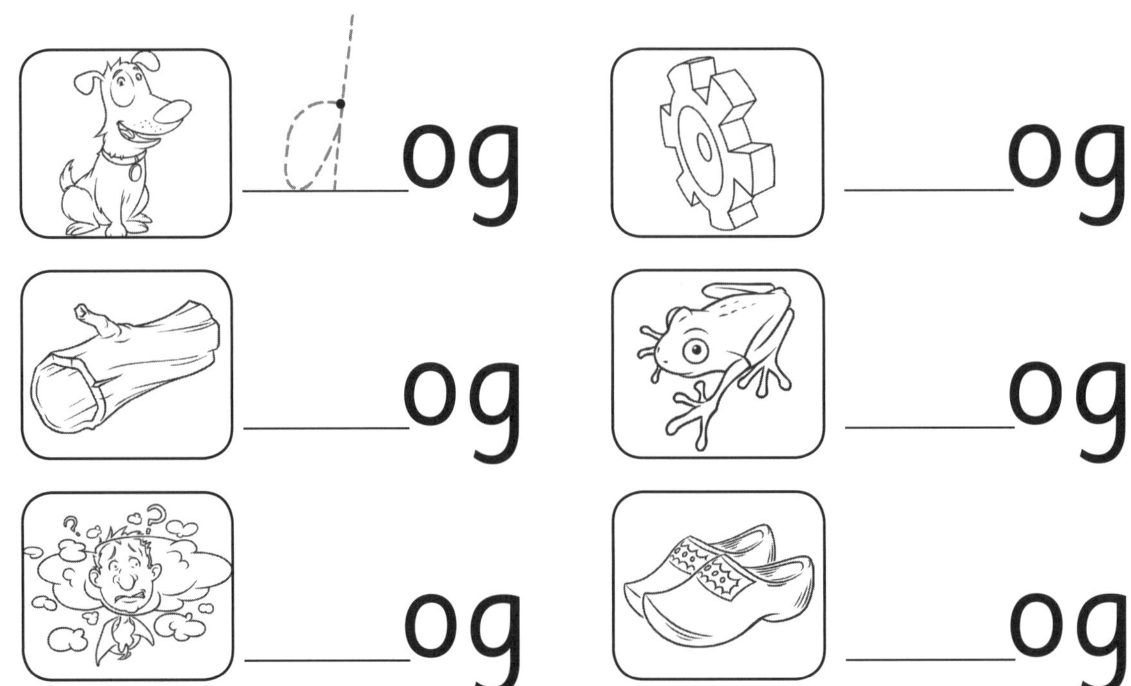

Name

Read and write

Review

Lesson 60 · Worksheet 2

1 Complete.

---.

2 Complete the sentences.

her hop said

"I can see the big dog," ________ Sam.

This frog can ________ and hop!

The Queen likes ________ pink hat.

Review

Lesson 60 • Worksheet 3

Name

Word families 2

1 Make word families. Complete each word.

od words

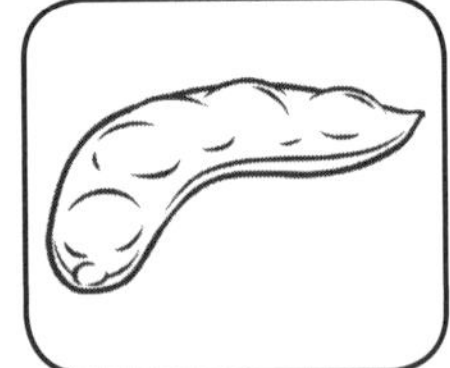 ____od

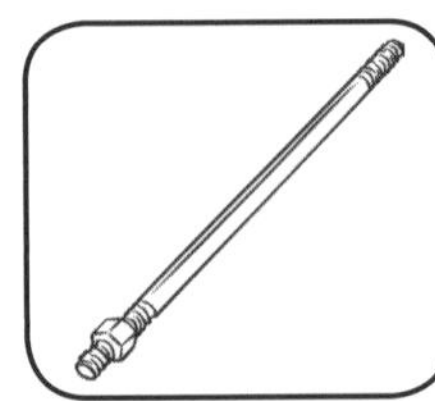 ____od

op words

 ____op

 ____op

ock words

____ock

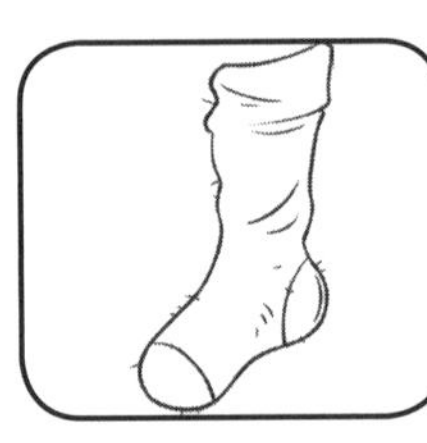 ____ock

2 Say the word for the picture. Find the word that rhymes.

hat

rock

mix

hop

fog

dot

clock

Name

Check

Review

Lesson 60 • Worksheet 4

1 Complete the crossword. Use the picture clues to help you.

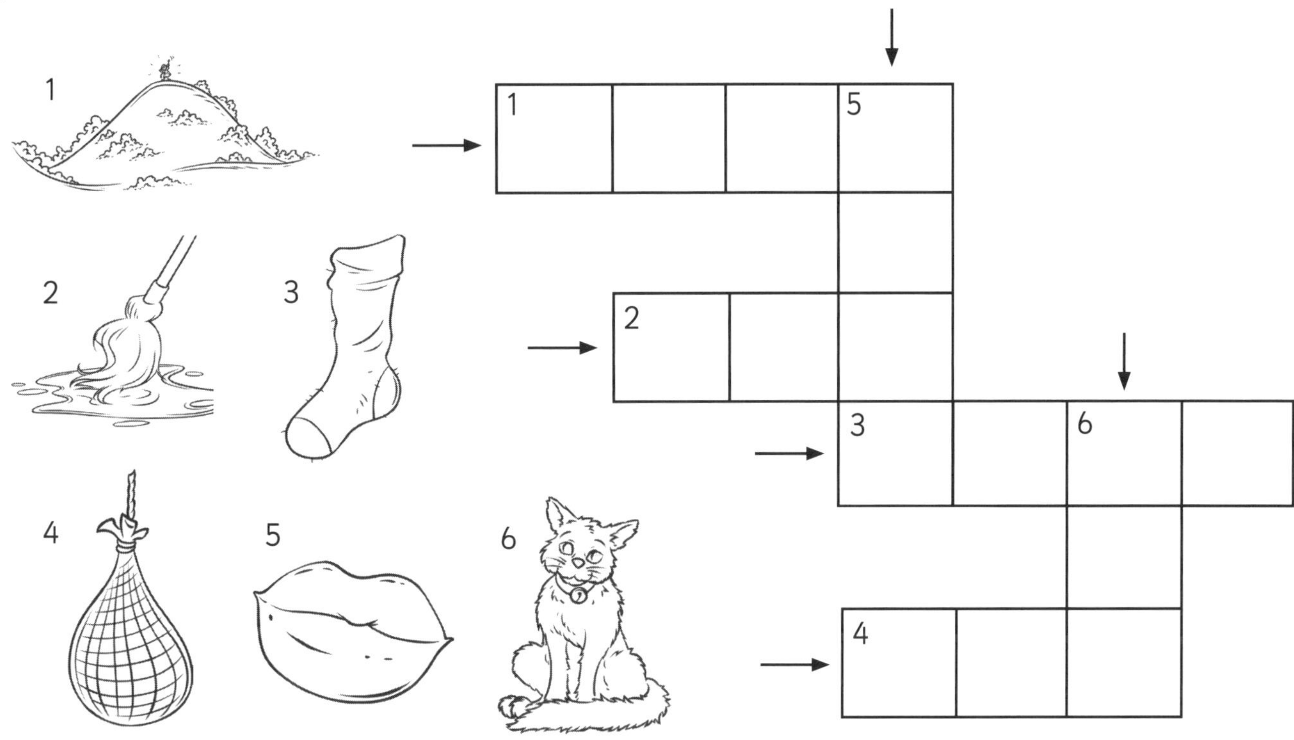

2 Say the name of each picture. Colour its beginning sound, then its end sound. Write the word.

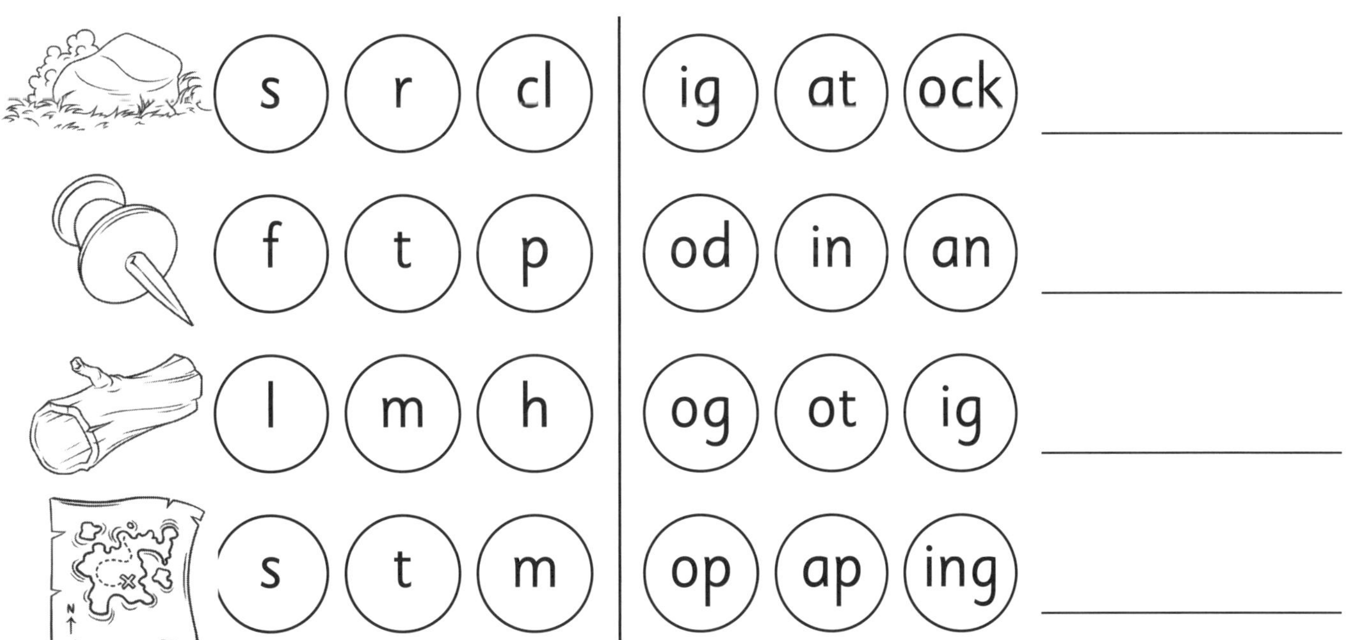

Reading Eggs Posters

In meeting the demands of the Australian Curriculum we have created a poster series as a teaching tool. These full colour, engaging posters can be used on Interactive Whiteboards and tablets as well as printed on A3 or A4 paper for classroom use. The series covers the broad scope of curriculum outcomes including language, literature and literacy.

Here is a sample from the series that address reading literature at a fiction and nonfiction level for Kindergarten.

Purpose

To give teachers a reference point to explain how to read and write a wide range of fiction and nonfiction texts.

The posters address fiction in narratives, poetry, nursery rhymes, fairytales, folktales and fables. They also cover key nonfiction texts: discussion, description, explanation, procedure, information report and recount. Teachers can use descriptions of the text types, sample texts, text type structures and scaffolds to teach text recognition and writing. There are also posters to give students strategies for approaching the reading and spelling of new words.

Australian Curriculum Content Descriptions

Literature and context

Recognise that texts are created by authors who tell stories and share experiences that may be similar or different to students' own experiences (ACELT1575)

Examining literature

Recognise some different types of literary texts and identify some characteristic features of literary texts, for example beginnings and endings of traditional texts and rhyme in poetry (ACELT1785)

Teaching notes

- Cut the high frequency words into smaller lists and play word detectives to find the words in books you read together as a class. Be sure to practise these words often. When students are writing independently direct them to this poster to help them spell common words.
- As teachers choose texts that suit their class and topic area, the posters explaining common text features are designed to support the teaching of how texts fit a certain genre and the special features they use. The posters provide interesting starting points for discussions of texts with students.
- Annotate the text samples together as a class. These provide a succinct, grade level appropriate text sample that can be used to highlight key features of the text.
- Each type of text is supplemented with writing scaffolds. Print and laminate class sets of these to be used by students for planning their texts (with whiteboard markers) or as prompts for writing specific text types.
- Use the posters' examples of fiction and nonfiction texts to help learners brainstorm the key differences between the two major types of texts.
- Print the Reading and Spelling Strategies posters in A3 format to put up on the wall. Use them as a reminder before students begin writing or reading activities. Refer students to the strategies during writing and reading activities to build independence.
- You could make a class book of helpful story writing words using the posters for Sequencing, What to write about, Ways to begin a story and Joining words. Refer students to the book when they are stuck in their writing.

The posters

Phonics

Reading Strategies

Spelling Strategies

Literature Texts

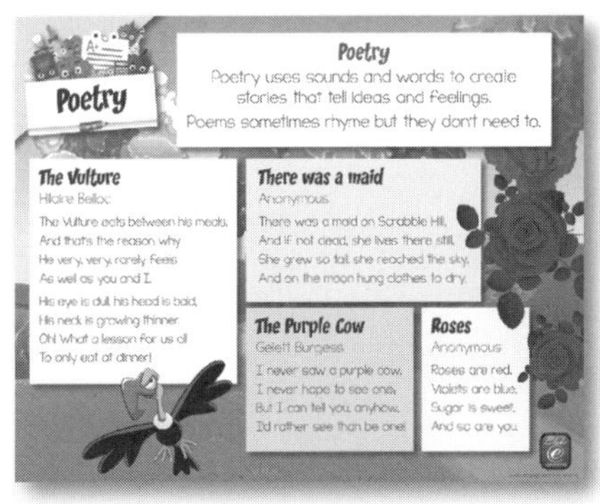

Samples

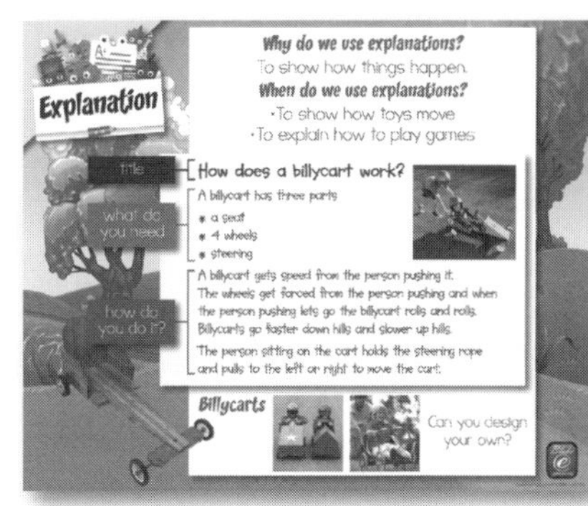

Text Structure

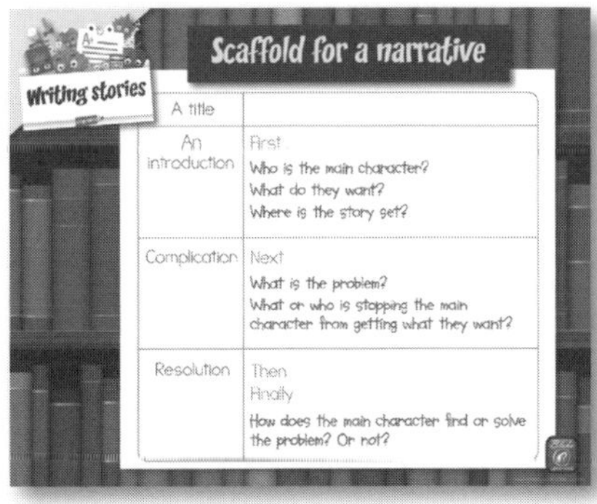

Writing Scaffold

Sequencing

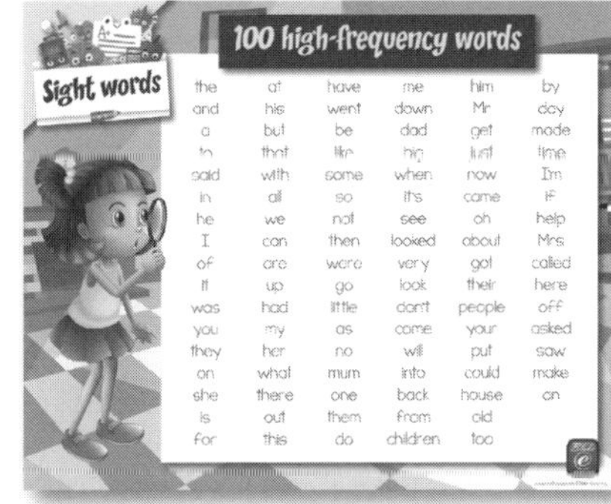

High Frequency Words

Alphabet

Vowels

Consonants

Skills Checklist Lessons 31-60

Name

Lesson	Skills	Check
31	Identifies words which start with the sound /g/. Writes the letter g. Recognises beginning sounds – a, b, c, g.	
32	Identifies words which start with the sound /l/. Writes the letter l. Recognises beginning sounds – b, e, g, l.	
33	Writes and identifies the sight words he and she. Comprehends sentences. Identifies -at, -ap, -an, -am words.	
34	Identifies words which start with the sound /k/. Writes the letter k. Recognises beginning sounds – s, a, b, n, e, g, l, k.	
35	Writes and identifies the sight words as and has. Comprehends sentences. Identifies -at, -ap, -an, -am words.	
36	Identifies words which start with the sound /y/. Writes the letter y. Recognises beginning sounds – s, b, v, g, k, y. Recognises end sounds –n, p, g, y.	
37	Writes and identifies the sight words yes and you. Completes sentences using short a words. Identifies rhyming words. Writes short a words.	
38	Identifies words which end with the sound /ks/. Writes the letter x. Recognises beginning sounds – r, d, g, k, y, x. Writes words with x in them.	
39	Identifies words which start with the sound /w/. Writes the letter w. Recognises beginning sounds – s, r, w.	
40	Identifies rhyming words. Comprehends sentences. Writes and recognises sight words. Identifies words that begin with g and k.	
41	Identifies words which start with the sound /u/ or /ue/. Writes the letter u. Recognises beginning sounds – c, g, l, u. Writes and recognises short u words.	
42	Writes the letters of the alphabet in order. Matches upper and lower case letters. Writes and recognises short a words. Identifies rhyming words.	
43	Recognises -id words. Uses -id words in sentences. Writes -id words.	
44	Recognises -ix and -in words. Writes -ix and -in words. Comprehends sentences. Writes and recognises sight words – you, can, see.	
45	Recognises -it and -in words. Writes -it and -in words. Completes and comprehends sentences.	

Name

Skills Checklist Lessons 31-60

Lesson	Skills	Check
46	Recognises -ig words. Writes -ig, -it and -in words. Completes sentences. Writes and recognises sight words – said, like, big.	
47	Writes and recognises the sight word – this. Completes sentences. Recognises short i words. Writes -ig words.	
48	Recognises -ip and -in words. Writes -ip words. Writes and recognises sight words – little, pink.	
49	Writes and recognises -ill words. Completes sentences. Writes and recognises short i words.	
50	Writes and recognises -ing words. Identifies sight words – two, has, bird. Recognises short i words.	
51	Writes and recognises sight words – go, by, can, you. Completes sentences. Identifies colour words – red, blue, pink, green, yellow.	
52	Writes and recognises sight words – look, got. Identifies theme words – the sea. Writes and recognises -ot words.	
53	Recognises short o words. Completes sentences. Writes -ot and -og words. Recognises -og words.	
54	Writes -op, -ot and -og words. Recognises -op words. Completes sentences. Writes and recognises the sight word – play.	
55	Writes and recognises short o words. Completes sentences. Writes and recognises sight words – lots, got. Recognises end sounds -ot, -og, -op.	
56	Writes and recognises sight words – are, not, said, happy, sad. Comprehends sentences. Identifies colour words – red, yellow. Completes sentences.	
57	Writes and recognises sight words – his, her, like, this. Comprehends sentences. Completes sentences. Identifies theme words – royalty and the sea.	
58	Writes -ock and -od words. Identifies use of plural -s. Completes sentences. Recognises -ock and -od words.	
59	Writes and recognises short o words. Identifies theme words – animals. Writes and recognises sight words – very, her, said. Completes sentences.	
60	Writes and recognises short o words. Completes sentences. Identifies and writes short vowel sound words.	

READING ASSESSMENT
Lessons 31-60

Name

Read the text.

This is a bus. The bus is big.
This is a truck. The truck is big.
This is a car. The car is little.
This is a little horse. This is a big horse.

Underline the correct answer.

1 What is little?
- the bus
- the car
- the truck

2 What is the bus?
- big
- little
- a car

3 What are the horses?
- big
- little
- big and little